Dr John Irvine is one of Australia's most
ogists, with daily radio segments on m
articles in magazines and newspapers and
shows. He also undertakes extensive
throughout Australia on parenting and i.
Day Care, Kidsafe and NAPCAN (National Association for the Prevention of Child Abuse and Neglect).

Because of his belief in the *prevention of child abuse*, Dr John will donate a significant percentage of the proceeds from the sale of *Who'd Be A Parent?* to the work of NAPCAN.

Dr John has a very busy clinical practice at the R.E.A.D. clinic in Gosford, NSW, for children with behaviour and learning problems and he has written three other books: *Coping With the Family, Coping With Kids* and *Coping With School*. He lives on the Central Coast with his wife, Jean, and their three daughters.

Other Books by John Irvine

Coping With the Family
Coping With Kids
Coping With School

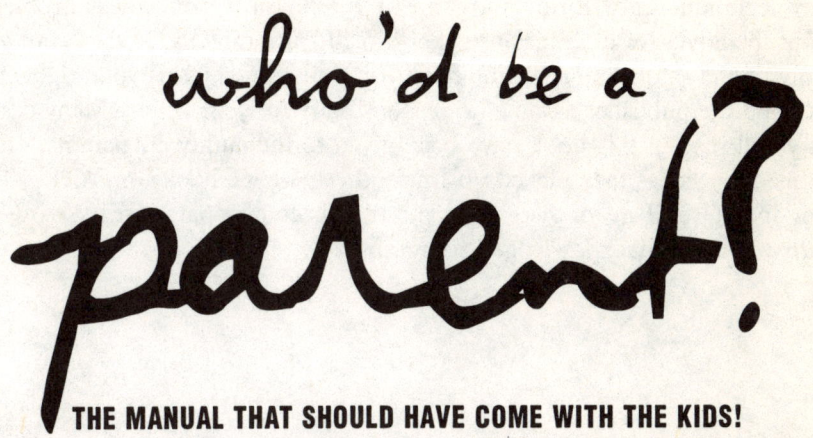

THE MANUAL THAT SHOULD HAVE COME WITH THE KIDS!

DR JOHN IRVINE

Pan Macmillan Australia

DISCLAIMER

The author of this book does not dispense medical advice or prescribe the use of any technique as a form of treatment for physical or medical problems without the advice of a physician, either directly or indirectly. In the event you use any of the information in this book for yourself, which is your right, the author and the publisher assume no responsibility for your action. Many of the ideas you'll read in this book have been given to the author by parents, often modified from ideas they picked up from other parents, books or articles. The author apologises if any of these suggestions, in becoming part of tribal wisdom, directly replicate unacknowledged sources.

First published 1998 in Macmillan by Pan Macmillan Australia Pty Limited
St Martins Tower, 31 Market St, Sydney

Reprinted 1998

Illustrations Copyright © Brad Baker 1998
Text Copyright © John Irvine 1998

All rights reserved. No part of this book may be reproduced or transmitted in any form or by any means, electronic or mechanical, including photocopying, recording or by any information storage and retrieval system, without prior permission in writing from the publisher.

National Library of Australia
cataloguing-in-publication data:

Irvine, John (John Forsyth), 1942– .
Who'd be a parent? : the manual that should have come with the kids.

ISBN 0 7329 0929 5.

1. Parenting - Handbooks, manuals, etc. 2. Family - Handbooks, manuals, etc. 3. Child rearing - Handbooks, manuals, etc. I. Title.

649.1

Typeset in 11/13 Life by Midland Typesetters Pty Ltd
Printed in Australia by McPherson's Printing Group

Table of Contents

INTRODUCTION	**Why do We Need a Manual?**	1
	The Top 20 Behavioural Problems	3
	Introducing Sandy	4
	Famous Footnote—Pat O'Shane	7
CHAPTER ONE	**Management Instructions**	9
	Classic Kids' Styles	9
	Classic Parent Styles	12
	Classic Management Styles	14
	The 10 Rules of Effective Punishment	18
	Alternatives to Smacking	20
	Ages and Stages of Learning	22
	Parental Depression and Anger	24
	Balanced Management	26
	Famous Footnote—John Howard	29
CHAPTER TWO	**Up-Top Problems**	31
	Depression	32
	Anxiety and Worry	37
	Separation Anxiety	46
	Panic	50
	Obsessions and Rituals	53
	Perfectionism	57
	Stubborn Thinkers	59
	School Sick	62
	Hypochondriacs	64
	Mind Muscle Summary	67
	Famous Footnote—Janine Shepherd	68
CHAPTER THREE	**Ear and Attention Problems**	71
	Attention Demanding Disorder	72
	Attention Damaged Disorder	78
	Attention Disabled Disorder	82
	Attention Digested Disorder	82
	Attention Deficit Hyperactivity Disorder (ADHD)	85
	Listening Problems	91
	Interrupting Problems	96
	No-Alls	98
	Attention Summary	101
	Famous Footnote—Kim Beazley	102

CHAPTER FOUR	**Eye and Sleeping Problems**	105
	Sleep Interruptions	106
	Bed Departure	109
	Slow Sleepers	114
	Night Monsters and Bad Dreams	117
	Early Wakers	120
	Daydreamers	122
	Forgetful Kids	124
	Sleeping Summary	127
	Famous Footnote—Bryce Courtenay	128
CHAPTER FIVE	**Mouth and Eating Problems**	131
	Fussy and Slow Eaters	132
	Throwing Up—in the Car!	139
	Food Refusal	140
	Older Kids' Food Refusal	142
	Overeating and Junk Food	144
	Biting	148
	Restaurant Rebels	151
	Eating Summary	153
	Famous Footnote—Kathy Lette	154
CHAPTER SIX	**Tongue and Communication Problems**	157
	Crying	158
	Whingeing and Boredom	162
	Screaming	166
	Car Whingeing	169
	Swearing	173
	Back-Answering and Arguing	176
	Lying	180
	Smutty Talk	184
	Teasing	188
	Silly Talk and Showing Off	192
	Communication Skills Summary	194
	Famous Footnote—Bronwen Daddo	195
CHAPTER SEVEN	**Heart and Relationship Problems**	197
	Self-Esteem	198
	Lonely Kids	203
	Friendships Summary	206
	Bossing	208
	Jealousy	212
	Selfishness	216
	Cuddle-Shy	219
	Self-Esteem Summary	223
	Famous Footnote—Suzanne Chick	224

CHAPTER EIGHT	Hand and Aggression Problems	227
	Aggression	228
	Anger and Bad Temper	233
	Fighting (Sibling Rivalry)	238
	Destructive Kids	242
	Competitive Kids	245
	Bullies	248
	Stealing	252
	Aggression Summary	255
	Famous Footnote—Greg 'Wiggles' Page	256
CHAPTER NINE	'Down There' and Immaturity Problems	259
	Poo Refusal	261
	Sneaky Poos and Soiling	265
	Bed Wetting	268
	Sex Play and Talk	272
	Bad Habits	276
	Masturbation	278
	Thumbsucking	280
	Nailbiting	281
	Immaturity Summary	283
	Famous Footnote—Jeannie Little	284
CHAPTER TEN	Foot and Cooperation Problems	287
	Disobedience	288
	Cooperation	289
	Job Refusal	290
	Shopping	295
	Time Out Refusal	298
	Dawdling	302
	Dressing Difficulties	305
	Tantrums	309
	Laziness	313
	Bath Battles	315
	School Refusal	319
	Late for School	322
	Phone Problems	323
	Homework	327
	Messy Rooms	330
	Discipline Summary	334
	Famous Footnote—Cheryl Kernot	335
CONCLUSION	Who'd Be A Parent?	337
	Parents' Bill of Rights	340
	Famous Footnote—Peter 'McDonald's' Ritchie	342

Acknowledgements   345

Appendix   349
Phoebe's Story   349
Preferred Social Rewards and Punishments by Age   350
Fridge Disk Discipline   351
Fridge Make Up List   352
Success Charts   353
Practice List   354
Think Light   355
Travellers' First Aid Kit for Families   356
Children's Interest Inventory   357
Boredom Beaters   358
Web Sites   359
Pocket Money Chart   360
Family Meeting Form   362
Angry Parents' First Aid Guide   363

Contact Numbers   365

References   367

Index   369

INTRODUCTION

Why do We Need a Manual?

Being a parent is hard. You have to learn to say no and that is sometimes very hard. It takes courage and parents really knowing themselves to have the confidence in their own standards so they can say no when it needs to be said. I subscribe to the view that there's too much emphasis on children's rights without an equal emphasis on their responsibilities.

PAT O'SHANE, Children's Magistrate
[READ MORE OF PAT O'SHANE'S INSPIRING STORY AT THE END OF THIS CHAPTER.]

This is an adventure. I hope you can share it with me. After 35 years of working with kids I have picked up many clever little tactics. I have so many stories to tell and so many great families to share with you.

So where do I start? Who wants to know what, and more to the point, who'd be a parent anyhow if they had their time over again? Maybe it's no coincidence that Australians are raising more pets and fewer kids. And why not—pets don't answer back, they're always pleased to see you, they don't think you're an embarrassment, they don't interrupt, they don't bring their mates home and they don't mess up their room. Of course there's another possibility; maybe it's just easier to handle *tail waggers* than *tongue waggers*.

Whereas kids, well, from the time they're born, they've been described as one long alimentary canal, with a loud noise at one end and no responsibility at the other! And they cost: not only in sleep, sex and sanity, but in cold hard cash. Kids used to be an asset; they saw you through your old age and they took over the family business. But now they're a liability. It's estimated that the cost of the first born in lost wages is $350,000; the cost of the second is an extra $50,000; with an additional $30,000 more for each child after that.

It sure is a strange age for families as we take a turn into the twenty-first century. Parents are having fewer kids and spending less time with them. More kids are being cared for outside the extended family and more kids are being abused.

Why, with all the media campaigns and all the slogans, is child abuse still so rampant? Let me share what I think. Parents, in this crazy technological age, are fast losing one key thing. They're losing control, not just of the kids, but of life itself. Life is faster than ever before, our expectations are higher than ever before, there are more outside pressures than ever before, more options than ever before, but there are fewer family supports than ever before.

In order to cope with these stresses we tend to become very selfish, but kids require the very opposite! Kids need down time, goofing-off or nothing time, play time, lap time, cuddle time, talk time, reassurance time, and time is something that we just don't have. Our response to this is to 'disengage'—we're opting out, it's all becoming too hard, and a rapidly rising divorce rate (from one in five marriages 20 years ago to almost one in two marriages today) is evidence of that. We're losing contact and confidence as we hand the kids over to the experts to bring them up. And because we're losing contact with our families and communities we're becoming islands within our own homes. We're not being nurtured so it's becoming harder and harder to nurture our own offspring.

The good news is that our kids are bursting to re-engage with us, to have some family fun again, and the way to do that is to recapture the capacity to play! As we become adults we lose the child within us, but the wonderful thing is that we're never too old to enjoy our childhood. And as we do, we not only boost our immune system and use the best destressor life has to offer, but we live longer and healthier and we rebond with our own family. We can learn to manage the kids with *playfare* not *warfare* without losing a drop of discipline.

So that's where this book is different. It tries to tackle children's behaviour problems with playfare not warfare. But it's different, too, in that it also addresses the problems that *parents* said were hurting *them*.

'The problem is,' said one mum on her way out the clinic door, 'that everything these days comes with a manual, but not kids, and they're the hardest of the lot!' So I decided to write a manual. But I first needed to know where parents needed and wanted help, so I collected some initial reaction from over 2000 parents at seminars I ran around Australia over six months.

The Top 20 Behavioural Problems

The top 20 behaviours that made parents feel like hitting their kids were as follows:

1. Answering back
2. Cheekiness
3. Car misbehaviour
4. Defiance
5. Lying
6. Bedtime misbehaviour
7. Shop misbehaviour
8. Bullying
9. Homework Problems
10. Biting
11. Cruelty
12. Delinquent behaviour
13. Mealtime misbehaviour
14. Refusing to accept 'NO'
15. Seat belt refusal
16. Screaming
17. Tantrums
18. Teacher insulting
19. Swearing
20. Running away when called

When I looked at the survey results it suddenly hit me how many of them related directly to parts of the body—not just an arrogant mindset, but, for example, such things as a hard heart, a curled lip, a sharp tongue, light fingers, vampirish teeth, a manic mouth, ears immune to parents, eyes immune to mess, hands immune to nothing except a stack of dirty dishes and feet that play hard to catch. So, in keeping with my aim to be practical and playful, I invented a generic unisex child called SANDY!

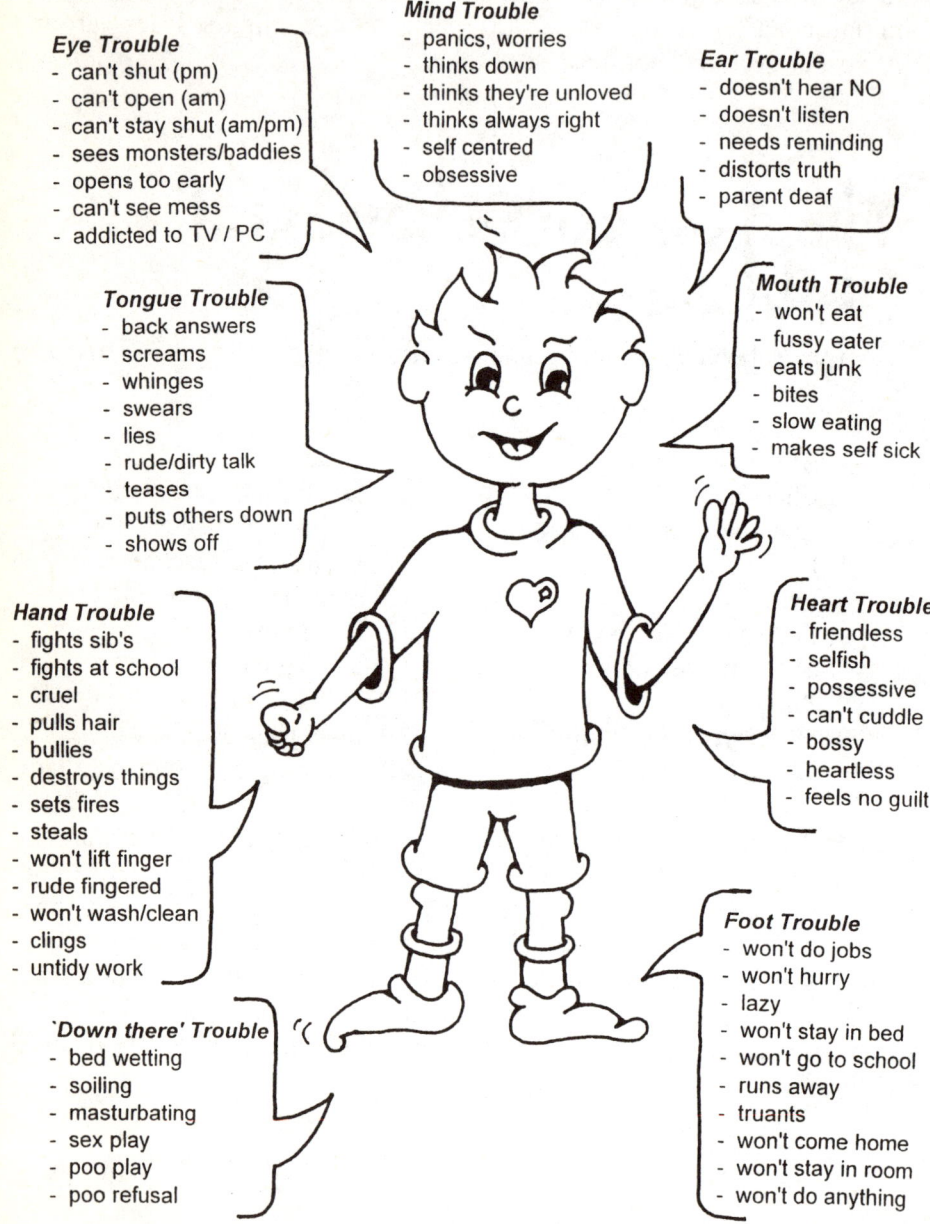

I'll refer to Sandy as 'he' or 'him', not because males are more important but, as four out of five behaviour problems are with boys, it makes more sense. I then took Sandy with me to every talk I gave to get parents to tell me which *parts* were causing them the most problems.

This time the question was not which *behaviours* make you feel like hitting your kids, but which *parts* cause you the most problems. The top 20 problems (after canvassing several hundred parents of children aged between one and 12 years) turned out to be the following:

1. EAR—Doesn't hear 'NO'
2. TONGUE—Whinges
3. TONGUE—Back-answers
4. EAR—Doesn't listen
5. MOUTH—Fussy eating
6. HAND—Fights brothers and sisters
7. EAR—Needs constant reminding
8. MIND—Panics, worries
9. TONGUE—Teases
10. FOOT—Won't hurry
11. FOOT—Won't do jobs
12. MIND—Thinks they're always right
13. MOUTH—Slow eating
14. EYE—Inability to shut
15. TONGUE—Screams
16. HEART—Bossy
17. MIND—Self-centred
18. EAR—Parent-deaf
19. EYE—Can't see mess
20. EYE—Addicted to TV/PC

What surprised me was that kids not hearing the word NO and kids not listening were consistently the biggest frustrations. Maybe in this technological age where everything is eyes-on and hands-on, it might be that it's also ears off! Maybe kids are becoming poor listeners!

So here is my manual on the most common problems facing parents in controlling kids. **The manual is meant to provide tried and true, practical and sensible advice for the parents who don't want to be experts, but want to enjoy their time with their children for the few short years they have them.**

I've included stories and wise words from ordinary parents trying to do the right thing by their kids. And I've also included stories from some special families, some famous and some that should be. I'm sure you'll be as inspired as I am by:

—the commitment of John Howard;
—the honesty of Kim Beazley;
—the motherly pride of Cheryl Kernot;
—the heart-wrenching comments of Bryce Courtenay;
—the self-disclosure of Peter Ritchie;
—the courage of Janine Shepherd;

—the wisdom of Bronwen Daddo, mother of the famous Daddo family;
—the humour of Kathy Lette;
—the frankness of Suzanne Chick;
—the attention to parenting of Greg Page;
—the strength of Pat O'Shane;
—and the sobering common sense of Jeannie Little.

I've also included a list of Do's and Don'ts for each of the problems. **These are not meant to be prescriptive solutions, nor am I suggesting that they are the *only* solutions**. The Do's and Don'ts are suggestions, based on what I have found to be the most effective, non-violent methods for altering children's behaviour. They are tried and true, but not every method will work for every child. You may have to try a few before finding the one that will work for *your* child.

So that's how this manual came about and my one wish is that you enjoy it and in so doing, enjoy your kids just that little bit more. Of course, not everyone would view a manual as requiring the detail that follows. For some, such as Kathy Lette, it's simple:

> The only instruction manual a new parent needs contains five points.
> 1. A balanced meal is whatever stays on the spoon en route to the baby's mouth.
> 2. The only way to find missing Lego is to turn off the lights and saunter around in bare feet until you crush your instep.
> 3. If your partner asks you what you want in bed, the only reply is 'breakfast'.
> 4. The answer to 'Who's Mamma's lovely baby boy then?' is—your husband.
> 5. And, most vital of all—*Don't listen to the parentally correct.*

With the help of the Bush Remedies, I'll try not to be too parentally correct!

FAMOUS FOOTNOTE

A COMMUNAL MUM

Pat O'Shane

CHILDREN'S MAGISTRATE

I'm constantly amazed and saddened by the number of parents I talk to, often sole parents, who see their children as their enemies, so many who seem to be afraid of their children, afraid that if they take a stand they won't be popular. But in my view I'm the parent and being a parent carries very clear and important responsibilities. I had no hesitation in making it clear to the children that I was in charge. This was my house, my rules and my consequences. They didn't always like it but as they've grown up they've told me that they respected me for it. That might sound authoritarian but my daughters accept that I always tried to be fair. But I was the parent, it was my job to discipline and teach responsibility to my children.

Being a parent is hard. You have to learn to say no and that is sometimes very hard. It takes courage and it takes parents really knowing themselves to have the confidence in their own standards so they can say no when it needs to be said. I subscribe to the view that there's too much emphasis on children's rights without an equal emphasis on their responsibilities too, and that includes housework. We work together.

It was also very hard as a sole parent, which I was for many years, to carry the whole load, to cope with the misbehaviour. To cope with the constant challenging of your authority without a break, without anyone else to turn to, even though they might play one off against the other. In two-parent families the children have someone else that they can turn to and that you can turn to, and that can give you a break.

What sustained me through their growing years was the absolute belief that I wanted them to be responsible *to* themselves and *for* themselves, as well as being aware of their responsibilities within the community. I had to make sure that they were ready and capable of doing that.

I feel that a lot of strength came through my Aboriginal background, because in our culture everyone was responsible. There were times I had to call upon the extended family to help me through. It wasn't very often but I knew they were there and would support me if it was needed. One time when one of my daughters was giving me the normal adolescent hard time, I was finding it very hard to know how to handle her. I called on my extended family and my father and my brothers came and talked to her and told her that her behaviour was hurting the whole family, not just her mother. It had a huge effect on her at the time.

We are not just individuals responsible to ourselves. We are a community and we need to be responsible to that community and the community needs to take responsibility for each person within it. In a community everyone has to work. Maybe some of my commitment to the role of the family stems from my own upbringing and the fact that my mother died when my children were very young, so I've needed to draw on the wider family group.

I also believe you need people, family, around you to tell you who you are, where you came from and reaching right back to the beginning. It's enormously dangerous to live as an isolated individual seeking satisfaction just for the individual, without seeing and finding your place within your own family. To me individualism is a total denial of our nature, we're social animals. I may not like what my brothers do or my daughters do but in the whole scheme of things that isn't important. What matters is that we have each other. I think we must make allowances for individual differences but that does not mean individualism.

My advice to every family, is to keep reaffirming your love for each other. When Tjandamurra was burnt, as you probably remember, that was a very hard time for us all. We were a family in crisis, but we kept trying to affirm our love for each other, and it's not easy. Unless you nurture it and hug and say loving things it won't be there for you when you need it. I hear so many parents blaming, ridiculing, attacking their children and that's so corrosive. It cuts me up to hear the way words are used to abuse children, they're so destructive.

We must treat our children with respect, but they also have to learn how to earn that respect. It all comes back to parental responsibility. There is nothing more important or more urgent than that in today's families.

CHAPTER ONE

Management Instructions

I believe that bringing up children is the most important thing most people do in their lives and nothing replaces time spent with your children.

JOHN HOWARD, Politician and 1997 Father of the Year
[READ MORE OF JOHN HOWARD'S COMMITMENT TO HIS FAMILY AT THE END OF THIS CHAPTER.]

So, the book begins and ends with the little character above, Sandy, who's a creation of all the trials, triumphs and tribulations that parents face day in, night out. But Sandy comes in more than just one model. Have a look around at any group of kids and you'll get a sprinkling of several kinds of Sandy that pose problems for parents.

Classic Kids' Styles

FASHIONABLE FIONA

This is the one in the group that has to wear the latest gear, and who judges everyone by how good they look and what they're wearing. It's a style which is sometimes caught from parents, sometimes taught by magazines, and sometimes it is just that they have an eye for what looks right. Deep down Fiona's scared that if she doesn't have faultless fashion, she'll be an outcast. The Fionas are lovely kids but they are awfully uptight, very expensive and they seem to tackle life and relationships so superficially.

Try to help them unwind, spend time on a farm, get them involved with animals—and help them find work so they can earn what they yearn (see Chapter Two).

WILHEMINA WORRY-WART

Wilhemina's the worrier in the group, often an intelligent, good-looking kid but ever so anxious about everything, and sensing a disaster around every corner. Wilhemina's a great kid, does everything right, but carries such a load that she's exhausted by the end of every day and edgy from the time she gets up.

By far the best answers for Wilhemina are good 'worry-tossing' tactics, good friends and a confident family (see Chapter Two).

SHY SERENA

You may not see Serena at first glance. She's the one on the edge of the group, hand in mouth, who would love to join in but would die if the kids asked her to. It's often genetic and so painful for watching parents who probably had the same problem. Serena shrivels under the spotlight, flushes, blushes and hates herself doing it.

Try to give her time to find her own ways to beat her shyness and time to find her talents so she feels she's not an ugly duckling. Break down big social hurdles into small steps to help build up confidence —handing out nibblies at a dinner party, saying just 'hello' to visitors, saying hi to five kids at school, etc (see Chapter Seven).

BOSSY BIANCA

This is the kid that most other kids wish hadn't turned up. She takes over any game—everything has to be done *her* way or she gets very upset and can't understand why she gets left out. It's often just a carry-on from home, where she's allowed to be bossy, but, when it doesn't work with other kids, she panics and her bossing becomes worse.

Some social skill training and role play are urgently needed before she's totally rejected. Often the Biancas just don't know how else to handle other kids (see Chapter Seven).

PERFECT PATRICE

This one hangs about with Fashionable Fiona but her problem is more general. It's not just clothes that must look good, everything has to be right—hair must look right, Mum must wear *this* gear, we must do *this* first, project must be perfect, night-time routines must be in *this* order. It may be part of a fearful nature and it may be copied from fussy parents. Whatever the cause, life is a living hell for Perfect Patrice because every day she's imperfect.

Rewarding fun, effort and enjoyment, and not rewarding perfection, is one way to make it easier later in life. Another way is to help her set kinder goals for herself (see Chapter Two).

SHOWMAN SID

You can't miss this one in the group. The other kids don't mind him in small doses but parents have more trouble. Sid suffers from the other ADD, not Attention Deficit Disorder like Sam, who I'll introduce shortly—but with Attention Demanding Disorder. Sid is the big attention seeker who makes a pest of himself wherever he goes, a problem often started by too much attention because he was a special baby for some reason, or maybe by busy parents only giving him attention when he makes a nuisance of himself so he comes to think that's the way to go.

Smacking and shouting at Sid suits him perfectly as it's still attention, what he hates is *no* attention, time out, attention to others, etc. Try to shift his game plan by paying attention to the behaviour you like, and isolating behaviour you don't like (see Chapter Three).

COOL KYLE

This one's got his sights set on being a clone of some older role model. He's your sleek super-cool kid, the powerful trendsetter, the eight-year-old going on 18. Kyle's behaviour is often copied in the anxious effort to feel more secure, but the image attracts so much attention from other kids all wanting to be older that it sticks.

The way to handle Cool Kyles is to just give them the responsibilities that go with the image—big enough to make their own bed, get their own lunch, save their own pocket money, do big jobs around the house, etc. If they're given low-key attention this way in a loving family that can ease them back to reality, they'll be okay and can be taught to cooperate (see Chapter Ten).

FORGETFUL FRED

Fred's gorgeous, he means well, never does the wrong thing by anybody, but he can be so frustrating. He has a one-track mind (if he's thinking about something he forgets everything else), he dawdles (you send him off to his room and he gets lost on the way), he doesn't know what day it is or what's going on. For some Freds it's neurological, but many are the youngest or the most dithery in very busy families where being forgetful is one of the best ways to make sure someone else does it for you.

Fred only changes his behaviour when the responsibility flicks back his way—he has to carry the consequences of forgetting so the pain pricks his brain into gear (see Chapters Two and Ten).

ANGRY ALEX

This is the one in the group I most worry about. He puts a shield up to stop any hurt, but it also stops any healing—'teachers suck', 'it's not my fault', 'why do I always get the blame?', 'he made me'. Alex rejects the good things people say, latches onto the bad, and believes it. Often he comes from an angry family or he hasn't found fun with his father. Because Alex can't or won't see the mote in his own eye, he ends up with a huge chip on his shoulder.

Alex and family need to see a professional early so the family can find ways to shift their game plan before it is too late (see Chapter Eight).

CYCLONE SAM

You can't miss Sam—he's your 100 kmh kid who's always on the go. He fiddles, teases, doesn't know the meaning of NO, he's into everything, has an engine much bigger than his brakes, he's impulsive, never listens, interrupts, but is the most adorable model of a child when he's asleep.

Many Sams have ADHD (Attention Deficit Hyperactivity Disorder) which requires good routines, strong rules, perhaps a bland diet and maybe even medication to help them settle (see Chapter Three).

Classic Parent Styles

The other problem in managing Sandy, or any of his mates for that matter, is that their parents aren't perfect either. But although we go about our kid management in different ways, we do have so much in common and so much to share. For a start, we all suffer from the same sexually transmitted disease (kids), we all cope with horrific hours, with service that's thankless, and for the same pathetic pay.

But there are four main styles of managing kids that I constantly see through the clinic.

To show how they vary, let's take a normal behaviour problem and see which way you'd handle it. The kids are watching TV and you ask Sandy to clean up the mess on the dining table so you can get it ready for dinner. He barks back, 'Why do you always ask me? I'm always asked to do all the jobs—idiot face never does anything.'

At this point do you:
A) scream at him for not doing as he's told, and order him to get his backside mobile before it wears your imprint;
B) quietly tell him that he might think he's being badly treated but you want it done anyhow so please help;
C) shrug your shoulders and do it yourself rather than have an argument;
D) feel guilty that maybe you didn't ask him the right way or that maybe he really believes you treat his sister better.

Probably you'll feel you do all four, simultaneously, but honestly ask yourself which one is more likely, or, if you're not sure, ask your partner or family for their comment ... and then give them heaps if they don't give you the answer you want!

OPTION A—AGGRESSIVE

If this is your style you're more likely to have kids who operate the same way, so expect lots of power struggles. Most behaviour is caught rather than taught so the kids would catch the idea that toe-to-toe is the way to go.

OPTION B—ASSERTIVE

If this is your style then the kids would again follow suit. That probably means they won't be too timid to say what they think, they will assert their point of view (commonly called arguing), but it's the style that probably gains most cooperation.

OPTION C—SUBMISSIVE

If this is your style then the kids will sense a leadership vacuum at the top and fill it in as they see fit. They won't need to argue, they just won't do what you ask. Because you lack respect for yourself then so will they. On the other hand if they identify with you, then they will become submissive too.

OPTION D—GUILTY

If this is your style the kids will be quick to exploit it. Every request will be thrown back on you till you feel that you are to blame, if it's not one thing it's a mother! These kids will be more interested in power than protest but either way the parent has lost power.

Classic Management Styles

Whatever your personal style every parent seems blessed with a range of instinctive tactics that are guaranteed to make the job harder. Tactics that make us wear the problem more than the kids do. Just for the fun of it see if you can see yourself in any of these 'parent wear-it-all' management styles.

1. DENIAL

Some parents use denial as their staple discipline tool to manage their kids. They say 'NO' to the kids to show their power and then give in to show their compassion.
'No you can't, ask me once more and you'll go to your room.'
'But Mummy, Mummy, can I, can I?'
'Oh all right,' says the loving parent, 'just this once and no more.'
Kids are quick learners so guess what will be their top tactic next time ...

2. INTELLECTUALISATION

Some parents go to their grave believing that kids are rational, reasonable creatures. The typical effort at intellectualising might go something like this: 'I'll explain again why Mummy and Daddy don't like you poking your sister in the eye.' Kids quite like not only the poke but the attention it received so they will repeat the behaviour. With young kids, words have little impact on behaviour, and with older kids, unless they are linked to consequences, words won't be heard.

Always give children a reason for your punishment, especially if you've thought of one in time.

3. INQUISITION
This is a technique loathed by adolescents, not just because we're trying to run their life, but because we know the answers before we've asked the question—'Whose shoes are these in the lounge room?' It's seen as a power game and is one of the reasons we are developing a generation of 'I dunnos'—they're asked an idiotic question so they learn an idiotic answer.

4. SATURATION
This technique uses repeated small jabs to the eardrum. It's commonly called nagging, and is used in the belief that if you gnaw away long enough the kids will do anything to relieve the pain. Homework is often a good spot to find saturation being used: 'Just get your homework out. Why have I got to tell you to get your homework out? You know you've got homework but every day it's the same thing... nag, nag, nag.' And on and on it goes. Research shows that kids switch us off in 0.5 seconds if there's nothing new in it for them.

5. MARTYRISATION
This is where parents assume that children's behaviour is ruled by moral responsibility: 'That's right, leave your clothes on the floor, off you go and play, the old slave will pick them up because that's my job isn't it.' It's almost as if we expect them to suddenly see how immoral they've been and come begging at our feet for mercy and forgiveness for being such an unprincipled and thoughtless child. It doesn't happen.

6. INCARCERATION
This is also known as grounding, and is intended to slow the kids down till parents can catch up. It's useful for tired kids and attention seekers. It doesn't work if it's done in extreme anger or if it lasts for hours, days, weeks or months. And the other problem is, once they're grounded, how do you police it and how do you stop them making their time behind bars so incredibly annoying for others that you give in anyhow?

7. SHOUTING
This works on the idea that the loudest voice contains the most truth and so everyone ups the decibels in the argument to make sure that their truth wins out. The fact is that kids will hear a whisper (and a

lolly wrapper) at 40 paces, but they won't hear a shout at two! If you're a shouter, drop it to a whisper and notice the difference in their attention (and in the general level of noise pollution around the house).

8. SMACKING

Some parents feel that a good smack never hurt them so that's the way to go—give the kids something really bad so they'll be good! They think that belting kids teaches them a lesson, but if you think about it, the lesson they are learning is that if you're stronger you use force and if you're frustrated, you hit. The problem is, as we'll see below, that smacking tends to create more problems than it solves, has some nasty side effects if it's used at all regularly, and breeds in us the idea that force is the answer to friction and frustration.

PAUL'S PUNISHMENT

My mother left when I was three. Dad tried with me but he started to lose it just by having to do it all by himself. I was shoplifting and stuff when I was at primary school, but I got caught so I gave it away till I got older, till I could do it properly.

Dad only bashed me when I deserved it. He used bits of the garden hose, but it ran out so then he used jug cords because nothing else hurt. He only ever hit me once around the head. I called his wife a slut to his face and he punched me and I hit him and he hit me. He was right to hit me for that—if one of my boys ever said that to me I'd knock him unconscious.

My mother found me in the end. I was pretty out of it when we met at the airport. We hugged. Hugging your mother for the first time when you're 18—it felt strange and good. A mother would have made a lot of difference. A father's discipline gives you something to look up to, but mothers give you love, show you how to love.

Are men meant to just be the fathers for all floggings and women the mothers for all meaningfuls? And did Paul learn discipline from Dad or was it how to hurt when you punish? In spite of all his dad's strength, and all of his punishment, it was only when a parent used their arms in affection, not aggression, that Paul learnt his lesson.

Paul's is a sad story but such a powerful one. Although no sane parent would think of belting their kids that hard it still shows just how much kids do accept and copy. And with 95 per cent of parents reported to be smacking their kids, that's a lot of aggression being copied and continued. I recall one interesting university study that compared two groups of preschool children. One group contained parents who used smacking to 'discipline' and one group that didn't. The findings were that 100 per cent of the first group of kids were hitting other kids, compared to only 20 per cent of the other group.

Probably we all use most of the eight problem management styles sometime—sometimes simultaneously! But they're not all that clever for the simple reason that we wear the problem more than the kids do. Even if you get the techniques right the effect can still be stymied so easily. Here are a few of the little nasties that need to be mentioned if we're going to be able to get any warranty on their behaviour:

ACCIDENTAL REWARDING OF MISBEHAVIOUR
This can happen through the attention the behaviour gets, or if, for example, they've stolen, the goodies they gain may outscore the punishment.

MISMATCH OF WORD AND ACTION
Sometimes what we are trying to teach may be undermined by what we do or what their friends or siblings might do. Children may not listen to our best advice but they will tend to copy the worst.

FORGETTING TO REWARD GOOD BEHAVIOUR
This means it is less likely to be repeated.

BAD COMMUNICATIONS
Too many, too bossy, too hard, too long, too vague, too angry or bad timing are all likely to spoil your efforts at discipline.

The 10 Rules of Effective Punishment

Children need punishment to steer their behaviour, and they need encouragement even more. Below are 10 ways to punish effectively, without raising your hand or your voice.

1. **Aim your punishment at the action**, not the ego.
2. Make it **logical**—if they can't be home at the time they promised then they're not ready for the freedom of unsupervised time.
3. Make it **sensible**—a list of jobs on the fridge might save some silly punishment when you're angry and help your workload too.
4. Make it **inescapable**—con merchants are bred in watery rules. If the punishment seems too hard after you've cooled down then soften, but don't disobey yourself.
5. Make it **noticeable**—some families become so negative that an extra punishment isn't noticed.
6. Make it **acceptable**—if rules and penalties are clear and fair then the kids are more likely to accept the consequences.
7. Make it **respectful**—insulting or bashing just makes them think about revenge not remedy.
8. Make it **consistent**—as the ancient Greek author, Plutarch, said, 'perseverance is more prevailing than violence'.
9. Make it **reasonable**—give a reason and sometimes maybe even give a bit of choice on when and how they're going to fix things up.
10. Make it **private**—public punishment hits the ego not the action and they'll hit back to save face.

Just remember that discipline is not punishment. Discipline refers to the rules, the code of conduct. It's taught and it's caught. It's caught by copying and it's taught by *encouraging* behaviour you like and *discouraging* (punishing) behaviour you don't. But we're all egomaniacs, we learn much more from praise than punishment, so as a general rule try to keep the ratio of positives to negatives about nine to one. If you don't believe how much more kids respond to praise than punishment, spend the day encouraging your kids for every little thing they do right rather than pouncing on them for everything they do wrong and notice the difference.

But let me share Rhonda's letter just to show how easily punishment-based management can descend into something quite scary.

MANAGEMENT INSTRUCTIONS

Dear Dr John,
We have a three-and-a-half-year-old I just can't stand. Ben had open heart surgery as a baby but recovered beautifully. Then at 20 months, just before my second child was born, he changed. Even if I smack or yell or hit him with the wooden spoon he just looks at me as if to say, 'Who the hell do you think you are, telling me what to do?'

I hate him. Even when I go to pick him up, I find my fingernails digging in to hurt him. Have you come across this before? What can I do about it before it's too late?
Yours,
Kaelene

Kaelene, hating your own kid is a sign of real stress; having the courage to ask for help is a sign of real love. Probably the early heart scare made you idealise the little fella. Then at 20 months when he found his ego you lost yours. With number two due you were probably exhausted just at the time Ben needed you at your bounciest best. Then you disappeared from his life and brought back a newer nicer model.

Join a playgroup (your local Community Information Services will have a number to contact), and maybe link into a parent-toddler group through your local health centre straightaway. If none are available then catch up with a local child psychologist, get your husband to become a leading light in Ben's life, get some time away from the kids, and then focus on all the big beaut things he can do and you'll get more of them.

Often the hate we harbour for others is the reflection of failure we feel in ourselves. Kaelene, you haven't failed, you're fallible that's all. Now you've asked for help be just as determined to get it.

Alternatives to Smacking

I've yet to meet a parent who *wants* to hit their kids. According to Stephen Juan in his book *Only Human*, there are a number of unpleasant and unwanted follow-on effects of smacking. These include anger, aggression, suicide, delinquency, low self-esteem, poor relationships, and drug and alcohol abuse.

An American book, *Redirecting Children's Behaviour*, offers nine alternatives to smacking. These are listed below.

1. **Get calm**. If you feel out of control, either leave the scene or suck deep breaths as if you were on mental marijuana.
2. **Take time for yourself**. If you're angry then walk away till you've worked out how you want to handle it.
3. **Be kind but firm**. Instead of raising your hand, drop your body down to Sandy's level and then gently, but firmly, get your message easy over, that hitting hurts and he has to make it better.
4. **Give choices**. Maybe try just two—he can either go to time out or he can say he's sorry to the other boy.
5. **Use logical consequences**. For example, if he hit the other child with a toy, then that toy goes away until he knows how to use it.
6. **Do Make Ups**. Instead of smacking, give the kids some jobs they can do to make the other kid feel better and get back into your good books.
7. **Withdraw from conflict**. Once the course of action is determined there is no argument. If he starts to argue, either walk away yourself or send him to some time out to cool off.
8. **Use a firm hand**, not to hit, but to take Sandy by the hand and firmly make sure he does or goes where you indicated.
9. **Give forewarning**. If you see the behaviour heading for danger, use a special signal you've practised to stop the action.

I smacked my kids occasionally, out of frustration, when I was tired, when nothing else seemed to work. I don't think it did permanent damage—they still see me as fairly harmless actually—but it certainly didn't do any good either. Probably in small doses and with lots of love and fun and good times thrown in it does little harm but the message has to be that we need to find other ways to control our kids. And as Steve Biddulph (author of *Raising Boys*) points out, it isn't fair.

> Like every parent I learn as I go along. For instance, I used to believe in 'quality time' and now I think that is a big cop-out. Kids need *quantity* time too. I am proud that I do spend lots of time with my children, and they know I love them. When my son was two I decided never again to hit or smack, that as a big strong man I had no place hitting small and defenceless children, and I have never done so since. We made a Men's Declaration for NAPCAN and it takes the form of a promise: 'I will not harm or intimidate a child.'
>
> Steve Biddulph

SMACKING PREVENTION

The following ideas can also be used to prevent smacking.

1. **Stay in close contact with your kids**.
   The best way to avoid the need to smack is to be in close contact with our kids so that we don't have the need to hit across the gap between us. A very recent study has found that parents who worked on good communication and close contact with their kids in the very early years tended to have good kids. On the other hand, parents who used force, threats and smacking on kids had more problem behaviour four-year-olds; kids lived *down* to expectations.

2. **Use the tribe**.
   It's pretty hard to stay in close contact with your kids when you're tired, frustrated, sick of their whingeing and fed up with their fighting. That's where we need the tribe, as Pat O'Shane reminds us in the Introduction, to give us support, reassurance and time off.

3. **Take it a day at a time**.
   We have to stop taking kids' problems so seriously. Life is a struggle, we do worry about how we'll cope but the good thing about the future is that it comes one day at a time. That has to be our focus, and if we can make the most of each one then the rest will have to look after themselves. Life is a mystery to be lived not a problem to be solved. ALL kids will test parents, that's their job, they have to manipulate us to survive. Our job is not to take the test trials too seriously, the kids don't. We may not be able to control kids as well as we'd like but it is our choice as to whether we'll treat their challenges as playfare or warfare.

4. **Try some of the ideas outlined this this book.**
   Believe it or not there are hundreds of ways we can punish kids without having to raise our hand or our voice, or engaging in hand-to-backside combat. Every time we say NO to kids, every time we ignore them, every time we give them the hairy eyebrow, we're in fact punishing our kids.
5. **But if you're too angry to think, then before you do anything else, turn to the Appendix, and read the Angry Parents' First Aid Guide (page 363).**
   Tear it out and hang it somewhere near the phone so it's handy when you're tempted to use your hand. Remember, your child will be all right if you're all right, so look after yourself first.

Ages and Stages of Learning

If we understand *how* kids learn behaviour then we can work out effective ways of changing their behaviour.

Here are some guidelines on how children's behaviour is modified.

BABIES

Babies learn by sense and feel. Cuddling, talking, holding, stroking, singing, praising all register and will reinforce whatever behaviour preceded it. If a reward meets a child's need at that time it will reinforce the commitment to the person who initiated it. On the other hand, a sharp no, no attention, a sad face, a stern voice or a hairy eyebrow will weaken that behaviour.

TODDLERS

This special little period is a testing one for parents because children are finding their own ego. They quickly learn to do those behaviours that feed their ego and not do those that don't and this is why they will deliberately repeat annoying actions—the negative attention makes them feel powerful and independent. They will deliberately not do poos on demand or eat on demand because that puts them in control.

TWO TO FOUR

This is the egocentric learner in full flight. They can now store memories and images in their minds, so they like to role play, act out, act powerful, experiment, test and generally just check out how powerful this new creature really is. The terrible twos are the result of this need to ego-satisfy and many parents mistakenly believe that their child is personally rejecting them.

Because of their inflated ego they respond to being told how big they're getting and how good they're getting. This can also work to your advantage because every time you reward them for doing the right thing, it makes them feel good, up jumps their ego and they'll do more of it—not out of love for you, but out of love for themselves! At this stage anything involving their ego or their imagination will work wonders. But their world is immediate, so if they're to be rewarded or punished it must be as close as possible to the action so they link the two together. Waiting is one of the things they need to learn but start it in small chunks they understand, eg when the oven timer goes.

FIVE TO SIX

These kids still have their lovely imagination but their ego has settled and they're now keen to make others feel good. If you capitalise on their thirst to be told they're good then you can develop the most adorable kids. Their behaviour can be reinforced even by abstract symbols of parental approval, such as stars and charts, and their behaviour can be shaped by consistently reinforcing behaviour you want and consistently punishing behaviour you don't. Because they believe in their world, things that shatter that faith hurt hard. If a dog is nasty to them or somebody hurts them then they can wear the scars for a long time.

SEVEN TO ELEVEN

This is the age at which kids start to think logically, so logical natural consequences are the best teacher. It's also the age at which their brains can handle add-ups and take-aways, and where they can see things from other points of view. Reasoning can be used to some effect, but bear in mind that their reasoning may not agree with yours. As they get older and their mind starts to manage their behaviour, so the management of their behaviour has to make sense to their mind. Their mind has to be engaged with reality-type choices and options, eg 'If you help me then I'll have time to read you a story, but if you don't then we won't be able to.' Charts are still useful but at this stage a significant shift is occurring; what parents say matters less and less, what their mates say or think matters more and more. Rewards and punishments that take into account that they have a capable brain that needs respect and which acknowledges their peer approval need will be most effective.

Because they have good logical brains, they can be involved in setting up the rules. Involve them, consult them and respect them, and deliver logical consequences, good or bad depending on how they've handled their own rules. It's very hard for kids to disobey their own rules.

TEENAGERS

Physically, socially, sexually and psychologically the teenage years are a time of enormous change. Parents tend to get left way behind as a reference group as teens struggle to find their life membership with their peer group. This means behaviour, attitudes, values and clothes must pay homage to peer values which more often than not clash with parents'. Children see themselves as young adults and the old management techniques of power, control and coercion no longer work. At this age their management has to respect their self-image as young adults and must involve communication, negotiation, respect, responsibility, trust and all the other principles we would use with other adults. It does not mean that parents should just give up or give in, teenagers are adaptable and can adapt to our values and standards if these are seen as being consistent, authentic and which we stand for rather than making them bow down to.

Parental Depression and Anger

DEPRESSION

It's so easy to get depressed when you look at all you have to do, the never-ending nature of the work, the lack of support, the lack of gratitude, the feeling of being trapped and not in control of your own life any more. Dorothy Rowe, author of *The Depression Handbook*, says that parents try so hard to please that they start to think they're only good if they're pleasing others. When it all gets too much they hide in their prison as a safe refuge from all the forces that threaten to destroy them. Once inside it's even more scary because they're not only the prisoner, but they're also the jailer, punishing themselves for being bad and causing the problem.

The first step out of the depths is simply to reach out as far as a friend or phone. For those parents constantly struggling with depression, here's a self-survival guide.

- Immediately get a good eating and exercise program.
- Get a full medical check-up in case there are physical, biochemical or hormonal factors at work.
- Contact the local health centre as most communities are now running very effective depression management groups.
- Do some urgent rethinking. Rowe suggests that when we feel we're falling apart it's *not* us that is but our conclusions about life. We feel that we should be rewarded for good and punished for bad. Once we can accept that that's not how this world operates then we're on the way to a healthier frame of mind.
- Another way to fight a way out of the pit is to decide to act 'as if' we accept ourselves, warts and all, because then we have the right to exist and to be treated with respect. That means we will no longer accept disgraceful behaviour from our nearest and dearest and we'll start to notice now that other people do not despise us as we once despised ourselves.

Here are 12 decisions to help you beat depression.
1. Because I accept and value myself I will end my loneliness.
2. I shall take the risk of approaching other people.
3. I don't expect instant results.
4. I will be interested in other people.
5. I will improve my skills in listening and asking questions.
6. I will become skilled at seeing things from other people's point of view.
7. I will try to improve my understanding of the consequences of my behaviour.
8. I will be more accepting of other people's anger and not take it personally.
9. I will improve my skills in distinguishing real and imaginary enemies.
10. I will learn how to receive graciously.
11. I will let go of envy and allow myself to be sad.
12. I will learn to share my sadness with others and to share their sadness.

The depth of our depression is often a measure of the size of the gap between our expectations and reality. It's worth remembering that in the long run the kids won't remember what or how much we did for them but they will remember how we felt on the way.

ANGER

If you feel that anger is more your problem than depression then here are a few suggestions. Work on where the anger is coming from—in busy families the anger is often angled outwards from the feeling of being trapped! Housework, homework, spouse-work, work-work can make us feel cornered and caged. So here's a seven-point plan out of anger for working parents.

1. Stop thinking of yourself as trapped. Work out freedoms you do have or could have and ways to make sure you will have.
2. Set some goals. How would you like to see yourself and your family five years from now?
3. Remember that anger is often emotional energy unearthed. Give the hugs you would like to get back and there's every chance the family will respond.
4. Don't try to be the perfect parent. For instance if you're busy don't try to be the best cooker and cleaner in town. Stick to a repertoire of about 10 standard meals that you do well and the kids love.
5. Don't expect your family to help. Train them to help! Work out with them what each can do in terms of time and talents, teach them how, hug the helpers and pull out of any favours for the shirkers.
6. Give yourself some quiet child-free time at night.
7. If you have a partner, make sure you get some time alone together.

Balanced Management

Not only do we want to avoid depression and anger and not hurt our kids—we actually want to enjoy having them. What's needed is not the child-centred model nor the parent-centred model, it's the balanced model. A *balanced model* gives us the chance to parent the way we'd prefer to, it injects peace and fun into our parenting, makes kids so much easier to handle and the role so much more satisfying. Picture your kids or Sandy in the centre of a love triangle—all parts of which we have the capacity to deliver.

PARENT ROLE

At the apex is the parent part of our personality. This is the protective part that watches and worries over the kids' day-to-day survival—what they eat, wear, say, moan and groan about, who they play with, how they're going at school, and how happy they are. This part demands much and depletes much of our emotional energy, day in and night out. This is the part that nurtures, but the role becomes very hard if the parents have not been nurtured themselves or if they haven't had good role models to show them how. This is the part of the personality that is trying to guide the kids in their journey forward. It's the part that all the management ideas in this book rely on for delivery.

ADULT ROLE

On the left base angle is the adult part of our personality. This is the part of the love triangle that provides the sense of self and of peace. It works on replenishing the system with soul food—through prayer, meditation, yoga, music, art, waves, tea leaves or whatever form the parent finds their inner peace. Without this dimension being cared for we are angry adults unable to cope with the crises that sometimes face us in parenting. This sense of peace is something children can't give us, it's our own voyage inwards to our inner self. If this part is in harmony it is the part of our personality that is very attractive to other adults and to children. If you feel this part is undernourished read Louise Hay's *You Can Heal Your Life* and the sequel *The Power is Within*, Maureen Garth's book *The Power of the Inner Self* or talk to a person who is making that journey and find out what has helped them along the way.

CHILD ROLE

On the right base angle is the child part of our personality. This is the playful, funful, risk-taking part of our nature, the part that gives us energy to manage our kids the way they like; it helps us to use playfare rather than warfare as our management style. To satisfy this need, we must make the journey backwards to our childhood, to find, accept (heal, if necessary), enjoy, relive and remember and then share the ageless child within each of us. If the child is alive and well within us then play is never far away, no matter how serious the situation. It's the part we must be in touch with if we want to stay in touch with our kids and if we want to handle their problems with optimism and energy. Play also involves exercise, which is the best possible protector against stress, exhaustion and disease. It's also the part of our personality that kids love best. It knows no generation gap. If our 'child' is nurtured, it can nurture a happy, healthy childhood in our kids.

The advice given in this book relies upon this model of balanced management. None of us achieves the best balance, but it is that search that allows us, not only to manage our kids well, but to make our own journey towards understanding ourselves.

Now we're armed with a few principles and one Sandy, let's see if they help us get our kids into good shape without having to belt them into shape. I'll try to tackle it top-to-toe.

FAMOUS FOOTNOTE

A PUBLIC HIGH-PROFILE FAMILY

John Howard

POLITICIAN and 1997 FATHER OF THE YEAR

When Janette and I first discussed the realities of a political career and the possible effects on our family, we resolved that the most important consideration was to provide a stable and loving environment for our children.

In our case Janette chose to stay at home full-time with our children when they were young. This has been a decision that has worked well for our family and a tribute to my wife who is largely responsible for the three young adults who are proudly our children today.

Keeping close contact with the family when I am away is important to me. I often recall the advice given to me as a new Member of Parliament by Peter Nixon, a former Minister in the Fraser government. Speaking of the importance of the family, he said, 'Stay in touch every day and if you say you'll be home for something, be there.'

I am sure that anyone who has a job that takes them away from their family would agree that one of the highlights of the day is that phone call or two to the family to catch up on their day. It is important for families to share their triumphs and challenges. That means staying in touch. Sometimes, especially in public life, members of your family are the best people to trust, giving an honest opinion, no matter how difficult.

Weekends have always been a special time for our family, where we are able to spend some time together, and I look forward to football or cricket matches on a Saturday where we join the other parents on the sidelines, lending support to the children and their teams.

We are a close family, we share things and we talk about things. Politics is such an all-consuming thing for a family, we have also shared the successes and the challenges of my political career. Some of the hardest times for Janette and me as parents were to see our children disturbed by the publicity surrounding me during the difficult times, but as a family, we have always discussed the issues and got through them together.

Very often the hard times begin to look like the good times because they are the times that people who love each other really pull together. Most parents find that their children do get caught up in their challenges or problems. This is inevitable, naturally children do worry about their parents—probably more than many parents realise, and more than some parents deserve. As parents we all have to watch this and make sure that our children know that we value their love, help and concern.

I believe that bringing up children is the most important thing most people do in their lives and nothing replaces time spent with your children. Encourage them in their endeavours, cheering their successes, giving them your shoulder when they don't succeed. We have always been part of our children's lives and they have been part of ours.

Good parents teach their children the values they will live by. This might be ordinary things like the value of work, earning a living, preparing for the future, managing what they have and sharing it when they can, and facing reality front-on in the good times and the bad. For example, we have encouraged our children to have some degree of self-sufficiency that comes with earning their own pocket money through after-school jobs and I know that they have learned through this.

There is probably only one thing more important than teaching your children and that is learning from them. A great many of the valuable lessons that I have learnt in the past 23 years have come simply from talking to my children and watching them grow. You must always take the time to talk, no matter how busy you are.

CHAPTER TWO

Up-Top Problems

I always say you have to learn to love the hills because I loved them. My nickname was Janine the Machine. People used to laugh about it because I was a tough little nut, I always trained really hard and the results did pay off. I believe you not only have to take on the hills but you have to learn to love them because that's what makes a difference.

JANINE SHEPHERD, athlete, author and pilot
[READ MORE OF JANINE'S GRITTY STORY AT THE END OF THIS CHAPTER.]

Everyone worries about 'Up-Top' problems: 'he's ten cents short of a dollar', 'he's as thick as two planks, and they're both warped anyhow', 'off with the fairies', 'schizo', 'psycho' and 'got a few kangaroos loose in the top paddock'. And some parents and peers have special labels for kids with these problems. The labels named by the kids as the ones that hurt most included dumb, idiot, stupid, lamebrain, cretin, brainless, useless, dork and peabrain.

Sandy had several 'Up-Top' problems that his parents found hard to handle:
- sadness and depression
- panic and worry (eighth highest overall)
- stubbornness—thinks they're always right
- self-centred
- obsessive and perfectionist

Depression

Depressed kids are depressing! There's no other word for it. Nothing you promise, no treats you deliver, no holiday you take them on, nothing seems to make any difference. It's usually linked with self-esteem (which I've tackled as a problem of the heart in Chapter Seven). It's becoming a bigger and bigger issue with kids who find little to latch them into life.

CHECKS

- **Symptom Check**
  If Sandy's showing signs of more than six of the following symptoms then chances are that he's depressed and in need of an urgent psychological lift.
  - worries a lot
  - feels worthless
  - seems and looks sad
  - talks about killing himself/herself
  - sulks a lot
  - cries a lot
  - needs to be perfect
  - tries to hurt himself/herself
  - anxious about everything
  - feels no-one loves him/her
  - feels everyone picks on him/her
  - feels guilty about everything
  - very self-conscious
  - worries that he/she might do something bad
  - lonely and feels he/she has no friends
  - very nervous

- **Medical Check**
  Get sad kids fully checked out medically as there could be a number of things depressing their systems—anaemia, thyroid, glandular fever, allergies or food intolerances ... anything which makes them feel off the pace or not coping.

✻ Perception Check
Check them out through the eyes of others who know them well and know how they behave away from home (eg teacher or grandparent). If the symptoms shrink away from home then a thorough check by a psychologist may be all that's needed.

✻ Situational Check
If the depression is *all the time* then a psychological check-up is needed. If it's *just after exertion* (exercise, game, sport, playgroup, full day at preschool, etc) then a medical check is needed. If it's *after school* then an educational check is needed. If it's *just at home* then a marital and parent depression check is needed. If it's *just before meals* then it may be blood sugars are down and the answer may be having healthy snack food easily available. If it's *just when brothers and sisters are around* then it's quaintly called sibling rivalry.

✻ Home Tone Check
Check out the home tone. From my clinic experience the more common depressors are divorce, fighting, no time with favourite parent, new baby, favouritism, parents too busy, or 'special' brother or sister.

DO'S AND DON'TS

✻ With little kids
- Use your body language to convey the feelings that you care, you love them, you want to listen, and that there's no problem that Mum's or Dad's strong, loving arms can't fix.
- Let them talk if they want to about things that make them sad, but don't put words in their head.
- If it's just an attention-seeking habit then don't use sad behaviour to attract extra attention.
- Suggest that their teary sad behaviour is because their battery is run down and they can have a rest in their room until they feel strong and happy again.

✷ With older kids

Often depressed kids fall into two categories—verbal downers and visual downers.

Verbal downers

These are older kids who talk their way down to depression. In this case you can use the 'Magic Macaroni Tin'.

MAGIC MACARONI TIN

Get some tube macaroni, put them in a special tin and place beside the bed. When family or close friends stay over, get them to write on a thin slip of paper one thing they like about Sandy. Each thought is placed inside a different piece of macaroni so when the kids are 'down' they go to their magic macaroni tin, unravel a few, read the messages and get the lift and the memory to shift their mood.

If they feel that wouldn't work then work out with them good thoughts to intercept the nosedive and make a bit of a game of working out which ones work. In other words keep them on the job helping to solve *their* problem.

Visual downers

- These kids can see the whole thing unfolding as a catastrophe. If that's their style then that's how we need to intercept it too.
- Help them to think about an image or action that intervenes and stops the catastrophic nosedive.
- If they say that they can't, then try to challenge them with this thought—'Just as your mind is so clever that it can create the problem, so, too, if we work hard enough on it we can make up the image to beat it.'
- Some kids enjoy that challenge, but if they don't then it may be they need to talk about what they will do. It is *their* problem and it's only by *their* success that they get the lift out of the depression.

✷ Parental depression

If this is the problem then that's the urgent priority. See suggestions on page 24. It's hard to give kids a sense of fun and optimism when it's just not there.

Kids won't remember all we did for them as they were growing up, they will remember how we felt on the way.

Maybe the best way to beat the blues is to change the colour of your glasses.

UNTYING THE KNOT

Peter's parents broke up. His mum got custody and got depressed, his dad got mad and got out, and Peter, as you could guess, got both mad and depressed and got the tummy aches that wore his inner pain. Later on, Dad and his new partner asked to have Peter for the holidays. Many solicitor bills later it happened, it worked well and Peter asked his mum if he could stay. Mum threatened to get rid of his dog, Sally, if he didn't come back. So back came the tummies, tears and even suicide threats.

Fortunately, his step-mum stepped in. She got a stay of execution on the grounds of intestinal insanity and got a few things started with him. Peter was feeling much better and asked me to share with other kids the tactics that worked for him.

For mild tummies, he recommends the 'falling leaves' method. Get the uptight kids to imagine a desk diary page dated one floating down to the bottom of the tummy, then number two, then number three—a bit like sheep over the fence but these land on tight muscles.

If it's a tough tummy, Pete says to get them to imagine and build up one fantastic peaceful scene in their mind then fly into it till they feel more relaxed.

Then for night-time tums he says to use one of those lavender-laced heated seed pillows or get Dad to record some stories the kids like onto a cassette—reckons that was the best fix of all.

Divorce, badly handled, doesn't really untie the knot, it just shifts it.

Bush Remedies

- We would only ever buy chocolates when one of us was down. It sounds silly, but as long as we didn't eat too much, it was a little lift that we could look forward to on a bad day.

- I think a lot of depression comes from parents expecting kids to be perfect, maybe because they haven't got the time to fix things if they're not. We weren't perfect so why should they be? I think our job is to find something special to love even if the child is difficult, and surely that's not too hard.

- When they're sad we talk about how cute they were when they were born, how loved and wanted they are, and the funny faces they'd pull. Things like reminiscing really crack the face up from a frown and would often end up with us all breaking out into uncontrollable laughter.

- Uncle Pete died and then Snoopy, Nan's dog, died. We talked about how old things die and I told Taylor (aged four) that Uncle Pete and Snoopy were in heaven and still watched her and still loved her and that she could talk to them, cuddle them and play with them in her dreams. I told her that she could see them watching from heaven, and that they looked like stars as they were so far away. She is happy with this and can now talk easily about people dying without getting upset.

- When my kids are sad I just give lots of cuddles and talk to them but most of the time I just listen. That's all they want most of the time, just someone to know how they feel, then things seem to be a lot better.

- I realised part of her depression was my doing as I really went down after my husband went off with a younger version. So I decided to do something about it. We worked out that we both liked dancing so we've both started (in different groups of course). It's made us both feel better.

Anxiety and Worry

Anxiety is reaching epidemic proportions in our community and it's catching—I seem to be treating more anxiety problems in kids now than ever before. Maybe the weakening of our social glue (families and communities) is making kids feel more isolated and less secure, or maybe it's the level of fear in the community. But whatever the reason, it's a worried world we live in and the kids know it and show it.

CHECKS

* **Symptom Check**

    Use this symptom checklist as a guide to the level and extent of their anxiety.
    - dry mouth and swallowing difficulty or hoarseness
    - rapid breathing and heartbeat
    - twitching or trembling
    - muscle tension and headache
    - appetite changes
    - sweating
    - nausea, diarrhoea and weight loss
    - sleeplessness
    - hyperventilation
    - irritability
    - fatigue
    - nightmares
    - frequent urination
    - memory problems
    - constant seeking of attention and reassurance

* **Self Check**

    Check out your own anxieties, as kids soak up the atmosphere and tend to copy. I'm prepared to guarantee that there's at least one worrying adult if the kids are worriers.

* **Situation Check**

    Check when and where their worries are at their worst. If you can get a pattern then you can work out counter moves. For instance, if they seem less worried and happiest doing ballet, then maybe it's the movement, the music or particular kids that are good for them, so cash in on that. If they're more worried before and after school then follow up that lead. If they're constantly worrying then get them checked out by their doctor in case there are medical reasons (eg lacking energy, can't keep up).

✷ Environment Check

Is the pace too fast? Is there down time for them to take stock and just be, not do? Are they being exposed to excess adult worries (news, current affairs, scary TV programs, horror videos)?

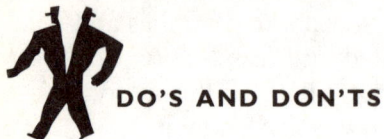

DO'S AND DON'TS

✷ Try the 'What If' Worry-Winning Game

'WHAT IF' WORRY-WINNING GAME

- ◆ Kids work out ways to handle some of their fears so they become winners—eg What if a bully was to say he'd get you after school? etc.
- ◆ When they've come up with possibilities, you add a few of yours.
- ◆ They choose the best that suit their circumstances. This game builds up the feeling that it is worth sharing their worry, and that a worry shared is a worry spared.

In other words they become what Stephen Covey (author of *7 Habits of Highly Effective Families*) calls 'inside out' kids rather than 'outside in' kids; that is, they make the move and they force the outcome rather than hopelessly and anxiously waiting for the fickle finger of fate to crook her digit.

✷ Play the 'As If' Game

'AS IF' GAME

For the kids who feel trapped by worry sometimes I'll ask them to act as if they were one of their friends who is very confident and notice the difference. Or if they're animal lovers, I might ask them to feel like their favourite animal.

- **Use the bit-by-bit 'desensitising' technique**
  If, for instance, they're worried about sleeping with the light off, then start with a lower wattage light in their bedside light, then they might be ready for a passage light or a night light or just the bathroom light. Many fears are beaten this 'bit at a time' way.

- **Use Charts (see Appendix)**
  The charts are a way of recording the child's worry-beating progress but they're not much use below four years or over 10. For the littlies, use hugs, kisses, comments of approval and letting them know how *big* they're getting.

- **Have fun with the Worry-Winning Ladder**

G·A·M·E·S

WORRY-WINNING LADDER

- Kids list or tell you all their worries.
- These are each rated out of 10 by the worrier, with highest scores being the biggest fears.
- The fears are then arranged on a ladder with the lowest-scored worries on the bottom rung. (Make sure that the lowest is such a little worry that they can't help but succeed.)
- The kids work their way up, but they need some worry-beating aid to make it easier (worry dolls, squeeze ball, images, power stone, etc).
- If any step is too hard break it down into smaller steps so again success is ensured.

- **Watch your body language**
  Be reassuring. That sounds easy but kids read our body easier than our lips. The words might be saying 'it's okay' but the shoulders and eyes might be saying, 'What a wimp you are, you're just like your father!' If you try pushing square pegs into round holes you're bound to produce a misfit.

✷ Some kids are Word Worriers

They think their way with words down to disaster. This needs to be met with 'Word Lifters'.

WORD LIFTERS

- Help them find some signal that they're going down the worry road (eg starting to think a bad thing about themselves).
- Call a stop to that angle.
- Find some other way of thinking about it so it shifts their expectation from negative to positive (eg because the last thing that happened was bad now I must look out for the next good thing that happens to balance it).
- Reinforce how clever they are if they manage the shift, or help them with ideas if they can't.

✷ Some kids are Imagination Worriers

They can see the disaster in their mind's eye.
- These kids need to construct counter images that are much more friendly than their worst vision.
- With the help of your own childish imagination you can help them visualise a better image to replace the worrying one.
- Practise and practise this new image until it is powerful and comfortable.
- Then, when they're ready, call up the nasty one and see if they can switch to the new one, which may be a whole different image or a different ending.
- This technique can be used to remedy bad dreams too.

✷ Try using muscle relaxation

- Hands and arms—get them to pretend to be squeezing an orange. When it's all squeezed out they let it drop and let their muscles relax.
- Arms and shoulders—get them to pretend they are a cuddly cat that's stretching, raising their arms high over their head, back to their side, out in front, up to the ceiling, and finally dropping down by their side.

- Shoulders—let them pretend they are a turtle sensing danger, pulling their head in tight into their shoulders, right up to their ears if they can. When the danger passes they relax and come back out into the warm sunshine.
- Jaw—let them pretend they have a hard caramel in their mouth. They bite down on it hard and then let their jaw relax. Repeat.
- Face and nose—let them pretend an annoying fly lands on their nose and they have to get him off by wriggling and wrinkling their nose. He flies away but comes back so they repeat it.
- Stomach—my favourite here is to let them imagine that the muscles in their tummy are all gnarled and knotted like the roots of a tree. Then they imagine little leaves falling to the bottom of their tummy, one at a time, gently landing, and each one unknots the muscles a bit. Sometimes I might get them to feel that someone is about to walk on their tummy first, so their muscles are tensed up ready.
- Legs and feet—let them pretend to push their toes down into soft mud that's oozing around. They push down, spread their toes, then they step out and relax, then back they go again.

Other ways for kids to relax are listed below
Just get to know what works for your family.
- Sharing and cuddling around a storybook.
- Repeatedly throwing a ball against a wall.
- Playing with pets.
- Taking a walk.
- Spending time in private space such as a cubby or room.
- Daydreaming.

Try breathing relaxation
Use a bubble wand (teach the kids to take deep breaths and breathe slowly into the wand to make the world's biggest bubble) or blow a tissue held in front of their face till it's horizontal and they can see your face. Sometimes I'll get the kids to breathe in through one nostril (usually the dominant one even though they don't know they have such a thing) and breathe out the other to encourage deep breathing, relaxation and to settle mind panic.

✸ Try water relaxation

Most kids love water to unwind their little systems. If that's what they like then maybe have a special relaxation bath. That might include bubbles, soft music (but no electric cords in reach), and a plug-in night light, so they can lie still and soak up the ambience of music and dim lights. Of course parents can try the same thing, but it doesn't always work out the way you intended!

BATH BLITZED

Tracey has one hectic household, so on Anzac Day, when her husband was working and all five kids were frollicking with friends, she decided that this was the time to take a well-earned bubble bath.

While she was having this heavenly hiatus in her hectic day, suddenly 12 kids burst into her bathroom with her third child, Michael, holding his head, which was bleeding from a friend-inflicted flesh wound. Tracey snatched at a towel and with one hand clutched onto her modesty while with the other she washed Michael's mess into her beaut bubble bath. Then in raced the friend's dad (having heard of the horror) and he caught Tracey still towelled up with nowhere to hide. Apologising profusely, the neighbour took over the first aid in a now overcrowded bathroom while Tracey dived for her dignity.

Tracey recovered, her son recovered and it was a lot funnier in the retelling than it was at the time. Kids often do the unexpected. If we can accept the unexpected, expect the unchangeable and respect the rare easy times in between, then we can cope with kids.

✸ Try music relaxation

Make your own relaxation tape of music that makes them feel good. Some go for nature sounds, some just like their favourites and some families use composers such as Bach, Grieg, Mozart, Vivaldi and Pachelbel to help settle restless kids.

✻ Try the 'Worry-Unloading' Game

> ### GAMES
>
> #### 'WORRY-UNLOADING' GAME
>
> Have a special drawer in some little keepsake or jewellery box, which you mark 'Give it a Rest' drawer. Before bedtime, let Sandy draw or write what's worrying him and then put it in the drawer for thinking about the next day, not then. I use those little worry dolls or guardian angels the same way. I give each a name and a job (like making sure Mum doesn't die or whatever else they're worried about), stand the dolls on Blu-Tack on their dressing table and each doll carries special worries.

✻ Have a calming corner somewhere out of the way

It must be a corner with no noise or interruptions where *anyone* can go when stressed, to listen to soft music, read a book or magazine, do a puzzle, brush hair, or anything to help them unwind on their own.

✻ Try a worry burner

For a bit of reverse psychology on uptight kids needing a tension reliever use an energy outlet such as the rhythm of the trampoline or just let them burn it off somewhere safe like a park or beach.

✻ Play the 'Face Lifter'

> ### GAMES
>
> #### FACE LIFTER
>
> You probably know that if you're down or worried, one technique that works is to just lift the corners of your mouth into a smile. The brain can't tell what's fake and what's fact. The 'Face Lifter' is a clock-type chart on their wall with the hands pointing to one of six faces—happy, sad, angry, worried, peaceful and thoughtful. Train them to pick the face they'd like or if they come out with the wrong one on their dial then send them back in for a face lift.

✻ **For younger kids who like being massaged, do the 'Weather Report Massage' on their backs.**

GAMES

WEATHER REPORT MASSAGE

◆ Firstly, snowflakes: tap fingers rapidly and lightly on the head, shoulders and back.
◆ Secondly, raindrops: tap fingertips at the same time, but a little harder than snowflakes.
◆ Then thunderclaps: with cupped hands, clap hands across back and shoulders.
◆ Now, the eye of the tornado: put your hands on their shoulders and circle your thumbs down either side of the spine and across their shoulders.
◆ Then comes the tidal wave: slide your hands in long strokes up and down their arms and across their back.
◆ Finally, the calm after the storm: rest your hands on and then above their shoulders for a few moments. Then step back.

It's easy to learn, feels good and it's one weather report that can accurately forecast a cool change.

Some kids tell me they pretend they're a tube of toothpaste and they try to squeeze all the nastiness right out the top.

Be *playful* in the way you handle it so the atmosphere as well as the message helps them to handle their anxieties. That means parents need to find fun in their own lives, taking time to play and re-energise their systems. That not only reduces their anxiety, but it helps kids find ways to handle their problems more playfully and less stressfully. The best results will come if we get the anxiety out of the air. The problem is that worry works; as one little kid said to me, 'When I worry real hard the thing I worry about never happens.' Unfortunately, as anxiety and worry are the parents of temper and disease, one day it will.

If you're not getting any worry lift then consult a clinical or child psychologist.

IMAGINATION MAGIC

Young Tahlia was one of those intelligent sensitive kids with a very vivid imagination. Her parents were wise enough to know that she should not be exposed to anything scary because she internalised it, elaborated on it and made it a monster of the mind. So they didn't let her watch the movie 'Child's Play', but her friend, Hannah, told Tahlia the plot. A Chucky doll was brought back to Australia, and its nails continued to grow. During the night it scratched Dad and Mum to pieces so the little girl fled to Aunty's and the next night she was found all scratched to pieces too.

Tahlia's mighty imagination did the rest. She could not only see this doll, she became possessed by it. She would panic if left alone, wouldn't be in her room by herself, and it got worse every night until she couldn't go into her room at all. She was so spooked by this Chucky doll that when I met her she was shaking with fear and her little eyes were sunken. Even to mention its name made her mouth quiver and she would start to get short of breath.

Her parents said they had tried reasoning, but panic and obsessions are not reasonable so no bribe or punishment would work. Too often adults forget that kids are kids. They don't reason like we do, they imagine like we don't.

I found out that Tahlia's favourite fluffy toy was Simba the lion, so we decided that Simba was the most powerful of all creatures, king of the jungle and a great Chucky chewer. Anytime Chucky or his clones appeared Tahlia would call on Simba to 'go chew Chucky' and Simba would gobble him up and grin for more. Tahlia's magic mind could see this; we practised the combination of Simba and the hated doll word a few times till Simba was deadening her pain.

The message to be gained from this story is to keep an eye on what they see, an ear on what they say, and a lap for what they fear. Remember that to a child who lives in fear, everything rustles.

Bush Remedies

- We bought a set of worry dolls in a tiny case. Kerri told the worry to the doll, put it under her pillow and the doll took her worry away by the morning.

- We talked to them at the table about everything and that kept things down to manageable proportions.

- All kids worry, we make it worse if we constantly worry about their worry. Every kid has anxieties and they usually don't last long. Just put up with it and reassure them; after all, you are a parent.

- We used meditation and worked through the fears step by step. Also, we wrote worries down and put them in a balloon, then we went to the top of a cliff and let the balloon go.

Separation Anxiety

If you have a child who won't let go, clings, grips onto your hair, screams if detached from you, etc, then here are some checks and repair suggestions.

CHECKS

- **Check your own anxieties** about separating from the kids. Research shows that 60 per cent of the separation problems kids have is caught from parents.

- **Check which signals bring the panic on** getting into the car, putting make-up on, getting into good clothes, cutting lunches, etc. If we know these there may be ways we can do the routine a little differently.

✯ **Check whether it's a general problem or just a problem separating from a particular person** (usually the one they're closest to).
If separation from you is the key then maybe use someone else or change the group dynamics—eg Dad takes your child to school or you collect other kids and go together with them.

✯ **Check if it's just a problem going to a particular place.**
If it's a problem going to school or preschool then check how things are in the playground and classroom to make sure there are no scary pressures there (eg bullies).

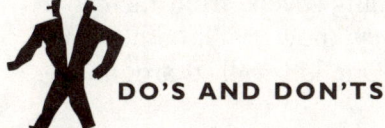

DO'S AND DON'TS

✯ **If it's a problem everywhere then Mum's not the answer!**
Soften their dependency on Mum with some time at Nan's or with Dad. If they won't go, then Mum takes a break from them (that time apart will also test whether the problem is the parent or the child). Read Melissa's case study over the page.

✯ **Arm them with their own 'Magic Power Stones'** or some other imaginative keepsake. These are just stones which we imbue with magic power. Take Sandy to the shop that sells rocks and crystals and then follow this ritual:

GAMES

MAGIC POWER STONES

- Get Sandy to choose six rocks that look and feel good in his hand from those on display and place them on the counter.
- Sandy then shuts his eyes, feels the six and selects the two that make him feel good.
- These two become his power stones—one for travelling and one for home, or one as the main stone and the other as reserve.
- These stones are given special power by Sandy thinking of all the things that make him feel good.
- Sandy keeps the stone with him, so when he's worried he clutches that instead of Mum and, with his imagination, brings the force in the stone to help him walk into school, etc.

✻ **Always take success in small steps**
  If it's a problem separating at school then reward letting go at the bubblers, at the front gate, at the car, etc (always best if they're also armed with friends or teacher on stand-by to make sure they're not left alone).

✻ **If you're confident, just leave them with someone secure**—like a friend, family member or teacher—say goodbye and take off. If *you're* anxious then you make the separation much harder.

✻ Some families let the kids pick something special from their handbag like a scarf or a hankie so they know you'll be back, but just be careful with what they select. One kid walked around preschool all day clutching a tampon.

✻ Here's a novel idea I picked up from a parent. I call it 'Stretching the Friendship Chain'.

G·A·M·E·S

STRETCHING THE FRIENDSHIP CHAIN

- Get a whole series of long strips of colourful paper ready to play paper chains. The idea is that the chain will grow with their growth in independence.
- Because all little kids like to be big, start sharing all the big things that they can do, like helping to set the table, doing wees on their own, sleeping in their own bed, feeding themselves, colouring in on their own, etc.
- Write each of these achievements out on a separate strip of paper, using different coloured strips to keep it bright and attractive and maybe to help them remember the achievement.
- Link all the strips together into a chain. Then get the child to hold one end while you hold the other and talk about how big they're getting.
- When they manage something new the new link goes in and they can show other people all the independent things they can do.

MELISSA'S MESS

Melissa's in a mess. Towards the end of the year she just couldn't cope with school, not because she wasn't bright, but because it meant being away from Mum. Every morning it would be the tears and tummies, the choking and chuckies so bad that she would force Mum to stay home with her. Melissa had avoided the problem, and because Mum resented her she was more insecure than ever.

Now the family is so fed up they have dropped their plans to do anything at weekends. They just stay home and be miserable to teach her a lesson. What Melissa needs is time out with friends and with Dad, building up her confidence away from home. If that doesn't work she may need to stay with family or friends for a while and go to school from there till she builds up her confidence, because her problem is *not* school, it's separating from Mum. Once kids get the sniff of success there's no stopping them, so success rather than punishment is the name of the game. But they will sniff out our every anxiety so if you're clinging on and choking their confidence then work on that. When it comes to adult problems it's always best to lean on someone our own size.

Bush Remedies

- I went back to casual work so she had to be left with the babysitter, like it or not—she got to like it.

- Tell your child when you will return in terms of *the day's events* rather than the time.

- Set an example. If your child sees that you are not made anxious by a situation then the battle is half over.

- When going to a new carer, take them to meet the carer for 10 minutes before you leave them for a whole day.

- If the children won't let you go out at night without a major performance then don't sneak out. I used to give them a kiss into the palm of their hand so if they felt lonely they knew there was always one left in there for them.

◆ My first three were no trouble, but the fourth was a nightmare. I'm not proud of this, but what I ended up doing was to tell the baby-sitter to stay outside in her car while I got changed into my pj's, with make-up on. I'd get into bed, wait until she was sound asleep and then flick the lights back on—that was the signal to the baby-sitter, who then came in as I got dressed and went out.

◆ My daughter just would not let me out of her sight, she always wanted to be picked up and wouldn't let me get on with anything. What I found worked was a bit of reverse psychology. Every time I went anywhere—to the toilet, to make the beds, anywhere—I picked her up and took her with me, even if she was watching TV. 'You'll miss me if I leave you on your own,' I'd say. She got so sick of it and being dragged away from TV that she used to run when I came near her. We've now reached a truce, she doesn't bug me and I don't bug her.

Panic

Nearly every family seems blessed with at least one panic merchant: it's not lost, it's been stolen; hair won't go right; clothes don't look right; homework won't be right; everything's a bother. Some seem born that way while others have panic thrust upon them by an overanxious family that sees every issue as a threat to survival.

I recently did a survey on things that kids aged between seven and 12 panic about. Here's their list:

- things under the bed
- the water
- going to school toilet
- breaking something precious
- when friends die
- nightmares
- having to talk in front of class
- bushfire
- spiders on them
- parents getting drunk
- parents fighting
- having to go to hospital
- doing something wrong
- getting lost
- losing something
- divorce
- exams
- storms
- choosing between parents
- running late
- strangers

CHECKS

* **Check whether it's real panic** or just strong/rewarded anxiety. Panic tends to have *some* of the following symptoms: sweating, nausea, pupil dilation (if you can get close enough to see), rapid heartbeat, hyperventilation, twitching or trembling, muscle rigidity, wetting or soiling.

* **Check whether it's being copied** from other panickers in the family.

* **Check when and where it's happening** and see if you can get a pattern or common culprit.

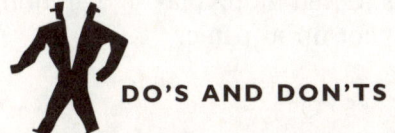
DO'S AND DON'TS

* To beat panic that is being copied from panicky parents, we must first get that panicky parent trigger under control. That probably means hypnotherapy or clinical psychology for the panicky parent. But for mild panickers there are few easier books to help than *Living with IT* then *Living IT up* (by Bev Aisbett). Both books put the problem out there, where it can be handled and challenged, this way you make IT, the panic monster, easier to deal with. Maybe both parent and child can make up their own picture or image of the panic monster and share ideas on ways to beat it.

* Teach and empower their control over their panic with breathing relaxation (see page 41).

* Arm them with images like walking in the garden with the wind gently making little waves in the lush green grass (see Maureen Garth's books for more of these images).

* Arm them with a few positive stock phrases and some proud parent around to notice and record their success.

✻ If Sandy fears he's failing the peer approval test or if he feels like a square peg in a round hole then finding a team or hobby that loves square pegs can work wonders.

✻ Use some of the stroking massage techniques outlined on page 44 when their body is really tense. If they won't let you touch them then try some of the following:
- Talk softly, and if possible take them to a change of scene as that generally changes their act.
- As you talk softly, throw in the names of pets and people they like, so you chip away at their psychological spasm.
- Encourage deep breathing by getting them to pretend to blow up a balloon.
- If they like animals practise 'going turtle'. Get Sandy to imagine putting his head back inside the shell where it's safe and nothing can hurt him.

A lot of these kids and their parents have never learnt to play with their problems, everything is dead-set serious. Often more 'playful' parenting can unwind those worries before they knot up in panic.

TALCUM TENSION

Tiny Tina was in the other day. She was only five but she had already absorbed Mum's panic attacks. She couldn't sleep in her bed, couldn't go anywhere without Mum, couldn't sleep at Nan's, couldn't catch a bus; she was literally petrified.

Mum had always been worried about Tina—being molested, being sick, not coping with school—but admitted that her own school days may not have helped. Apparently at school she was always made to feel guilty about sin, life, boys, and even her own body, to the extent that the girls had to put talcum powder on their shiny black shoes so the boys couldn't see their underwear in the reflection.

With the help of the book *Don't Panic*, Mum started to use visualisation of peaceful scenes to help her control her panic and get her breathing back in order. For young Tina it was a matter of little steps to success, with the added help of those neat little worry dolls to take on her worries each night before bed. She'll be okay, as soon as Mum manages to feel back in control. Each night when Tiny Tina goes to bed, Mum strokes her back with the soothing feeling, believe it or not, of some talcum powder!

Obsessions and Rituals

All little kids have rituals; it's their way of getting order back into a booming buzzing world that's pretty scary. But some rituals don't disappear with age. Little kids get obsessed with the oddest things—the colour red, Thomas the tank engine, fans, even the vacuum cleaner. Then there are the softer rituals like 10 kisses before bed, always doing routines in a strict order, always sitting in the front seat of the car. In older kids, if the rituals are still there and interfering with their day, then they're probably labelled as OCD (Obsessive Compulsive Disorder) and any tricky treatment must only be attempted after consultation with a psychologist.

CHECKS

Symptom Check
- obsessive thoughts (eg 'My hands are covered in germs.')
- can't get to sleep
- walks or talks in sleep
- talks too much, hard to shut up
- has strange ideas (eg 'If I don't say goodbye to Dad he may not come back.')
- strange behaviour (eg carries out lots of odd rituals as if talking to someone)
- stares
- hoards things
- doesn't sleep much
- does compulsive repetitive acts (eg washing, touching, switching, checking)
- seems overtired
- anxious
- many nightmares
- twitches
- daydreams
- seems confused

If your Sandy registered strongly on more than five of these, then it's worth getting checked out by a clinical psychologist or psychiatrist as medication may be helpful. I should add that many of our very successful leaders admit to some degree of compulsive behaviour.

❋ **Check if it's a family style**
If so get assistance from the doctor and make contact with the Obsessive Compulsive Disorder support group in Adelaide on 08 8231 1588.

❋ **Check if it's a management style**
- Are you being too tough on tidiness and cleanliness so that it has become a family habit?
- Are there family pressures that may make Sandy feel that some order and ritual is a way of controlling the chaos he feels?
- Is the home a fairly tense scene?
- Are you playing along with the ritual and in a sense making it worse?
- Have you tried changing the ritual in some way?

DO'S AND DON'TS

Here are some repair suggestions for parents to adapt.

❋ **Use music** to soften the scene if home stress is part of the problem.

❋ **Try changing the ritual in some way** For instance you might limit the number of times he can wash, or turn the taps off tight so he has to ask for permission to wash.

❋ **Teach simple relaxation techniques** (see relaxation ideas on pages 40–44).

❋ **Help Sandy develop a few 'Compulsion Crushers'.**

GAMES

COMPULSION CRUSHERS

- Get him to actually do the compulsive act while he thinks of something yukky like eating brussel sprouts.
- Teach him to change to an opposite act, eg a compulsive hair twiddler can play with a neck chain instead. If he has some particular bed ritual let him sleep in another room, or keep his toothbrush somewhere else so the sequence loosens up.
- With older kids keen to be habit busters, quietly count the number of times they do it, let them know their score then see if together you can work out tactics to get their score down.
- Sometimes you can get success by flooding. That means instead of asking him not to do it, make sure as soon as Sandy starts that he must keep doing it until you give him permission to stop.
- With young kids' obsessions with red cars or red stop lights or Thomas the tank engine, reward them each time they respond to another colour or another of the Thomas fleet.

Whatever you do don't blame devils or evil forces beyond their control or that's exactly what they'll blame too.

Bush Remedies

I don't know whether you'd call this a compulsion, but my daughter never shuts up. Her father says he's finally found a support group to help her, it's called AN-ON, AN-ON, AN-ON!

COMPULSIVE CARLOS

Carlos was not your average 10-year-old because he liked to keep clean. At first it was just regular washing before he ate anything, then it had to be with his own special glass and cutlery and then his own water bottle for school. Rather than cause a scene his parents went along with the rituals. However, when he started spitting out his saliva and keeping his hands under his jumper to avoid germs, they realised he had a problem. Carlos had become obsessive-compulsive, obsessed by the thought of germs ready to destroy him and compulsive in the rituals he had to follow to stop them. It was chewing up more and more time and was getting everyone down, including Carlos who really wished with his parents that he didn't have to do it.

He was started on Anafranil medication but he needed something strong in his thinking framework to challenge and replace this obsession with germs.

I first showed him photos of kids I know whose bodies have never learnt to fight germs and how sad their life is. Then I challenged the obsessive idea that avoiding germs has kept him safe. We talked about how our bodies wanted and desperately needed soldiers to fight the battle of the bug. We pictured the good soldiers in hiding waiting for germs to attack. Then, like in the game Bull Rush, they attack those germs and win them over to their own army so the army gets bigger and the body gets stronger. 'That's why doctors rarely get sick,' I said, 'because their bodies have lots of soldiers from winning so many wars over so many germs.' So what we needed to win the Battle of the Bug were plenty of soldiers and that meant meeting lots of germs so we had a stronger army. Occasionally if it was a new germ with new guns and artillery it might take a day or two but in the end the good army wins and takes over all the beaut big guns and artillery. Then they're stronger than ever.

Having got the chemistry in line and his thinking straight then it was important that his parents played their role very differently. No longer would they wash his bottle for him every day, including three rinses of the top. If he wanted it, he did it. If he got a bit of dirt on his towel then no longer would Mum put her mouth over the dirt to suck the germs out before he would use it. If he wanted the same glass and cutlery then no longer would Mum wash it for him.

Carlos is less compulsive, I think. I should add that he has now rung me five times to make sure his story is in the book!

Perfectionism

Perfectionism is a subtle but ever so demanding form of OCD if it's overtaking their life. It means that the poor kids like Perfect Patrice (see page 10) have to do everything perfectly and pity help everyone around them if something isn't right. It's a trap for good kids, often made worse by teachers and parents rewarding it. The problem is that because they're human and imperfect, the perfect goal is never reached so they're never satisfied with themselves.

CHECKS

- **Symptom check**
  - Must they have everything done perfectly?
  - Are they unable to leave anything unfinished?
  - Do they get very distressed about every challenge or project?
  - Do they always find fault with everything they've done?
  - Are they constantly worried that they might get something wrong?
  - Does not finishing or getting something wrong distress them?

- **Check if they're wanting to be perfect at everything or if it's just related to school performance**
  If it's school-related then chances are they're under a great deal of pressure—either they feel they're not coping or they're not matching up to someone's standards.

- **Check on parental anxiety.** If parents are setting super-high standards then the kids soak up the style.

DO'S AND DON'TS

- Have a conference with the teacher and agree to reward effort, imperfect and incomplete work only (don't worry about standards slipping, these kids provide their own pressure). For instance, see if they can be strong enough to get work wrong and not let it bother them, or to stop doing something they haven't quite finished and not worry about it.

❉ For this form of habit and for all fear-related problems, give them a weapon to beat their worries (eg the 'Magic Power Stones', see page 47) and encourage every little success. If your Sandy is aged 4–10, record his mind muscle success on a chart of some sort, such as the 'Mind Muscle Chart'.

GAMES

MIND MUSCLE CHART

- ◆ This is just an ordinary chart, similar to the ones outlined in the Appendix.
- ◆ Kids love developing muscles, especially boys. So what I do is to give Sandy an arm wrestle or look at how strong his body is for sport and then comment on what a shame it is that his mind muscle is so weak.
- ◆ When he looks at me in horror and anger, I remind him that although he wants to break some habit (eg being perfect) he can't.
- ◆ This throws up the challenge and sets him up to find tactics to prove me wrong.
- ◆ Then we work out ways to help him beat the habit and ways we will record it so I can see his progress.

❉ Encourage messy play, getting dirty, water play, rhythm, playing with pets ... anything to get their bodily defences down as I find many of these kids are fearful of messy or free-for-all play.

Bush Remedies

🍃 I told her 'if you knew everything then no-one would tell you anything new, and to learn, you have to try and sometimes when you try it doesn't work—but that's okay.'

PERFECTIONISM PAINS

Helena lived in fear of her daughter's next school project. Any time her ego was on the line, Perfect Patrice panicked, screamed and threw in the towel because she couldn't live up to her own expectations.

If you have a perfectionist like Patrice then maybe get them to list the things they'd like to be good at (like dancing, reading, soccer) and make a deal that if they want to be good at lots then they must have on their list being good at handling mistakes.

For younger perfectionists maybe give them a magnifying glass so they can see that even things that look perfect aren't really when you look closer, maybe let the family say what they're not so good at and how they handle it. Just be careful what they magnify. One family used the magnifying glass to show their perfectionists that even after washing hands perfectly there were still teeny specks of dirt under the skin. Now they have a compulsive hand washer.

Some parents expect their kids to be perfect to the point that they can even understand why their parents aren't.

Stubborn Thinkers

This is a problem of all growing kids. Once their ego lands at the age of about two, they're the centre of the universe. As they grow they gradually learn to see things from other points of view.

CHECKS

* Check if they've **copied the style from parents**.

* Check if they've **developed the style** because parents were too

preoccupied or too lacking in confidence to cause a scene so they've given in to the style in the past.

✸ Check if it's **part of a rigid personality** where everything must be done their way or they freak out and can't cope. These kids have a lot of trouble adapting and adjusting to changes.

✸ Check if **it's a defence mechanism** they've developed to protect themselves from threat—they're too scared to give ground or let their guard down in case they lose control.

 **DO'S AND DON'TS**

✸ Read the suggestions under Back-Answering and Arguing in Chapter Six (page 176).

✸ Don't label them as stubborn or that's what they'll be as we all tend to live life by our labels.

✸ Don't lock horns if you're in a hurry. Stubborn kids have nothing to lose by digging in. You have your sanity and family at stake.

✸ Do expect stubborn behaviour from every young child. They've suddenly found their feet and their freedom so saying 'no' is really just their ego saying 'hello'. They can't see other people's point of view.

✸ Do learn how to harness it.
- Divert or distract two-year-olds.
- Give a small, limited choice to older kids so it's hard for them to buck their own decision.
- Be clear and quietly determined about what you want. You don't need to shout to prove you're right.
- Quietly and firmly ride out their objections till the dust settles.
- Remember that determination and perseverance are much more powerful in controlling kids than violence.

- ✷ If it's not their normal style then do a scene check.
  - ◆ Is the pace too hectic emotionally or physically? If so, cut back the pace, put on some music, read a book to them, make some lap time or just down time to do nothing—in other words cool things off a bit and treat their behaviour as a useful reminder that home life has become a bit overheated.
  - ◆ Are they tired? If so, some time out in their bedroom could be an easy answer (if they won't go, see suggestions on page 298).
  - ◆ Are they freaking out because something they're facing is new or scary? If this is the case, save yourself some frustration by walking them through changes slowly.
  - ◆ Is it pride? Older kids with strong ego defence are sometimes too proud to fail and too proud to say they might, so they dig in. If this is the case then preguessing their fear and reducing the hurdles are the tactics to help them save face.

- ✷ Do remember that some stubbornness is in their heart, not their head so trying to reason it out just doesn't work. All young kids need to say no to prove that they've arrived. If you take it on as a personal battle you're bound to lose because they know no other way to prove their point.

SOPHIE THE TALKING MULE

Sophie was so stubborn her mum had nicknamed her the talking mule. When Mum said 'Come to the table', the answer was a swift sharp 'no'; 'Pick up your toys'—'no'; 'Do you love your mum?'—'no', 'What do you love then?'—'no'.

Some parents call it 'strong-willed', outsiders call it 'spoilt', but Sophie's mum called it anarchy, a deliberate plot to destroy her sanity.

Sophie's family had just split up, Mum was totally distraught and distracted and she was looking to her two-year-old for reassurance. Sophie was determined to get her mum's attention one way or another, as long as she got it. Had Mum read her a little fairy story it would have made them both feel better.

So, shrug it off if they're young, change your tone, drop the pace and pay attention to the good things they do and you'll get more of them. If you see it as a battle of wills that's exactly what you'll get. Remember that for most kids the bouts of stubbornness are temporary—it's only the grey hairs that are permanent.

Bush Remedies

- You have to negotiate with them on things. If you talk it over you can generally con them into cooperating.

- Be consistent with your demands as sometimes kids get stubborn when they're tired or it's all too much for them.

- If they won't cooperate befriend them and they'll generally be happy to do things for a friend.

- Stick to your decision and just change the topic of interest easily and gently. With most young kids they can't be dissuaded but they can be distracted.

- Use gentle firmness, *no* anger because they love a scene.

- Praise other kids who do as they're told in front of them.

- Sometimes they just need a cuddle and a little help in doing the task requested of them.

- Be kind and gentle, this type of child is often stubborn because they fear making a mistake.

School Sick

Some kids feel sick in the head long before it gets to their body, but it will if they keep thinking that way. School sick is a favourite amongst kids. I've known kids with biro marks on their tummy, headaches that keep coming and going every Monday ... one kid even claimed premonition of a bomb threat!

CHECKS

🕴 **Symptom Check**
- Have there been other symptoms or is this a sudden onset?
- Does the sickness happen every morning or is it only on certain days (eg sports day)?
- Do the symptoms show a regular pattern? (If not, get a medical check. If so, get a psychological check.)
- Does Sandy get miraculously better by about 9a.m.?
- Does the teacher indicate that Sandy was ill at school?
- Are there more tears than would normally happen with an illness?
- Is there more anger than sadness if he's forced to go?
- Does it make a difference who takes Sandy to school?

🕴 Are there other indicators that it's emotional rather than physical, eg nightmares, loss of energy, etc?

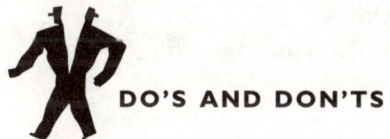
DO'S AND DON'TS

🕴 Send them to school each day if at all possible.

🕴 Check with the school receptionist on their health by recess.

🕴 If they stay home then make a clear rule that school sick means bed—no TV, no mufti gear, no special treats, no play, no computer, just bed!

🕴 School sickness can become quite serious, so get up to the school and check it all out. There could be bullies they're scared of, work they can't do, or a teacher that 'hates' them.

🕴 Don't take sides against the school, or you'll reinforce the avoidance.

- ✨ Make sure that sick thinking is not a family style. If there's a lot of sickness floating around in the family, kids think that's the way to win attention.

- ✨ If it's being repeated then even if the sickness isn't real, the fear is, so get help from the school counsellor or a child psychologist.

Hypochondriacs

All kids, including Sandy, will complain loud and long about feeling sick, headache, tummy ache, backache—anything to grab attention, get out of work and capture sympathy. This is not Hypochondriasis.

CHECKS

- ✶ **Is there a parent or sibling who is always or often sick?** If so, Sandy may feel this is the way to capture attention.

- ✶ **Does the family worry a lot about sickness** or focus on sickness, tablets, medications, germs, etc? If so, the vibes may be the virus that has caused Sandy's problem.

- ✶ **Has Sandy had a serious health scare or medical condition** that has promoted excess anxiety and sensitivity to any aches or pains?

- ✶ Sandy's problem can only be classified as genuine Hypochondriasis if:
    - ◆ Sandy has an ongoing preoccupation with having some serious illness,
    - ◆ he does not suffer from an Anxiety Disorder, Obsessive Compulsive Disorder Panic Disorder, Separation Anxiety Disorder, or Depression (see page 32),
    - ◆ his preoccupation persists despite medical reassurance,
    - ◆ his distress or concern about his sickness is preventing him playing, interacting, sleeping, laughing or generally engaging in the normal activity of the household,
    - ◆ his 'sickness' has lasted for at least six months.

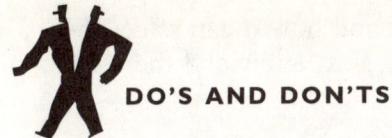
DO'S AND DON'TS

✶ Kids feel very vulnerable to nasties lurking out there so some think sick and can't shift their thinking unless we give them a way (see 'Imagining the Cure' below).

✶ Remember that all three-year-olds are dramatic, in fact I call three-year-olds the 'theatrical threes'.

✶ Use logical consequences. For example if Sandy is claiming sporadic sickness then stop him going over to a friend's place in case he gets sick there.

✶ If the kids want to beat the pain, then help them make it mind over matter by 'Imagining the Cure'.

GAMES

IMAGINING THE CURE

- Get them to feel where the pain is and imagine what it looks like down there.
- Spend some time getting to know what they love and like and what are powerful influences in their lives.
- Help them work out a way they can use those forces to beat the pain.
- The other day I had a girl drop her hip pain level from 9/10 to 4/10 by imagining she was sending little happy face balls down through her bloodstream to land on the nasty nerve ends, burst open and put out the pain that way. If more pain came she'd send more down.

For little kids it might be a matter of finding the magic cure that works wonders and imagination is all that's needed to create a special rub or a special cream.

✱ Be careful just how sick the family is and how it can affect the kids. Let me share the story of a very sick family and the lessons Mum learnt to survive.

TOUGH PARENTING

If you have done it tough in your family then you'll have more than a modicum of feeling for Jodi. She copes daily with two children, aged seven and five. There's nothing unusual about that, but her husband has a serious, dangerous heart condition, is in and out of intensive care, every day could be his last, and he has died *twice* on the operating table. You wouldn't be surprised to know that the kids are forever wanting days off and they always feel sick, so Jodi decided to put her thoughts in writing.

'When I am super-stressed I always go looking for a self-help book but this time I just couldn't find one. So I thought I'd write a few notes based on all my mistakes, and there are many.

- Right away forget about the rules of parenting. You are in a different situation to normal people where the husband works, wife is happy, and everyone is well.
- My biggest mistake was helping everyone else and forgetting about myself. Learn to be a little selfish.
- It is natural to want to help your partner and your kids. Society expects this and people will call you noble. But remember, most noble people are dead! Keeping this in mind has really helped me to get sleep and lots of it. I find it hard to cope if I am dead tired, but I can cope if I am well rested. At night this may be impossible, so try to catch up during the day—a pillow on the table or sitting in a chair can help.
- Beg neighbours, friends or relatives to mind the children for an hour or two.
- Try to budget and allow for small rewards. A little make up for yourself, hire some videos for the kids or maybe buy a book, some colouring pens or stickers. They're not expensive but it makes a big difference.
- Look at what you eat. I find coffee tenses me up and most cold and flu medications make my heart race. Find foods that calm the family. Get decaffeinated coffee.

- Stop volunteering for everything.
- Learn to jump up and down and say I have had enough.
- Be kind to yourself in the kitchen. Stock some easy foods for the bad days. Teach your kids the basic skills like getting rice bubbles and making a sandwich. My seven-year-old can cook toast. He learnt to burn it black and set off the fire alarm. Now he knows what happens when you forget about your toast. An electric cut-off switch is great.
- Learn to find friends. This was hard at first, but now I just love to talk. Listening to their problems makes me glad I've not got all that money to worry about!
- Have lots of fun. Laughter is God's present to all of us.'

It's no wonder we have so many 'up-top' problems. The mind is a magnificent instrument. If we can have a healthy home and give kids a healthy head and heart then that's probably the best legacy any of us can leave our kids.

'The mind is its own place, and in itself, can make a heaven of hell and a hell of heaven.' John Milton

Mind Muscle Summary

STRONG MIND MUSCLE IS THE KEY TO SUCCESSFUL INTERPRETATION AND MANAGEMENT OF LIFE'S CHALLENGES.

M Make the kids aware of how to use Mind Muscle to cope with problems.
I Imagination is a very powerful tool for kids to learn how to beat problems.
N Never label a child with any negative label or the label could last a lifetime.
D Do reframe the problem so the kids can see how to solve it.

M Make the steps to developing mind muscle small enough to guarantee success.
U Use visual tactics with kids so they can see (not just hear) how to tackle it.
S Self-check to make sure the kids aren't soaking up parental depression or anxiety.
C Create a home tone that is positive and as playful if possible.
L Locate the personal empowering tactics that work for each child.
E Ensure that a clinical psychologist is consulted if the problem is prolonged.

FAMOUS FOOTNOTE

BEATING THE ODDS

Janine Shepherd

ATHLETE, AUTHOR AND PILOT

My parents were very poor and we didn't have any money but we had what I think a lot of families lack today, and that is, my parents were always home and they were always there for me. My house was a home, Mum was always there and I never felt poor. I always felt like I had everything because my parents spent a lot of time with us.

Obviously in my adult life the most difficult time was my accident. It happened when I was out training on a pushbike for the '88 Winter Olympics, and it left me ... well, they didn't think I would survive, let alone walk. I broke my neck and back in four places, as well as my right arm, five ribs on my left side, my collarbone and some bones in my feet. I also had severe lacerations on my body, head injuries, internal injuries and I'd lost five litres of blood. Suddenly everything that I had ever, ever valued and worked for was gone in an instant. That was terribly difficult to deal with, especially the loss of self-esteem. I hated my body.

There were many things that got me through it. A recurring part of my life was that my parents were there for me again. They gave up everything to look after me and nurse me at home when I couldn't look after myself. Also I have always had a sort of gritty determination. I have always been a survivor, I've always worked hard and I think that that comes a lot from lessons I have learnt from sport.

I think sport teaches you lessons in life: that you have to work hard, that you have to stick with it, that you don't give up. I always say you have to learn to love the hills because I loved them. My nickname was Janine the Machine. People used to laugh about it because I was a tough little nut, I always trained really hard and the results did pay off. I believe you not only have to take on the hills but you have to learn to love them because that's what makes a difference.

One of the most important things I have probably learnt from my accident is that I feel everything is there to teach us something. When things don't work out the way I want them to work out I can now think, well I've made it through the toughest battle so I'll make it through this one. I look philosophically at things and think what can I learn from this? Sometimes you don't end up going the way that you wanted to go but you end up on a different tangent and it is usually a better one. Tough times never last but tough people do.

Life is all about the difference between an optimist and a pessimist. There is only one good thing about a pessimist and that is they are great to borrow money from because they never expect to get it back. We all need to be optimistic. I've read books such as *The Optimistic Child* and it is really important that we practise those behaviour patterns because we have to pass them on to our kids. Being optimistic is what's going to get them through. They have to look at things and realise that every problem has a life span.

People need to remember that our kids' emotional and spiritual development is just as important as providing for them materially. We are so busy paying off the mortgage that both parents are working, but we've got to be there for our kids and we have to work out what our priorities are.

My recovery has taken a long time. I can now look back and say that I can see a reason for it all happening but back then I couldn't. I guess the important thing to realise when you are in the middle of that, when you are in the tough times is that other people have done it, other people have survived and you will survive. That's got to give you hope—the fact that you are not alone.

CHAPTER THREE

Ear and Attention Problems

> *My mother was a very strong influence in my background. Basically she was very supportive; if ever there was something I wanted to do, she was right in there behind it. She was a strong mother, a good one, a very busy one and I was damn lucky.*
> *I'm not sure what made her so special, but I think it was attention.*
>
> **KIM BEAZLEY**, politician
> (READ MORE DETAILS OF KIM BEAZLEY'S VIEWS ON FAMILIES AT THE END OF THIS CHAPTER.)

Attention is a big issue for families, not just the amount we give or kids receive, but kids' capacity to pay attention. In every survey, in every age group, difficulties with kids' attention emerged as the biggest problem for parents. So I've linked it in with listening and blamed the ear! I'm now starting to wonder whether the literacy crisis that education authorities say is with us is not part of the same problem—kids whose listening and attention skills are shot to bits under the onslaught of noise, Nintendo, TV commercials, movies with special effects and the deadening effect of our 'visual Valium', the video.

Parents everywhere are frustrated with kids who are parent-deaf, don't listen, don't hear no and need constant reminding. Then there's the huge area of ADHD, Attention Deficit Hyperactivity Disorder (ADHD, also known as ADD), which appears from recent research to clearly be a genetic/neurological problem. There can be so many reasons why kids don't pay attention: emotional preoccupation, poor hearing, poor listening, too much noise, too much competition for their ears ... it could be so many things. I'm sure that ADHD has become more common because it is often confused with several behavioural look-alikes. This is very unfair on the genuine ADHD cases so I thought it might be worth sorting out the true ADHD from several look-alikes. I should add that there's a bit of tongue-in-cheek with these. I'm not seriously trying to create new disorders, it's complicated enough already. But here they are.

ADD
A. Attention Demanding Disorder
B. Attention Damaged Disorder
C. Attention Disabled Disorder
D. Attention Digested Disorder
E. Attention Deficit Disorder

Attention Demanding Disorder

Attention Demanding Disorder is a term coined recently by teachers who feel that every child being badly managed or with a behaviour problem is being labelled as ADHD. I call this one Attention Demanding Disorder.

Parents who are particularly busy, preoccupied, guilt-ridden or lacking in confidence are particularly prone to producing children with this problem. Dr Balson, author of *Becoming Better Parents*, sees the attention-seeking problem as taking two forms: active and passive.

- **Active Attention Demanding Disorder**—symptoms include clowning, showing off, misbehaving, embarrassing and endless questioning, interrupting, distracting or even being the model child to be noticed.

◆ **Passive Attention Demanding Disorder**—symptoms include laziness, bashfulness, shyness, tearfulness, helplessness, fussiness, vanity and even cuteness.

Attention Demanding Disorder (both passive and active) has many features that distinguish it from ADHD.

ATTENTION DEMANDING DISORDER	ADHD
behaviour has a goal (adult attention)	the behaviour seems goalless
behaviour ceases if unsuccessful	little change if behaviour unsuccessful
adult compliance reduces disruptive behaviour	adult compliance makes little difference
often enjoy books and listening if with adult attention	even with adult attention generally find it hard to concentrate or listen for long to stories/abstract information
rarely able to occupy themselves for long periods without adults	flits around activities, often doing dangerous things but can occupy themselves for long periods
often eager to articulate causes and blame for problem	rarely has much insight or even interest in causes
often carries grudges about being hard done by, etc	rarely carries grudges or even thinks about problem after the incident

You can see why it's confused with ADHD as many of the symptoms are common to both. Justin's case puts it in perspective.

JUSTIN—THE BOY WITH ATTENTION DEMANDING DISORDER

Justin was a real worry to everyone, particularly his teachers as his school reports indicated—attention seeking, rude and disruptive, needs constant supervision, demanding, never finishes his work, interrupts other children, calls out in class. His parents read Dr Chris Green's book *Understanding A.D.H.D.* and were convinced Justin had all the symptoms of Attention Deficit Hyperactivity Disorder so Mum took him off to the paediatrician for the proven ADHD alleviator, Ritalin. Fortunately the paediatrician was more interested in the problem than the prescription and referred Justin to our clinic for detailed testing. The results were astounding; on all the measures of distractibility, concentration, persistence and retention, Justin was way above average.

In Justin's case, the parents were after the quick fix, not the 'hard yards'. They were both ambitious, both in business, both workaholics, neither prepared to change their busy lifestyle. When they weren't home Justin beat boredom with the help of violent video games like 'Mortal Combat' and when they were home they gave him 'quality time'. This meant denying him nothing, being at his beck and call, tolerating the intolerable, and hating every minute of it. So they searched around for a paediatrician who would respond to their pill plea and were sure that this would fix everything. It didn't, so now they're getting chiropractic treatment for the problem. I'm just not sure whose spine is the problem.

If you have a child with Attention Demanding Disorder, the answers are easy if you have the confidence and courage to deliver them.

DO'S AND DON'TS

- **Focus on their needs more than their wants**. Their needs are for fun and friends, love and cuddles, learning and laughter, routines and rules. Their wants are for everything advertised on TV or owned by their mates.

- **Do allow kids to find their own way to beat boredom**. If they can't, use the 'Think Light' (outlined below and in the Appendix, page 355).

GAMES

THINK LIGHT

- They make up a list of things they like to do when they're bored (play on the computer, go for a ride, etc).
- They put these ideas onto paper and then Blu-Tack them onto a yellow-coloured cardboard circle which they put in their room.
- When they can't think of anything to do they consult their light or oracle and do one of those things listed.
- If they say they're all boring then that's the chance for them to think of a new idea and replace one on their light.
- If nothing appeals then it means they need time to recharge their battery by lying down on their bed.

- **Be consistent**. In a firm but friendly way help them understand that NO means NO.

- **Make sure you have enough down time in the family** so they can feel secure enough to explore and play without needing adults.

- **Pay attention to the behaviour you want, not to the behaviour you don't want**. As attention seeking is the Attention Demanding Disorder goal, then taking away attention is often the best management. Smacking and shouting don't work because that still gives them attention. Withdrawal of attention could be by ignoring, refusing to argue, or isolating them somewhere away from attention.

- **Instead of nagging them about behaviour you don't want, practise what you do want**. The 'Practice List' is in the Appendix, (see page 354). As you will see, the Practice List requires you to put the behaviour you want (eg zipping their mouth, going to their room) on the list with their initials next to the task. At a time to suit you, and before you give any favours or privileges, you get them to practise doing the task till they're sure they can do it on a certain signal from you. If they don't practise then pull out of favours you do for them till they do, or use the 'Fridge Disk Discipline' outlined opposite.

* Have a 'Busy List' (or use 'Fridge Make Up List' in Appendix, see page 352) on the fridge listing useful jobs the kids can do to win your attention in ways that please rather than pester. If they're too tired to be busy and they can't think of anything else to do, then they can rest in their room till they can.

* Use consequences, not shouting or smacking, to fix Attention Demanding Disorder.

* Take a good hard look at your priorities and the time you're giving to your biggest job on earth, being a good parent. Spend easy time together—find out areas of mutual interest and enjoyment and make these special. For a child, L-O-V-E is spelt T-I-M-E!

Children with Attention Demanding Disorder can be helped but it's a hard problem requiring firm solutions, firm love, firm marriages, firm rules and firm discipline. Discipline comes from a Latin word meaning 'to teach' and the best discipline is the kind that teaches, not the kind that hurts.

Controlling kids' clowning is a matter of steering, if it's out of control the goal is to curb it without driving it into the gutter.

GAMES

FRIDGE DISK DISCIPLINE

- Cut out the two disks in the Appendix or make your own, one red and one green.
- With preschoolers make two circles; draw a happy face on the green one and a sad face on the red one.
- If they're high school age, you may care to just use ordinary rectangles of paper with their name on each, one featuring a tiny happy face down the bottom right-hand corner and one featuring a tiny sad face.
- Paste them back-to-back if you like or use separately.
- Use one round magnet for the nose or hold to the fridge with any form of magnet anywhere unobtrusive.
- Have one set for each child over two years of age.
- When Sandy is cooperating, the disk is on the green/happy side.
- When Sandy doesn't cooperate tell him what you're sad about and then make sure he knows that the disk has been flipped to the red/sad side.
- Let him know you won't be able to give him any help because he's not giving you any help.
- Then pull out of any favours until he makes amends.
- The way to make amends is to do one or more (as nominated by parent) of the jobs on the 'Fridge Make Up List' (see design in Appendix, page 352) so he pays his dues and everyone is happy again. With under-eights it's hard work to order them to do 'Make Up' when they may not know how, or do it so poorly that you wish you'd done it yourself. I usually include the word 'help' in their Make Up List and you do the Make Up with them. They like that. This way the kids learn to Make Up or fix the relationship and cooperate. Then flip the disk back to the happy/green side again.
- If Sandy won't do the Make Up it means his battery is too run down to have a go so give him time in his room for a battery recharge. He can come out when he feels ready, when the oven timer goes or whatever system you decide on.
- If no Make Up, no favours until it's all sorted out. The line of attack is that he's a good kid and wants to be good, so what's gone wrong?
- The idea is to keep it fun and let the disks do the shouting for you.

Attention Damaged Disorder

Another ear and attention problem commonly mistaken for ADHD is Attention Damaged Disorder. Our kids live in a busier, noisier world; in many ways their world has become noise polluted, making it much harder for parents or teachers to compete. Recently there have been suggestions from researchers that the amount of stimulation and noise being foisted on young kids is one factor behind the apparent upsurge in children's attention difficulties.

CHECKS

The following are all symptoms of Attention Damaged Disorder.
- TV turned up loud
- TV obsession
- little physical activity
- computer obsession
- deaf to parents when watching TV
- cranky when told to stop watching TV or playing on computer
- talks about TV characters or computer games in preference to anything else
- has difficulty sharing TV or computer
- wants to eat meals in front of TV
- spends more than two hours each day in front of TV or computer
- freaks out if TV is turned off or will turn it back on again
- goes to TV first thing every morning

Okay, so most normal kids show some of these symptoms, but if you're getting the lot, you have an Attention Damaged Disorder problem. Attention Damaged Disorder is closely related to a disease called Parent Deafness which, from all my surveys, appears to have reached epidemic proportions in our community.

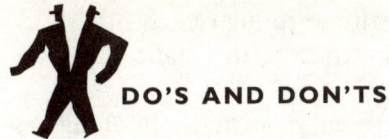 **DO'S AND DON'TS**

If you think your Sandy is suffering in silence then here are a few special ways to treat the disease.

❋ **Talk quietly**—if you're a shouter, draw up a family pact that nobody shouts in the house. If you're still not being heard then listening practice (see below) is the way to go. Remember that you'll stop a child at 40 paces with a whisper, but they won't hear a shout at two!

❋ **Have quiet time every night for everybody's sake**, even just one hour where there's reading, talking, board games—things which hopefully are a bit more peaceful and personal.

❋ **Read to kids**. The pace of life is depriving kids and parents of time to share stories, to get excited by books and bond together in fantasy. Legend has it that Einstein was asked by a mother what could she do to make her kid cleverer. He replied, 'Read him a fairy story.' She laughed and asked again, 'Yes, but after I've read him the fairy story, what do I do then to make my son more intelligent?' Einstein replied, 'Read him another one.' He wasn't joking; reading is the world of imagination that opens up kids' minds and allows them to be creative, self-entertaining problem solvers. And it teaches them to *listen* and to enjoy books.

❋ **Cut out unnecessary noise producers**, such as background TV, and cut back on volume generally to the point that people can still talk and be heard.

❋ **Limit the time children spend in front of TV, videos and computer games**. Some experts believe not only is our electronic media producing short attention spans, but maybe shorter fuses too. Because the electronic media are so stimulating, but involve no exercise, they're building a pent-up need for action which often comes out in random activity, hyperactivity, frustration and irritability.

- **Don't eat in front of the TV**. Use mealtime to hear each other's trials and triumphs and to just keep in touch with what's going on.

- **Use background music as a focus or to calm**—some school classes try classical music to fascinating effect, others use white noise (fans, melodies) to mask outside harsher noises that might disturb learning. At home or school let them try their favourite style of music but if it doesn't show evidence of helping them then suggest softer, guitar or semi-classical music instead. Just remember that different types of music might help at different times of the day.

Bush Remedies

- I just stood in front of the TV and turned the sound off.

- Kate always listens, she just pretends not to, so I pretend I'm talking to her nearby dolly. It worked until the other day when she said, 'Don't be silly, Mummy, Dolly's asleep!'

- I just stop, make them look me in the eye and make them repeat what I say.

- I put the stereo on very loud until they were forced to give me some form of attention.

- I'd just turn and talk to the wall or repeat 'Ground crew to Kyle, come in please,' to make sure he was tuned in before giving him the message.

- Any time I say Damien's first name and middle name, he knows I mean business and he'd better listen.

LISTENING LOUTS

Young Matthew was a woeful listener. He was only five but he had to be told a dozen times to do something by Mum before he cooperated and then it was only after she screamed 'Matthew, do as you're told' so loudly that Dad would go dotty in his den. You see, Dad was an older than average dad, a retired army major in fact, who had remarried to a much younger lady and now ran a consultancy from his home office.

There was of course the alternative that he back Mum up with a bit of firm love but bringing up the kids was not men's work. Meanwhile pencils were snapping in his office as the major became more and more flustered by this five-year-old's 'insubordination' as he called it.

Home habits are hard to break but everyone was unhappy with how it was, so they each agreed to change one horrible habit. Matthew's was having to be asked so many times, Mum's was telling him more than once and Dad's was to back Mum up, rather than back out. So they used a chart to record every time Matthew heard Mum the first time she called. Mum deliberately let him miss out on a few things when he didn't listen first time and Dad's job was to give Matthew some listening practice at TV time if Matthew had a problem with listening that day.

It started to work well but as Dad started to take a bit more interest in his little listening lout, he noticed that he never missed a whisper and never missed hearing the word ice-cream no matter where he was in the house. So in an effort to expedite the progress, Dad started calling him ice-cream, 'Excuse me, ice-cream, can you come for dinner now?' Young Matthew was furious. 'Don't call me that,' he moaned. 'My name is Matthew.' On this they both agreed and Matthew overnight became a better listener. But there is a sting. Any time Dad's preoccupied Matthew calls him Johnnie Walker!

Attention Disabled Disorder

Some kids don't pay attention because they just can't hear. Many's the young kid who gets off to a bad listening/attending start because of hearing loss or even just glue ear where there's too much gunk to let sounds come through clearly or easily. These I have called Attention Disabled Disorder.

CHECKS

The following are all symptoms of Attention Disabled Disorder:
- delayed or distorted speech
- don't startle to noise
- need the volume up high or sit up close to the TV
- seem uninterested in looking at the person talking
- seem uninterested in stories and music
- turn their head to one side when listening
- don't react to a whisper, wrapping paper, their name or the word 'chocolate'

DO'S AND DON'TS

If you have any concerns then see the clinic sister or your family doctor who can refer through to specialists if required. The secret to a good outcome for these kids is to get specialist help early before they get too frustrated with listening and turn off speech communication.

Attention Digested Disorder

There is another important cause of attention problems in children. I've called it Attention Digested Disorder to distinguish it from the other forms of attention problems. For some kids the impact of intolerances to certain foods can be enormous. Some kids are food-sensitive (not allergic) and this can affect their attention, not always immediately either. Sue Dengate, mother of children with ADHD and author of *Different Kids*, cites a study by Dr Schoenthaler of 6000 institutionalised juvenile delinquents, where all the authorities did was to cut out sugars and processed foods yet the incidence of rule breaking, attempted suicide and assaults was virtually halved!

CHECKS

These are some of the symptoms of Attention Digested Disorder.
- behaviour changes dramatically within a few hours of eating certain foods
- behaviour becomes consistently more restless, hyperactive, aggressive, noisy or irritable within a few hours of eating certain foods
- child has a particular obsession with certain foods (eg sugars, cola, sauce, wraps, sweets, chocolate)
- child complains of feeling edgy or angry after eating
- child starts to misbehave if he has a build-up of particular foods
- child has other allergies

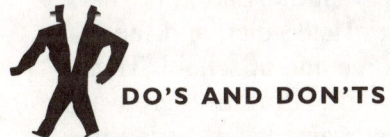

DO'S AND DON'TS

❋ Elimination diets are hard on the whole family, so if you're not ready to take that step, you can first try the gambler's approach—watch for reactions, make your best guess for culprits within the last 24 hours and see if you're on a winner in the following meals. If you're right, delete; if not, it's back to the drawing board.

❋ As you can see, this style is packed with problems so if you're not getting easy answers, consult a dietitian, get hold of Sue Dengate's book (see References, page 367) or, under a dietitian's advice try the Royal Prince Alfred Hospital's Simplified Elimination Diet. Here are some general steps:
Step 1—Prepare menus that contain only approved foods (meats, vegetables, fruit and nuts, rice and water, but no dairy

products, sugars, wheat, eggs, corn, chocolate, cola, oranges or tomatoes).
Step 2—keep a diary of child's behaviour symptoms, starting three days before the diet.
Step 3—eliminate suspected foods for 5–10 days or until the behaviour improves significantly for 48 hours.
Step 4—begin to add suspected foods, one each day.
Step 5—if a suspect food provokes behaviour reaction, delete it from their diet and await symptoms to subside before adding new foods.

It always works best if the child is involved in the decision and the diet so they cooperate with the restrictions.

Bush Remedies

While I was waiting for my son's Ritalin authorisation for his ADHD, I decided to try him on the restricted diet, and the difference was encouraging both at home and at school. Then I stopped the diet when the Ritalin arrived and again there was more improvement. But the big breakthrough came when I tried the combination of diet and Ritalin. This time the teacher commented on what an incredible change she had noticed. My son has not looked back.

ADHD children are a bit like a caterpillar. Not many can appreciate their inherent beauty and let's face it, they often leave behind a trail of turmoil and destruction. But if you nurture them, and make sure they don't get squashed along the way, wings with the most brilliant kaleidoscope of colours will slowly unfold. And they are ready to fly.
Mother of child with ADHD

ADD WANTED

AJ had all the classic ADD symptoms—he was fidgety, a poor listener, he couldn't sit still, he was easily distracted and disruptive, he never finished anything and, as you'd expect, he was driving his parents insane. So we tried some behavioural tactics such as strict rules, practising behaviour they wanted, and using water, music and the trampoline to soothe his system. We found that AJ had several food intolerances but red colouring was his worst. Then we organised a trial on Ritalin and that worked wonders.

AJ became a different boy, improved in both behaviour and schoolwork. He went up in the class and in self-esteem but football was the only exercise he yearned for so Dad sponsored the footy team and that got AJ in as a fumbly forward. But they noticed when they took him off his medication at weekends, as many do, that he was back to his old active self and actually ran, chased, tackled and played much better. The coach also noticed the difference and even more so when AJ added a red toffee apple to his pregame preparation so he put the whole team on red cordial at half-time and they cleaned up the comp. I'm not sure whether they're playing sport or uppers and downers. But it sure says something for the impact of food colourings for some kids, doesn't it? Anyhow, Dad thought that if he could make a go of footy, he might give cricket a go for summer—reckons he'll try chamomile tea at half-time.

Attention Deficit Hyperactivity Disorder (ADHD/ADD)

Just try to think of the ADHD (ADD) problem as information being conducted along the wires (neurones) of the mind. When the wires reach a connection point (synaptic gap) the message isn't relayed very well. It gets lost or weakened so other, more powerful, more visual information jumps in so the kids get distracted. It's worse at school because much of the information is in word form, it's abstract, it's not there, so it's easily lost. But, put them in front of the TV or a computer where the information is fast, visible and stimulating and it can keep them occupied for hours. There's the problem for schools! It's not the teacher's fault!

CHECKS

The typical problems referred to as ADHD include some of the following, depending on the type of ADD the child might have:
- poor concentration
- very impulsive, often takes dangerous risks
- can't wait
- doesn't finish the work
- easily distracted
- interrupts others
- doesn't listen
- difficulty taking turns in games
- tends to be bossy in games that have to be played his/her way
- tends to fidget, run about or climb on things
- trouble sitting still and staying seated
- often talks excessively
- often loses things

These symptoms are also easily confused with immaturity if the kids are still preschoolers and haven't built up their brakes yet. The difference, however, between young ADHD kids and just active kids is that active kids are generally better able to relax, can concentrate when needed (other than TV) and have more stable moods as a rule.

DO'S AND DON'TS

※ **Link up with your local ADHD support group.** If you're not sure where it is then look up one of the contact numbers (see page 365).

- **Get hold of the Raymond Terrace ADHD Support Group booklet** 'Our A-ngels D-isguised as little D-evils' (see Contact Numbers, page 365). It's just the most fantastic collection of parents telling it how it is and sharing ideas and frustrations.

- **Get some management help** through a clinical or child psychologist who has a reputation for understanding ADHD and who has practical advice.

- **Get hold of a good book on ADHD that is strong on management suggestions**, such as my book *Coping with the Family*, or Ian Wallace's very practical book *You and Your ADD Child*.

- **Ask your support group for the name of an understanding paediatrician** who can give Sandy a full check-up and prescribe medication if required. There are also some promising naturopathic mixes on the market at the moment but I have no scientific studies available yet that could allow me to recommend these with confidence.

- **Take the reports from the specialists to the school and ask their advice as to how best to handle it**. Sandy may benefit from being seated near the front or near someone very steady or he may respond to a task reminder. Try the following:

GAMES

DESK DISKS

- Put a green/red disk on Sandy's desk.
- The day starts with the green disk on the left-hand top side of the desk and Sandy's job is to keep it there.
- If teacher catches him 'off task', the disk is turned over to red and it moves one space across the desk to the right. If caught again then it moves across another space, etc.
- If teacher catches Sandy 'on task' then it can flip back one space onto green, and so on.
- If Sandy can keep it left of some agreed critical mark on the desk then he may get some privilege for good effort.

- **Teach problem-solving skills.** ADHD kids are not normally good at solving problems with words or with reflection but they need to learn. Many freak out because they don't know how to think their way through a problem. I like the 'Traffic Light' 'Stop Think Do' system (see opposite) which I use for a variety of problems but another method is to take it in four steps.
  Step 1—'What's my problem?' Help the kids to define as well as they can exactly what's going wrong—not 'He's annoying' but 'I don't like it when he pushes me'.
  Step 2—'How can I solve it?' Brainstorm answers together and let him select the one(s) that he feels will work.
  Step 3—'What's my plan?' After he has chosen his path, help him work out a plan to put it in action.
  Step 4—'How did I do it?' Talk about what worked so he's ready for next time.
  It also helps if parents can develop good problem-solving styles and show Sandy how they do it, so Sandy has a good model to copy.

- Occasionally, **with an older child with ADHD, I might try some reality ideas such as the 'Problem-Solving Signposts'.**
  - What are the signposts saying about the road you're on now? (reflects on present behaviour)
  - Do you want to be here or on a different road? (choices)
  - Where would you like to be heading? (goals)
  - How will you know if you're on the right road? (motivation)
  - What signposts will you be hoping to see? (improved comments, etc)
  - How can we make sure we head up the right road? (strategies)
  - When will we review if we're on the right road or what you will do if we're not? (structure)

- **Get the kids involved in real-life tasks.** ADHD children learn better in life than in the classroom and it also gives them some self-worth and motivation too. At school they can be given special practical roles that they can do well and help make them feel they have something to offer: watering, teaching another student, straightening desks, collecting lunch money, cleaning the board, sharpening pencils, etc.

- **Time out**
  Every family needs to be able to use time out and for families with ADHD kids it can be sanity saving. How to use time out is

outlined in Chapter Ten (see page 298) but there are a few special techniques to keep in mind when using it with ADHD kids.
- It must be used positively. Sending children to their room because they're naughty is likely to cause a revolt because they've been rejected and isolated in anger. Call it 'time to recharge', 'having a rest', 'cooling out' or just 'think time'. Some kids are quite happy to call it the 'sin-bin'. It should not be seen as imprisonment but as a chance to find some answers to a problem.
- For kids with ADHD, that time out must be boring, have firm boundaries of time and space, and must be 100 per cent non-negotiable or they'll worm their way out.

If highly defiant kids refuse to go then again it becomes their choice: they either do their brief time out or they suffer loss of some favourite privilege. The key is that the children know the rules, they choose time out by their behaviour and they choose loss of privileges by not complying with time out. That way parents are not seen as the evil ones. It's also important that the way back into the good books and out of time out is also clear.

- One way I blend a few brakes on behaviour with self-control and choice is to use the '**Traffic Lights**' in connection with time out.

GAMES

TRAFFIC LIGHTS

- Have an agreed in-house phrase to let them know when their behaviour is heading the wrong way (ie you're heading for a red light).
- If it continues tell them to go and 'think' of something else to do. That means going to their room where they have a big yellow think light with ideas written or drawn inside the circle of useful or good things they can do instead of what they were doing.
- When they can indicate they know what they were doing wrong and what they will do when they come out then you may give them the green light to go and do it.

- **Good rules are vital for kids with ADHD** because they often don't have the brakes to stop and self-steer. Any rules should be:
  - *agreed*
  - preferably *worked out together*
  - *consistent*
  - *stated in a positive way* (eg 'walk through the house', rather than 'don't run')
  - *practised regularly* so they become automatic and don't need thinking about

---

TROY'S TROUBLE

Troy's trouble was that he was active, he kept losing things all the time, and he just couldn't concentrate for more than one minute. Mum knew exactly how long because he was in the BMX races that took one-and-a-half minutes. Troy would start with a vengeance but halfway around the track he would stop and talk to people—he forgot he was in a race! Medication had helped but still he couldn't plan or organise himself.

Because he couldn't hold ideas he needed easy and immediate feedback on how he was going. So the teacher organised a special BMX chart with some little pay-off at each checkpoint for any big wins like finishing his work, trying hard and staying in his seat. If he worked hard on all three he got a special privilege from the teacher.

So Mum organised a two-sided cardboard flag to be left on his desk. The teacher would flip to the yellow side for danger if his concentration dropped and then back to the chequered side for good concentration. If he got more than five yellow flags during the day he would have to do lunchtime duties, but if the chequered flags won he could add one more to his BMX chart. At the same time they watched his diet and put more routines and clearer rules into his day.

He actually finished a race the other day. The family was so happy, and the club was so happy they organised a special trophy. The only problem was Troy left it somewhere.

Bush Remedies

- If you can't get your child to sit still or focus or listen then put your hand or arm on the child (like an anchor), meet their eyes directly, then talk short and to the point.

- My son has ADHD and was hopeless to take shopping. I realised it was all too stimulating so I learnt not to take the kids there, I'd go on my own and I'd take them bushwalking instead which was good for all of us and their behaviour in natural surroundings is a lot better.

Listening Problems

Most of the kids I see with listening problems, memory problems or forgetting problems have faulty attention. Memory is stored in multiple sections of the brain—one part might remember the *person* who spoke, another part might remember the *sound*, another part the *words*, and another the *meaning*. When we recall something we actually have to put all these parts together, so you can see why peoples' memories (eg of accidents) often vary so much. It also depends on the amount of stress or stimulation to our system. If we're preoccupied, thinking of a million things at once or worried about something, then our attention to what's coming in will be very limited. If we're overfocusing on one thing then we'll block out another.

CHECKS

This listening section will be useful if your Sandy suffers from poor listening, poor communication or if he forgets what he has been told.

- Check for **hearing problems**—talking loudly, speech disability, always talking at high volume, turning their head to one side to listen, not hearing normal house noises, etc.

- Check for **intellectual problems**—slow to learn, can't keep up, slow to read, behind in schoolwork.

✮ Check for **emotional problems**—sad, preoccupied, bossy, feeling rejected, etc.

✮ Check for **social problems**—feels kids don't like him or won't play with him.

✮ Check for **Attention Demanding Disorder, Attention Damaged Disorder, Attention Disabled Disorder, Attention Digested Disorder and ADHD/ADD.**

DO'S AND DON'TS

✮ **If the problem seems to be in their hearing**, get it checked by a specialist on a referral from your family doctor.

✮ **If the problem seems to be intellectual** (ie they can't keep up), get the school counsellor or local child psychologist to do some testing. These kids shouldn't have a listening problem if the message is at their level.

✮ **If the problem seems to be emotional**, have a friendly chat at eye level, preferably when it's just the two of you (eg in the car or out walking). Just talk about things that make Sandy feel happy or sad and that may give you the remedy route. If it's deeper than that, then a child psychologist would be the person to consult. Kids that are overwhelmed emotionally tend to only listen to the things that will help them emotionally survive, and they cut out or short-circuit others.

✮ **If the problem seems to be social**, then a quiet word to the teacher or child care worker would be the best starter. It's hard to solve social problems in a one-to-one chat between parent and child. It needs to be done at the scene of the problem.

✮ **If Sandy doesn't appear to have any of the above problems**, there's a fair chance that he may either have ADHD or else have developed lazy listening habits. Treat it firstly as a poor listening habit and use some of these ideas.
  ◆ Give instructions in attention-grabbing ways.
  ◆ Make sure that Sandy is listening before delivering any message.

- Use some special tune-in phrase such as: 'Mum to Sandy, are you listening?' or a special listening-in signal such as first and middle names (eg 'Sandy Ridge, can you hear me?').
- Sing the message if you want novelty and to keep it fun. If you're tone-deaf, so much the better—they won't want you to do an encore!
- Mime what you want.

(I'm not suggesting that these be used all the time, but just to begin a new and better listening habit.)

✸ **If poor listeners have ADHD**, then it is even harder for the message to be relayed. It takes practice to oil the right connections. (See 'Practice List' in the Appendix, page 354.)
- Write the word 'listening' on the 'Practice List' (or tick it if you use my prepared list in the Appendix).
- Let them know it's not good enough straightaway.
- At a time to suit you, have them practise again and again till you both feel that it's under control (this enriches correct behaviour loops in the mind).
- To do the practice, choose your time, tell them to wait in their room until you call, then call softly to see if they hear. They then do whatever you whispered to prove that they heard it.
- Give them another practice from their room with another instruction, never repeating the message more than once.
- If successful, acknowledge improved hearing. If not, then (without malice) do more listening practice till they get the message that you mean business.
- If they refuse to do the practice, use the 'Fridge Disk Discipline' (see Appendix, page 351), turn it to sad/red side and give none of your cooperation (on any privileges) until after they have practised or shown you that they can get it right after being told only once.
- If they're really defiant and still won't cooperate then pull back on privileges (dessert, stories, TV) or, better still, if you have a partner, then get them to do the practice for you so you don't need to have constant confrontation.

✸ **Use good communication skills** (also see suggestions in Chapter Six). Many parents with a poor listener will get into the habit of saying things many times over, nagging, threatening, lecturing, criticising or ridiculing, with obvious results. Good communication is based on firmness, dignity and respect.

The worst communication killers are these:
- assuming ('I didn't tell you because I knew you'd be angry.')
- rescuing ('Don't forget your homework.')
- directing ('Pick up your clothes.')
- expecting ('I thought I could count on you to behave.')
- adultisms ('You know better than that.')

Instead we should be aiming for the following:
- checking ('What did you think I wanted you to do?')
- exploring the what, why and how ('What could you do differently?', 'Why were you so angry with me?', 'How did that happen?')
- encouraging ('I'd really like it if you could clean up your room before dinner.')
- celebrating ('I think you did a terrific job on your room today.')
- respecting ('I'd love to hear your ideas on this problem.')

✻ **Do some active listening** so you know where Sandy is coming from. If you can see the problem through his eyes, it not only makes him clarify his thoughts, but means you become an ally in problem solution rather than the enemy. Another important aspect is to use the honest 'I', how I feel, rather than the accusing 'you'! The way to do it is to give a clear description of the behaviour, the feeling it creates in you and the reason you feel that way. For example, 'When you dirtied the kitchen floor (the behaviour), I felt angry (the feeling), because I had spent the morning cleaning it (the consequences).'

✻ **Remember that poor listeners with ADHD have bigger engines than brakes—they can go but they can't stop**. So, for example, if you tell Sandy: 'Don't poke your sister', the word 'don't' stimulates the challenge, and then the words that followed actually tell him to do the very thing you don't want him to do! No wonder he's a problem, this poor kid!

It's natural to say 'don't' or 'stop', but follow up immediately with a direction telling them what you *do* want, not *don't* want. So, if Sandy is poking his sister, the follow-up command could be: 'Please come to me' or 'Come and sit on this chair till you've thought of something good to do' or 'Come and help me get dinner ready.'

Bush Remedies

- When my eight-year-old son didn't listen, do as he was asked or pick up his toys, I served up the family meals, called everyone to the table and gave my son his to take out and eat with the dog in the carport. I said, 'You seem not to want to be part of this family by pulling your weight so you don't eat with us.' I never had any trouble again.

- If he isn't listening I take him by the hand and make sure he gives me eye contact and I explain myself again.

- Time out in their bedroom always works.

- I kept on talking about what I wanted to tell him, then went off on a totally unrelated topic, then back to the issue, then off again, until he listened to what I wanted to tell him.

- If they don't listen to me, I don't listen to them, and if they don't answer me, then I don't answer them. It doesn't take long for them to get the message.

- I found that kids hear K words better, so I give things I want them to hear a K sound. For example, I might start a message, 'Calling car 42'.

- My problem is that sometimes kids listen *too* well, and I find my worst sayings or habits coming out in their play. One special phrase I've used in our busy family is: 'Let's relax and do our own thing', especially when they're hounding me while I'm on the move. I was getting ready one morning, putting on my make-up and Jack, my two-year-old, was in front of me quietly playing. 'Mummy, I'm doing my own thing,' he said. 'OK, Jack,' I replied, without looking down. But when I did, there was Jack with a pile of unravelled toilet paper as tall as he. How could I get upset when it was I who said to relax and do our own thing. Great tactic!

- I had a tape recorder at the ready in the kitchen. If they didn't listen, I'd tape what I had to say, turn off the TV and they would have to do what the tape said till it was finished.

In this modern age of communications, everyone's talking but few are listening. We have two ears and one tongue so we should talk less and listen more.

Interrupting Problems

Kids who interrupt and won't wait for anything really test their parents' patience. Most ADHD and Attention Demanding Disorder children have a huge problem with waiting, everything must be now.

CHECKS

- **Check whether it's bad manners or good copying.** Is interrupting a style used by others in the family?

- **Check whether it's ADHD-based.** ADHD kids have a lot of trouble waiting and worry that they might forget if they do.

- **Check whether it's Attention Demanding Disorder.** Attention-seeking kids will not be the least bit interested in lectures about bad manners—they seek attention, and interrupting is one guaranteed way to get it.

- **Check whether it's stress-based.** Frantic families have so many things on their mind that they have to blurt the thought out before it gets swamped by others.

DO'S AND DON'TS

- **Adjust your family style** if you're all talking over the top of each other. That can be done by new habit formation, using practice and the 'Habit Chart'.

GAMES

HABIT CHART

- Share with the kids that you want the family to hear each other (more positive than saying 'don't interrupt').
- Get their ideas on how the family will do it and what signal they'll use if they feel interrupted (eg 'excuse me' or stony silence).
- Try and encourage or give points on their chart to kids who were good listeners (more positive than saying 'didn't interrupt').
- Use the three strikes and you're out (to time out) if they break the family rule.
- Keep the new habit fresh with charts, rewards, listening, or whatever works, for one month and you may have something that will last the kids' lifetime.

Practise waiting

- If they can't wait at all then maybe tell them to keep remembering and going over in their mind what they wanted until you can listen.
- Train them to wait until you've done whatever you're doing (at first with something as brief as putting food back in the fridge).
- If they're a bit better than that, use your oven timer and they can wait one, two, three, four or five minutes or whatever time you feel you need and they can manage.
- If they just can't wait at all then put this on your 'Practice List' (see Appendix, page 354) and practise the waiting at a time to suit you (maybe not them) until they're sure they've got the message.

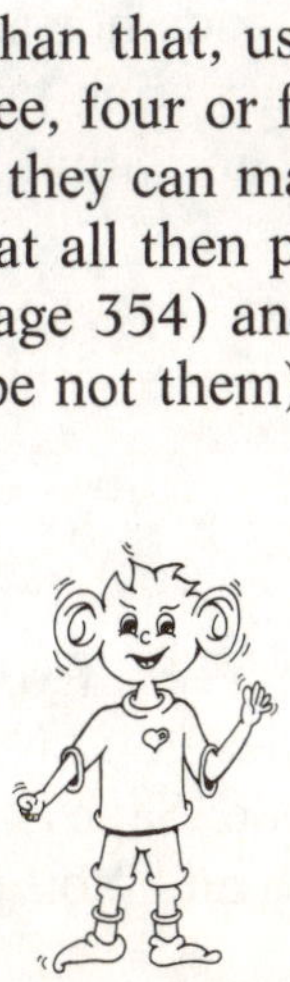

Bush Remedies

- I just pointed out that they would not like me interrupting their conversations or phone calls.

- I always found it a lot quicker to listen and answer them, than what it was to tell them to wait.

- If kids are interrupting or screaming at me, I say, 'I will listen to you when you lower your voice and talk nicely.'

- When my three-year-old interrupts I just take my cordless phone and lock myself into the toilet while he hammers on the door. It works.

- I just told them it wasn't fair and to prove my point I'd deliberately interrupt them when they were watching TV or playing with their friends. They got the message and we worked out an 'excuse me' rule.

No-Alls

Every survey rated this habit—kids not accepting NO for an answer—as *the* most infuriating and frustrating problem for parents, bar none! But for many no-alls the problem is that NO has not been used for an answer.

CHECKS

- Does the NO actually mean YES, if you push me? For example, 'No, you can't have any lollies now. No, Sandy, I said no and I mean no. Leave my bag alone. Sandy, give it to me. Oh, all right, you can have one, but that's all.' You just know what will happen next time.

EAR AND ATTENTION PROBLEMS

- Is the NO overplayed: sometimes inflected up as a warning; sometimes the Noooo is lengthened to signal keep asking; sometimes light and bright which means NO, but no offence; and sometimes bellowed, which means 'NO, are you deaf or just stupid?' where offence is taken?

- Is home just a mass of STOP or NO signs, in which case the kids won't notice them?

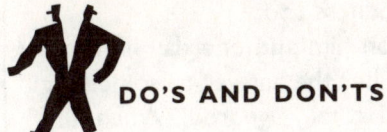

DO'S AND DON'TS

- Learn to not overuse NO. Only use it when you mean it.

- With little kids and toddlers, saying NO is like saying no to their ego so just expect, joke, divert or *con* them into cooperating. They adapt if their pride's not hurt.

- With older kids, follow the NO with a reason—if you've thought of one in time. For example 'We can't do that because . . .'

- Remember that NO will only work if life is not all NO and no YES. If they hear YES a lot then a firm NO rings through loud and clear. So make a practice of saying YES more often; kids of any age enjoy hearing that word. In fact, if you watch a boy win something or do something hard, he will often raise his fist or hand and say YES.

- If little ones won't accept NO try saying YES even to their silly requests; like 'Yes, I see your point but we can't because . . .' It sounds silly but it takes the edge off.

- Have some little rule like: 'Ask once and I listen. Ask twice and the answer's NO. Ask three times and the answer's no TV, because it's damaging your hearing.'

I recall one little girl I saw who would never take NO for an answer at home but would be as obedient as you like at school. 'Why do you do that?' her mum asked.

'Well, at school when they say NO they mean it but when you say NO you don't.' Maybe it's not just little kids that are easily conned.

NINJA VERSUS KILLER

How did you learn to master the nastier side of your nature? Maybe we're all still learning but young Tai had NO idea. He was a pain in the class, called out, would never take NO for an answer, disobeyed, gave smart answers, upset every teacher, but this teacher, Hallina, was a bit too good for him, she not only believed in the goodness in every child but because she was so genuine, she could get the kids to believe in their own goodness too.

In time her tactics started to work on him and one day he came up to Hallina in the playground and told her the answer to something she'd asked in lessons and which he'd totally ignored. When she showed surprise at him knowing the answer, his reply was interesting: 'In class you only see the bad side of me, which I call Killer. But Ninja my good spirit was trying to listen but Killer never lets him win.' This intrigued Hallina and they talked about how good he felt with Ninja in action and ways to make it stronger. So he decided to shift seats, to try and draw deep breaths when he was angry, and to try to suck up his Ninja back in his head and press a cancel button in the top of his head each time Killer started to take control.

The short-term change has been remarkable. It seems that now he had someone who believed he could be good and now he could see his problem he knew how to be good. As Hallina said to him, 'Anyone who has the power to be bad also has the power to be good, if he wants it.' Now Tai did.

Bush Remedies

- Our daughter became a real drama queen when she heard the word NO. I didn't really have an answer but when we go out with friends and have a good laugh, her little antics don't seem so bad after that.

Attention Summary

OUR CHILDREN ARE GROWING UP IN A WORLD COMPETING FOR THEIR ATTENTION.

- **A** Attend to behaviour you like and you'll get more of it.
- **T** Train good listening, don't expect it (talk time, story time, lap time, teaching time).
- **T** Time out from attention for attention seekers is more powerful than yelling or smacking.
- **E** Example of parents is the best trainer of good listening in children.
- **N** Nagging and negative comments teach children not to listen.
- **T** Try flooding attention-seeking behaviour so it becomes a less attractive option.
- **I** Instil some special signals that tell the child to stop and listen to what's coming.
- **O** Only say things once if you want kids to hear you the first time.
- **N** Noise (shouting, screaming, TV, videos) destroys good listening.

FAMOUS FOOTNOTE
A SECOND-TIME-AROUND DAD

Kim Beazley
POLITICIAN

In politics, you have many good acquaintances and the times you spend together are to be treasured, but you have few close friends. So your family is likely to be a bulwark, but it is a bulwark which you constantly shatter by your absence and the fact that you really oblige your wife to be almost a supporting parent in terms of the lifestyle she leads.

A politician's lifestyle sometimes means your family and close friends are all you've got because you lose all your other friends, the people that you went to school with, to university with, acquaintances you've made in the community. Even relationships with family and close friends are not well nurtured, and so you're a very psychologically isolated individual.

But it's also hard being the child of a politician. When you're in a bit of political trouble or your party's in trouble, your kids all carry those burdens. I can recollect when I was a kid in school in the fifties other kids all shouting 'Commo' at me and that sort of thing. You do get into trouble from time to time in politics—generally speaking, the community dislikes you intensely—and when you're in trouble they dislike you even more, and some will take that out on the kids. So the kids have to develop a certain toughness, and sometimes they are capable of bluff, and sometimes they blame you for the circumstances in which they find themselves.

One thing my lifestyle has imposed on my kids is probably a higher level of selflessness than most kids would actually possess. They've had their complaints, their bitternesses and their worries, but they've also—as good human beings and well-rounded characters—got deep and complex psychologies, and they have actually been able to arrive at a decision that they will look after me. I noticed that when I was divorced and the kids were quite young. The eldest one, in particular, tried to mother me, and they looked after themselves fairly well.

My mother was a very strong influence in my background. Basically she was very supportive; if ever there was something I wanted to do, she was right in there behind it. She was a strong mother, a good one, a very busy one, and I was damn lucky. I'm not sure what made her so special, but I think it was attention. I took it for granted at the time, there was no question about that, but gee it was nice to get it.

Dad, I think, always had the view that imposed morality was no morality. Parental imposition is just that, imposition. He believed that each of us is an individual moral being that has to arrive at our own conclusions. The duty of a parent is for a parent to say what they think is right, but then to also have underpinning that, at the end of the day, it was a matter of your choice. Parental love is not dependent upon the choices that you take.

My tips to parents would be answer all their questions. That's about the best you can do for them, I think. They may not ask the question, but if they do, answer them.

Something in my life is always being sacrificed—my electorate, my family, my party, the parliament, the policy. It is not possible to do all the things all the time and that leaves a residual dissatisfaction in you that is not easy to cope with. Sometimes you can sit down with pleasure and say, 'gee, I did this and this well today', then you pick up the phone to the family and you hear, 'Dad, you forgot this . . . ' I mean, I couldn't possibly have remembered or done something about it and done these other things, so okay, what I thought was a perfect day is in fact a flawed one. I haven't found a way around it and I never will I don't think.

CHAPTER FOUR

Eye and Sleeping Problems

It was always my job to wake up at night and attend to Damon. I don't know quite how this happened; I know that there were times that I resented it enormously. I'd be dog-tired after a hard day or I'd have arrived home a little worse for wear and having to wake up in response to Damon's crying wasn't easy. But the implication of Damon crying was that he had a bleed and this would inevitably end in his having to go to hospital.

If I said that I didn't often think that I'd gotten a raw deal, I'd be lying. I'd flop into bed exhausted only to be awakened two hours later by a Damon tug on my arm. Sometimes my head would be splitting and my mouth tasting like the inside of a parrot's cage. But I had no choice; I often found this hard and felt sorry for myself.

BRYCE COURTENAY, author
(READ MORE OF BRYCE COURTENAY'S FAMOUS FOOTNOTES AT THE END OF THIS CHAPTER.)

Very few kids have a sleep problem! It's their parents that have the problem with the kids' sleep! Sleep in fact is *the* most common problem according to one study of parents of 14-month-old kids. It's certainly the cause of more domestics than we'd care to own, and probably the reason I had more parent input on this section than any other in the manual.

When they're preschoolers the problem is to get them to stay in their own bed. When they're primary schoolers the problem is to get them out of their own bed. Before you can say 'help hormones' we're back to where we started.

But it's not just eye-shutting problems that drive parents demented. There are other eye-related frustrations such as eyes that can never find anything and eyes that forget where they left anything (this is called the 'Mu-m, where's me ...' syndrome). Then there are the mind's-eye problems such as bad dreams and baddies in their bedroom.

Sleep Interruptions

If your Sandy is a problem sleeper, no matter what others tell you about the worst ages being 0–10, 10–20 or 20–30 years, it doesn't come any harder than what you're putting up with right now—especially if you're doing it on your own, or as in Bryce Courtenay's case, your family is coping with some sleep-interrupting disability. In fact, a young baby is the greatest destroyer of sex, sleep and sanity known to parents.

Recently I had a couple in the clinic, worried about their relationship. When I asked them what was their biggest problem, the young guy shuffled, looked down, took a deep breath, and then blurted out, 'Well if you want me to be honest, Doc, since the baby was born my wife, ah ... how do I say this ... ah, she has lost, like, her libido!'

His wife turned to him, slowly, furiously, ever reddeningly, and spluttered, 'Lost my libido, have I? I'll tell you what I've lost ... I've lost my sanity, that's what!'

CHECKS

✱ **Is it just their age?** Some kids take longer than others to adjust to day and night or to sleeping through the night. So don't look at yourself as a bad parent; in fact, at the moment, don't look at yourself at all! And don't look at your baby as some sinister package sent by God to pay you back for your sins in your younger years. And here's a bit of comfort for you: some of the most gifted and talented kids I've met have been problem sleepers. So, if you can, snuggle in with them and adjust to their style, knowing that what you have in front of you is a great Australian in the making, and that's why they're difficult.

🏃 **Is it an emotional problem?** Are you so exhausted and angry about your own sleep interruptions (or your partner's oblivion) that you rattle the kids' confidence so they don't resettle as well?

🏃 **Is it a feeding problem?** Maybe you're giving too much nutrition (solids or milk) in night feeds so their brain expects a midnight party.

🏃 **Is it a social problem?** Do you make the midnight wake times so much fun, so stimulating or so special that they can't wait for the encore?

🏃 **Is it a physical problem?** Check that they're comfortable, maybe top-and-tail them or, if it's not the normal pattern, think about teething or tummy trouble. If it's a scream, then maybe something like middle ear infection, 'otitis media' (not 'Optus media' as one lady told me), could be the culprit. Any doubts like this should be checked out with the clinic sister as soon as possible.

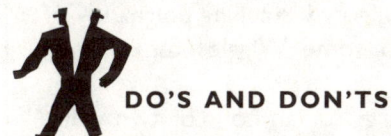

DO'S AND DON'TS

🏃 Link up with the clinic sister, the Nursing Mothers Association, playgroup, neighbours, family or friends for advice, support and reassurance before the problems get out of hand. We were never meant to do this parenting thing all alone.

🏃 Read Chris Green's book *Babies* and maybe try his ideas on controlled crying. I've also outlined a sleeping program in my previous book, *Coping with the Family*.

🏃 If the baby's anywhere near six months or more, then the waking is just for soothing and sucking, not for nutrition, so maybe weaken the mix to water over time so his system doesn't expect a feed.

- There may be other irritations that are the cause of the problem, so don't blame yourself or the baby. Check with your clinic sister and, if necessary, with a paediatrician.

- Get hold of a good novel or magazine and only allow yourself to read it when you're up for the midnight marathon.

- Talk to fellow sufferers. Every fellow sufferer would empathise with the sentiments in Mark's letter.

I tried leaving the light on, and turning it off, drinks, biscuits, toys in her room, no toys in her room, a pillow, more blankets, less blankets, less noise downstairs, more noise downstairs, leaving a ticking clock on in her bedroom, playing soft music on tape and ... yelling at her. None worked!

As I believe humour is the next best thing to a night off for coping with sleep problems, let me share a great little true story about my friend Stan.

Stan and I had started our lecturing careers together. I hadn't seen him since BC (before children). When I popped in on him for a surprise visit, I was confronted by one of the most pitiful sights known to man. There was this fine specimen of brain and brawn clumsily clad in his wife's dressing gown, smelling poignantly of perfume, mincing around the room to some Wiggles tunes while trying to interest bub in a wet washer.

Narelle, his wife, had left him in charge for an hour or two while she ducked out to fill up the fridge. Unfortunately, breast-fed Brad had woken and poor old Stan was found wanting. Stan had grabbed a small book called *Help* and on page 23 it offered ideas on what to do if bub's missing Mum. It said make sure the same music is playing, [the sitter] is wearing the same robe or cologne you wear when you feed him and if you suspect teething use a wet washer.

My bet is that bub linked feel and smell with Mum and was after Dad for the impossible.

Anyhow, we drained and dressed bub, gave him a suck of water or two and a bounce or two and talked between squawks until Narelle surfaced, then she got blasted for not leaving any breasto expresso.

But I was glad I called in; as Stan said, it was just a matter of minutes before one of them had hit the bottle.

By the way, if you'd like to know how much sleep you need to survive young kids, according to the experts it's five minutes more!

The fact is that every young kid has a sleeping problem: they can't tell the time, can't sleep long enough, can't tell when we're tired and can't whisper. So please don't blame the kids, maybe blame your own sleepless night some nine months before they were born!

So universal is this problem for parents that I've included it as the first event in my 'Parenting Pentathlon', for inclusion in the 2000 Olympics. Why not—the art of becoming a parent is the most widely practised sport in the community.

PARENT PENTATHLON
MIDNIGHT MADNESS SPRINT EVENT

RULES: The Midnight Madness Sprint requires all lights out and parents curled up in the foetal position. The event begins with a sleep-shattering scream. Parents immediately begin the battle for the bed by feigning deep sleep, claiming sleep deprivation, madness or murderous intent. The loser is dishonourably discharged into the darkness, risking life and limb as they weave their weary way through dangerous doors, furniture hazards and baby booby traps to effect a siren shutdown without waking anyone or doing any damage.

SCORING: Points go to the parent who can get back to sleep faster than the kids.

Bed Departure
Kids Who Won't Stay in Their Bed

This is the next game for slightly older, more mobile kids. In fact, it ranks as one of the top toddler tactics capable of converting placid parents into screaming, raving, demented monsters. And it's not as if they read your vibes, is it? No matter how angry you might be when you put them back to bed, back they bounce and re-emerge with that big grin that says 'Found ya'.

By the way, the record number of reappearances is 54, so if you're way short of that you're doing well.

CHECKS

- **Is it just their age?** All toddlers want more of the action but they've never had the legs to do it before, nor the brain to tell them how to find you. Now they can picture it all and are ever so pleased when they're proved right.

- **Is it an emotional problem?** If they have missed out on you during the day then they're going to want to get as much as they can at night. Or if there's anger in the air then they won't want to settle.

- **Is it a routine problem?** Kids settle better if they have been well bedded down in ways that make them feel secure: routines, whispers, a bedtime story, cuddles, kisses, etc. If they've been sick, sleeping elsewhere or if the routine has been disturbed in any way then they might try this one on a bit more. Don't fall for it; get them back into routine as quickly and confidently as you can.

- **Is it a social problem?** If everyone else is out in front of the TV, having a good time, then hey, why shouldn't they? That doesn't mean you should give in to it.

- **Is it a physical problem?** If they're usually good settlers then maybe there is something irritating their systems: teething, tummy, overtired, etc. Put them back down, but keep a close eye on their cry and their colour.

- **Is it management?** If getting up brings success—that is, they're allowed to stay up, even once or twice ... then that sniff of success will encourage encores for a long time.

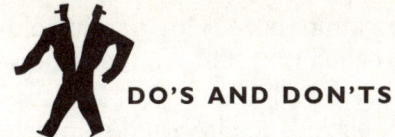

DO'S AND DON'TS

✸ If your kids have a settling problem then see this as normal if they're toddlers. The kids are so proud to be able to work out where you are. Keep putting them back down without a fuss and your put downs will plummet within a fortnight if you're consistent.

✸ If you need more help get hold of any good baby care book or the book *Teach Your Baby to Sleep Through the Night*.

✸ Every family will have its own ways of handling this problem but here's a general guideline called the 'Bed Settlers' Program'.

GAMES

BED SETTLERS' PROGRAM

◆ Put Sandy down after normal getting-to-bed routines—drink, toilet, cuddles, kisses and story—then say good night, switch the lights off (so if he wakes up he won't startle at the difference from when he shut his eyes) and leave.

◆ If he cries, just leave him for five minutes and then go in, no games, no fun, no yelling, no extra light, just give him a firm message to get to sleep.

◆ If he keeps on crying out, give him 20 minutes and then repeat the previous step.

◆ If he insists on getting up and up, then keep putting him back and back.

◆ Keep a record of your 'put backs' and your score will plummet with quiet persistence.

◆ If not, get him to practise the next *day* staying in his bed until the alarm goes. Set it for 5–10 minutes, or shorter at first if he's not familiar with the buzzer.

◆ Then use the buzzer technique that night and chances are he'll be asleep before it buzzes.

Give it a go, it sure beats telling kids to count sheep. One parent told me she tried that, but her smart alec son called out, 'Oh yeah, and how am I supposed to count them in the dark?'

Some parents will try anything to get their kids to sleep and so much depends on their personality.

The husband of a close friend actually climbed into the cot with the toddler. He said that the method works, but the rungs are murder on your back, so I don't think I'll try that one.

It is a hard time, there is a bit of 'soldier-on' in it, and as one parent said to me, 'Whoever it was that said someone "sleeps like a baby" has obviously never had one!'

Bush Remedies

- Our nightly routine consists of (1) 'Time for bed' ... she gets up again. (2) 'Go to bed now' ... she gets up, runs to us and smiles. (3) 'Naughty girl, time for bed' ... she gets up, smiles, thrusts her hip out, hand on hip and shakes her finger at us. (4) 'If you don't go to bed, you are in big trouble' ... I sigh and wonder do I smack her or hug her. I try to leave the room before I make a decision. Then she sleeps like a baby until 6a.m.

- I heard you suggest that kids settle better if there's the smell of Mum around so I sprinkle a bit of perfume around and put some lavender on her pillow to encourage deep breathing. I also recorded some stories onto cassette for her to listen to. Something's working, but I think it's mostly my determination that bedtime is bedtime.

- I had to install a lamp in the bedroom and have it on all night. I also had his favourite soft toys next to him in bed.

- At first I calmly put him back to bed and talk to him for a little while. After the fifth time I raise my voice and tell him I'm very cross.

- I'd suggest letting them help rearrange their own room or moving the bed. Keep putting them back quietly. It doesn't work to growl as it causes stress for both of you and then the child is scared you don't love them. Say: 'It's night-time now, give me a kiss and go to sleep.' Do this twice if needed. The third time, say 'good night' only and put the child to bed. Do not put on the light, hold a conversation or give cuddles. Just go for a walk outside if it's getting to you.

- When my second child started that business, I didn't have time for all the fancy stuff. If a kid's in bed he's in bed. I just took him out, upturned the cot and put him back in again with the cot on top. Visitors thought it looked a bit odd, but it did the job.

- I explained that after 8p.m. it was adult time and I would not pay attention to her.

- I put the toddler in with her sister and put the radio on.

- I just consistently kept her in her bed. It works!

- I set a regular bedtime to go to bed and read a bedtime story. If she was late for bed, then there was no story.

- I used meditation stories by Maureen Garth and also allowed a five-minute cuddle time in the child's bed ... it worked wonders.

- This is where you have to be firm. At the end of the day in our house they have to be in bed by 8.30. We start half an hour before—brush the teeth, toilet, bed, and then we read to them until 8.30. No TV after 7p.m. (unless it's the State of Origin). Instead, we have quiet reading, board games or talking. If they're still not sleepy at 8.30, we leave the light on and they can read for a while.

- Our very active child hated to sleep. In the end we just made his room safe, put a barricade across the doorway and let him run amuck as we had to have our sleep. Finally, at puberty, he discovered the joys of sleeping and staying in bed.

- *Twin Advice:*
My advice to multiple-birth parents is to put twins or triplets in the one cot right from the start. Either top-to-tail them or sleep them husband/wife fashion. In most cases they seem to settle down a lot easier than being in separate bassinettes. Mine did this for nearly

nine months before they started to wake each other up.

- My son hated going to bed. To avoid an unhappy night I would sing to him and he'd soon be asleep. Another good idea at bedtime was instead of me reading him a story, I'd get him to tell me a story and he'd soon drop off.

- My five-year-old, Nicholas, wouldn't sleep in his own bed and it had been taking me two hours to get him to fall asleep. Then I noticed how fascinated he was by the fish on the screen saver on the computer. So we bought two goldfish in a small round bowl. At night I read stories to Nicholas *and* the fish, we say our prayers and say good night, then I let him look at the fish and remind him not to call out because he'd startle the fish. I tell him he must stay in his own bed because the fish would be lonely without him but he could come into my bed when the sun was up and the fish wouldn't be scared. It has worked perfectly. Why didn't I think of it before? Those goldfish turned out to be better than a screen saver, they're a scream saver!

- I cuddled them in the lounge room till they went to sleep but they weren't allowed to sleep at Nan's or go to sleep overs till they could show me they could go to sleep in their own bed.

- I threw a sheet over their bunks and they made their own cubby house or tepee which they loved.

Slow Sleepers

Kids Who Just Can't Get To Sleep

The bed departure problems of the toddlers tend to give way to the problems of kids who will go to bed, will stay in their bed, but they just can't settle.

EYE AND SLEEPING PROBLEMS   115

CHECKS

✷ Do all the checks referred to in Bed Departure (page 109).

✷ Do they have plenty of energy in the morning? If so, chances are they're not ready to settle down. This doesn't mean they should stay up and intrude into parent time but let them read, listen or do quiet things in their room without bugging them to get to sleep.

✷ Check their bedtime routine.
- Are they having rich food too close to bedtime?
- Are they coming straight from TV to bed?
- Are they getting stirred up before bed with wrestles, etc?
- Are they waiting for a parent to come home or tuck them in, etc?
- Are they being sent to bed in anger? If so, they'll probably take longer to unwind.
- Are they just bouncy kids whose systems take longer to unwind (eg ADHD kids)? If this is the case, then clear rules and a bit of latitude to fiddle around (in their room) might be in order.
- Are they worry warts suffering from anxiety overload? If so, then use the ideas on anxiety listed in Chapter Two.

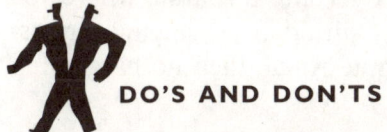
DO'S AND DON'TS

✷ Have a good regular routine before bed so they start to unwind before they reach bed. Hopefully, regardless of age, that routine should include a bit of reading or talk time with a parent just to settle the day down and talk through any worries they might have.

✷ Look closely at your evening routines. Maybe switch the bath to after dinner to unwind them, check that they're not eating a lot of rich food late, and be aware that many kids find it hard to come straight from TV and get to sleep.

✷ Check the atmosphere at home. If they haven't had some down time, cuddle time or lap time to touch base with you and feel secure, then they may kick on at bedtime because they're emotionally still hungry and not ready to settle.

- Other suggestions for younger children include:
  - have a good night parade for teddies then toddlers;
  - use the oven buzzer to tell them it's bedtime, it saves nagging;
  - tape-record stories (or nursery rhymes or songs if you're game)—that way they at least have your voice for company.

- If they like having their back massaged, make it more interesting with the 'Weather Report Massage' referred to earlier (see page 44) or with a 'Garden Massage', using different strokes for digging, raking, preparing the rows and planting fruit and vegetable seeds they've chosen. If they're teenagers, maybe you could even weed the zits!

- Put a dab of cologne on the back of their hand and tell them to sniff until the scent has gone . . . the deep breathing induces sleep.

- Let your child pick from a 'Dream Jar' (perhaps an empty tin you've decorated) a slip of paper on which you've written an idea for a pleasant dream. They can go to sleep with the paper under the pillow.

- If you want to save your sanity, don't get into a routine where you have to entertain them till they settle, with dances, singing, drives around town, etc. Just have a 10-minute ritual, then no bargaining, that's it, so they know the routine.

Bush Remedies

- I always read books to them, or had new books hidden away to make them enjoy going to bed.

- Tell them that their sleeping-with teddy is very tired and won't go to sleep without them.

- I turned off all the lights and went to bed myself leaving her sitting in the lounge in the dark—good night!

- We kept a taped story and book beside their bed, and did a comfort check of the room: windows, under the bed—we even moved the bed around.

- If kids won't go to sleep or lie down for their nap, use white noise such as fans or music, or, because kids love cubby holes, use a large cardboard box, decorated with stickers and cosily padded. Another good idea is to call nap time by a different name such as rest time or growing big time; I've convinced my kids that their bodies only grow while they're resting.

- If you're visiting and there's no cot, put the baby in the bath, and make it cosy with towels and cushions. But make sure that you remove the plugs and soap, and that you try this only if the baby can't reach the taps and if your host doesn't have a child old enough or mischievous enough to turn them on!

Night Monsters and Bad Dreams

Remember the golden rule about kids' imaginary problems: just as their imagination has created the problem, so it can solve it. Don't try to reason with them or give them logical answers; the problem is not reasonable! Most young kids will have monster trouble so don't overreact and give it time to see if it's settling.

CHECKS

- Are they using the monsters as an excuse to keep your attention? If so, treat it as manipulation and reply offhandedly with a comment such as: 'Well, monsters need sleep too, so keep your eye on them and see if any of them start yawning.'

✝ Are the fears and images worse after late nights, rich food, TV, etc?

✝ Is there any pattern to the type of monster or type of fear? If so, it might be worth creating counter forces to beat that image.

DO'S AND DON'TS

✝ If it's not manipulation but the genuine monster attack then try the following 'Monster-Munching Tactics'.

✝ If Sandy wants, you might allow him to leave a dim night light on.
- As his mind has made the monsters then sit with him and work out some fun ways he can beat the monster when it next visits.
- Instead of saying there are no monsters, join in the imagination and shoo them out the window. Let him select a crystal from a shop and give it special monster-munching powers but, if you do, make sure you've helped him visualise how it will work (eg emits a magic shield that monsters can't crack, has monster-disabling properties, acts like kryptonite on monsters, etc).
- If it's not improving, cut out rich food at the evening meal, shift his shower to just before bed, try burning lavender oil in his room and cut out all scary TV shows, videos and video games.
- This should fix 99 per cent of monster problems, but if you're still worried then consult a child psychologist; they're experts at handling little monsters.

✝ See suggestions in Chapter Two, page 31.

FEARS IN PYJAMAS

Katrina's cosy room became bedevilled with burglars and night nasties just with the creaking of shrinking boards. Each night she would wake up, convert the dark to demonic forces then scream her way down the passage, wake everyone on the way and hurl herself between Mum and Dad in bed. Her parents were angry and exhausted, and seriously contemplating divorce because they were arguing so much over her antics.

Everything else in her little life checked out okay, so the job was to harness this imagination for fun not fear. Although she was 10, Katrina turned out to be a great fan of Bananas in Pyjamas so we made up a Bananas in Pyjamas chart to record her wins, and then we practised imagining that the creaking boards were actually B1, B2, Morgan Ratina rat and crew playing hide-and-seek. I told her not to go to sleep that night but to stay awake (just a bit of reverse psych) to work out who was seeking who and where they were moving. If she was still awake when their game had stopped then she could wander quietly down to her parents' room and slip into a sleeping bag by their bed.

She was asleep within five minutes! Dad's really pleased; then with a wink in his eye, shyly suggested that he and his wife might have time to play bananas in pyjamas too. I'm not sure what he meant!

Bush Remedies

- If they're frightened, tell them about your fears as a child and how you beat them so they don't feel so bad. If they need a security blanket or teddy, let them have it.

- If they feared monsters in the bedroom we drew the worst monster face we could, and stuck it on the window facing out to frighten all the intruding monsters away.

- My son, Josh, was afraid of monsters so I bought him a magic blanket (electric blanket). Every night for four weeks I turned it to three before bed to scare the monsters away, and to make sure they stay away the blanket stays on one all night. Josh was so proud of himself he told everyone in the class for news. I'm not sure what I'd have done if it had been a summer problem.

- My son was scared of a monster in his room every night. So I got up in my boxer shorts and outside my son's room I shadow boxed this monster with all the sound effects. Eventually I won, of course, and my son was both very content and very proud of his monster-crunching dad. Ten minutes later, as I was just dozing off again, I heard this almighty shriek coming from his room. I raced in and there he was sitting up and quite petrified. 'You know that monster you killed, Dad? Well, his big brother's back and he's worser!'

- My daughter developed a great fear of monsters but she is also a fairy lover and has lots of fairy posters in her room. We tell her that the fairies come at night and sprinkle fairy dust over her so monsters can't get through and that the fairies use their magical fairy wands to fight off bad monsters.

- Our son, Josh, is a very excitable five-year-old and his sleep was bedevilled with bad dreams. We tried lots of things to no effect till my mum said to let him get up, go to the toilet and wee it out of his system. It worked.

- My son had problems with tigers in his room when he was almost three. We tried everything, but nothing seemed to work until we gave him a baseball bat to fight the tiger. He became the boss of the situation and the tiger was too scared to come back after only a few nights.

Early Wakers

Some people are fowl (tell me about it, I hear you say) and some are owl. That is, some are morning people and some are night people. If the kids are fowls but can self-entertain and are not overtired then that's them, they'll probably always be fowls. If they are tired and not getting enough sleep, then check them out as follows:

CHECKS

✸ Is it that they're going to bed too early for their sleep needs? If so, get them to their room at the usual time so you get a break, but let them fiddle around there for a while (reading, colouring, etc).

✸ Is it that being fowl means they get cuddly time with parents? If so, it's your call as to whether you want this special time together. If not, then make night time a special time instead and stick to firm rules (eg no shared bed before the alarm goes).

✸ Is it that early risers get the pick of the programs on TV? In which case you can choose your rules—no TV, TV on but low, no TV till the alarm, etc—and be consistent.

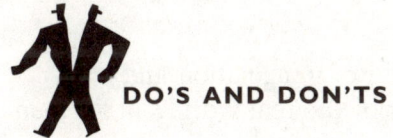
DO'S AND DON'TS

✸ Here are some ideas for toddlers who wake early.
  ◆ Keep a safe mirror for some self-entertainment when they awake.
  ◆ Have a surprise bag by the bed with some small items for quiet play.
  ◆ Put a few cloth books or soft toys in the cot after the kid's asleep.
  ◆ Maybe set an alarm clock as a get-out-of-bed signal.

✸ Some parents have a rule that when the sun is up they can get up and either climb in bed with the parents or play in their room.

✸ If you don't want them wandering out of their room then have a gate across their doorway and the damage they can do is at least confined.

Bush Remedies

🍃 We don't have an answer to this one. Our son wakes really early as bright as a button and ready to go. My husband thinks he'll buy Cain a milking cow as a job on the dairy looks a likely prospect.

Daydreamers

It's not just kids' eyes that cause problems, sometimes it's the mind's eye! Certainly, kids who daydream are a health hazard not only to themselves but to their family. As many daydreamers are loners or have some social problems, then the ideas in Chapter Seven (see page 197) would also be useful.

CHECKS

🏃 **Are they just shy**, preferring the world of imagination and daydreaming to the daunting realities of the real world? If so, then activities and hobbies that build self-esteem and social confidence might help (eg sport, joint projects, cubs, brownies, drama, ballet, etc). I remember one parent telling me that he was shy as a kid and used to daydream as that was the only way he could guarantee meeting kind kids! (See also Chapter Seven, page 197).

🏃 **Is their daydreaming temporary?** If so, it could be a form of epilepsy if Sandy also shows some of these symptoms:
- suddenly drifts off
- loses their train of thought
- forgets what he was saying
- eyelids flicker
- stares blankly
- the daydreaming is worse immediately after exertion or exercise

If Sandy has some or all of these symptoms then get a full medical check-up immediately.

- **Are they just what I call 'right brain' kids**, not interested in words, more interested in images, creations, mechanics, pictures, etc? If this is the case, then don't destroy their flair, but you can still expect them to shoulder their share of the work.

- **Have they been scared or scarred by life** to the extent that daydreaming is a form of withdrawing into a better (imagined) world? If so, these kids probably need professional counselling by a child or clinical psychologist.

- **Are they just one-track thinkers**, who focus on something in their mind and are oblivious to anything else around them? If so, then join the crowd, as every family seems blessed with at least one of these characters.

DO'S AND DON'TS

- Get them checked out medically or psychologically if the daydreaming is serious, shows no consistent pattern or if it's interfering with life (theirs or yours)!

- Use a lot more structure with these kids than you would your other kids. Set times, routines, jobs, so if their mind is on walkabout at least the automatic pilot can help them to survive.

- Sometimes for the bad-habit daydreamers, it pays to delay things that mean more to them (eg breakfast) until all other jobs are done. This way, although they may still dream, the growl of their tummy keeps them moving.

- Develop a new management habit. From now on try to tell them only once and mean it and then watch the dramatic lift in strike rate. These kids won't be getting ulcers so why should you?

Forgetful Kids

With these kids, nothing is ever lost, it's been stolen! It's not the early onset of senility, for many kids it's early learning of sensibility. They learn early that it pays to be useless so that someone useful does all the work. When I asked kids why the problem was so common, some said they couldn't remember where they put things, some said they just didn't look properly, some said looking was a waste of time, and one kid said: 'Well, my Mum's the best finder so I just ask her and she just finds things.'

And how do kids get that way? My wife's research over many years clearly indicates it's inherited ... from their father!

CHECKS

- **Is it a neurological problem?** If they're forgetting what they were doing, seem to go vague or to blank out, it could be absences (akin to what used to be called petit mal), a form of epilepsy, so treat it as you would for temporary daydreamers (see above).

- **Is it a social problem?** They could be so insecure in their social group that they're focusing on the interplay not on what they should be doing.

- **Is it their intellectual style?** Some 'left brain' kids think in words, rehearse in words and can't remember where things go or where they put things—their spatial maps are blank!

- **Is it an emotional problem?** Kids can be so panicky or worried that their little brain isn't processing what's going on around them and so they have poor attention spans.

- **Is it just learnt helplessness?** Some kids who live in a busy, efficient home know that parents will take over and find things if the kids dither or whinge for long enough.

Whatever the reason, mental blindness may be a reasonable excuse, but Mum's not the answer.

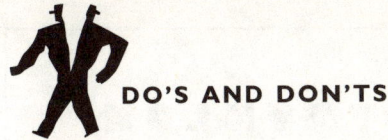
DO'S AND DON'TS

✸ For the learnt helpless here are some ideas to get their eyes back on the job:
- work out with them set spots for things to go,
- kindly insist that things go back in those spots,
- encourage their own efforts to put their own things away (with your help if they're young),
- have a regular tidy-up time so they can rediscover things they had forgotten and consistently learn where things go,
- never find things for them (sometimes *with* them, maybe),
- make them pay the cost penalty for forgetting (that may sound cruel but it sharpens up their priorities),
- practise, again and again if necessary, the sequence of some action that is proving the problem so the responsible action becomes automatic, till they're totally sick of it, but they will remember in order to avoid more practice.

For instance, if Sandy *never* remembers to get his lunch box out of his bag when he gets home and put it in the sink, then
- agree on a workable routine,
- get him to actually come in the door as if he was coming home from school,
- then, again and again, let Sandy go through the routine of dropping his bag, opening it up, getting the gear out, putting it in the sink, closing his bag and putting it in his room.

If he forgets the next day then more practice is needed.

✸ For your image-illiterate, your 'left brain' kids who can't get a picture on where things go—the same routine applies as for learnt helplessness. It's all very well to have their head in a cloud but their feet have to be firmly fixed on earth or they won't last the distance.

✸ For emotionally and socially preoccupied kids, whose heads are spinning with confusion (lost friends, lost love, lost confidence, etc) then something quite different is needed. These kids need hugs and cuddles to emotionally earth them. Many of the ideas in the depression suggestions in Chapter Two (see page 32) would be useful here.

PARENT PENTATHLON
DISABLED ORIENTEERING EVENT

This event is a special for children who can never find anything, children suffering from the 'Where's Me?' syndrome.

RULES: This event starts when everybody (except one) is in the car, the engine is on, you're running late and the horn is honking. At this point the disabled child will call out, 'M-um [as only kids can do], where's me jumper?', or some other ask that's entirely *their* problem. Sighing and seething, you pile out and go on the big man-hunt, retracing their last known steps, checking bathrooms, and being baled up at sister's bedroom (who won't let *anyone* enter). Then to choruses of 'she stole it' and 'no I never, you fat dork', the search continues until eventually the cat gets so distressed by the tension that she moves off the lounge and there it is, having been cuddled by cat.

SCORING: Points in this event go to the parent who can keep their cool longer than the cat.

Bush Remedies

- At the second loss of the same item I stopped replacing things and they had to pay for it. They soon learnt to value their own property.

- Put their name and phone number on a label on all their clothes and belongings. I even put a coloured texta mark on a particular finger to tell them which day it was.

- Jessica was always losing hats and jumpers at school, so in the end I said I was going to write her name in large letters on the outside of her clothing. There were no more losses because she knew I would do it!

> My friend just leaves this huge pile of washing on the table and simply says they don't eat till it's all taken and put in their drawers. I don't know why I just didn't do that.

Sleeping Summary

EVERY YOUNG CHILD HAS A SLEEPING PROBLEM, OR RATHER HIS PARENTS DO. IT TAKES TIME TO LEARN THE RHYTHM OF LIFE.

S Set up good bedtime routines and try to be consistent, parents need time off too.
L Let kids have a bit of settling down (lights-on time) after getting to bed.
E Every child likes a bit of one-to-one time at bedtime to unwind and unload.
E Every child has a desire to keep you by their bed as long as they can, 10 minutes will do.
P Practise getting them off to sleep in the same situation to the one they'll wake up in.
I If they keep getting up or calling out, practise the behaviour you want the next day at a time that doesn't suit them.
N Never give in to night performances or they'll rapidly get worse.
G Get help from a clinic sister, local health centre or Tressillian nurses if sleep problems are starting to sap your sanity.

FAMOUS FOOTNOTE
A GRIEVING DAD

Bryce Courtenay

AUTHOR

Dear Dr John,
I know that being a parent is without any doubt the greatest challenge I have ever faced. We reared three boys (which is a challenge in itself) but Damon, our youngest, was a haemophiliac with medically acquired AIDS, who died at the age of 24. Maybe the best I can offer has been said in *April Fool's Day*, which is Damon's book. Perhaps some of my early recollections of the long, lonely hours will strike a chord in those parents who've nursed a chronically ill child as Benita, my wife, and I have done.

When he began to crawl the wheels immediately fell off our nice, calm, family life. We kissed Dr Spock and all his good middle-class-American advice goodbye forever and started to learn the new reality of living with a child who bleeds internally at the slightest shock.

Throughout his life Damon was to have at least three blood transfusions a week and sometimes more. We would put him to bed at night not knowing how long it would be before we were wakened to his cry. Later, when he could walk, he would come to my bedside and tug on my arm, 'Wake up, Daddy, I've got another bleed.'

It was always my job to wake up at night and attend to Damon. I don't know quite how this happened; I know that there were times that I resented it enormously. I'd be dog-tired after a hard day or I'd have arrived home a little worse for wear and having to wake up in response to Damon's crying wasn't easy. But the implication of Damon crying was that he had a bleed and this would inevitably end in his having to go to hospital. Benita was genuinely scared of driving in the night and has never done so. Somehow along the way we'd negotiated that she did the days and I did the nights. If I said that I didn't often think that I'd gotten a raw deal, I'd be lying. I'd flop into bed exhausted only to be awakened two hours later by a Damon tug on my arm. Sometimes my head would be splitting and my mouth tasting like the inside of a parrot's cage. But I had no choice; I often found this hard and felt sorry for myself.

Even so, there is something that happens to you when you have a critically ill child. You learn, or at least I did, to keep things in separate compartments. Every task is clearly defined and kept in its own box. Damon's haemophilia called for an emotional neutrality. We decided it must never interfere with the opportunities available to Brett and Adam. They must not feel its impact on their lives. And so you couldn't in the end allow yourself to react emotionally to the circumstances around you, his bleeds and the procedure they involved took precedence over everything else—but they must not be seen to be doing so. After a while you simply gave up trying to work out who did what at home, what was fair and what wasn't. All the quarrelling and bickering and feeling sorry for yourself served no useful purpose. When you were in the Damon box, the haemophilia compartment, you simply got on with things and tried to create as little fuss as possible. There was an emotional price to pay for this, sometimes I appear very cold and unfeeling. However, the discipline involved in conducting one's life in this way is not good for the human soul.

Looking back, those long nights were my real time with Damon, the time a father should spend with his sons, but never really allows time for in everyday life. Damon and I grew up together in the dark hours when most of the world, and almost all the kids in it, were asleep. (P.48 April Fool's Day)

Sometimes seeing what others go through can be therapeutic for all of us.

CHAPTER FIVE

Mouth and Eating Problems

My high point in parental lows came at a dinner party in Glebe one night when I joked that I only hit my kids in self-defence.
The other guests shrank away from me as though I had slug larvae coming out of my nose. (That's what I love about the Politically Correct—their low anxiety threshold.)
'Have you thought about therapy?' asked the man opposite—a Tibetan Healing Chanter and trainee psychotherapist. ('Who are you training under?' I wanted to ask him. 'Doctor Seuss?')

KATHY LETTE, author
[IF YOU'RE GAME, READ MORE OF KATHY LETTE'S VIEWS ON PARENTING AT THE END OF THIS CHAPTER.]

Someone once said that kids are one long alimentary canal, with a loud noise at one end and no responsibility at the other!

I received so many Bush Remedies for this section—particularly on feeding toddlers—that I had to include it in the Parenting Pentathlon.

> ## PARENT PENTATHLON
> ### FOOD FOILS EVENT
>
> **RULES:** The Food Foils event commences with the barked command 'dinner's ready'. That battle cry forces the kids' gastric juices to retreat in fear, up come tight tummies ready to fight so when they get to the table they're ready for friction not food. Parents then respond with a bit of forced feeding and dire warnings about death, Ethiopia, eating it cold, never playing again till it's gone and other meal motivators. The contest ends 20 minutes later when the seething subsides, the gastric juices return and the kids announce that they're still hungry.
>
> **SCORING:** Points go to the parent who can get more food into the kid's mouth than Sandy can raspberry in your face, plonk on your head, fling onto the floor or paint on the wall.

Certainly more battles have been fought and lost over the alimentary canal than have ever been fought over Suez Canal, Panama Canal or Guadalcanal. That quaint custom we have of putting flowers on the dining room table is actually to commemorate the battles that have been fought over food. It's as if those three peas, mash and cold gravy are all that stand between our kid and death. So we throw down the gauntlet: 'No-one, I mean no-one, leaves this table till everything's finished. And don't think I'm enjoying it either. I can't even taste my food because of you. You said you wanted it, now you've got it and you're not getting another damned thing in your life till that's finished!' If this sounds a bit like your place then join the crowd because Australians have this obsession with food, little realising that when a child's ego lands he loves to exert his power in every way he can, especially what goes in the top end and when it comes out the other!

Fussy and Slow Eaters

Fussy eating ranked as number four in the parents' overall list of problem behaviours and slow eating ranked as second highest in the eating problems section. The level of concern surprised me a little so I got together with parents and nutritionists and here are some collective words of wisdom.

CHECKS

🛠 Is there so much fuss over food that the fussy eater is really not rebelling, just joining in?

🛠 Is there so much else going on around them that Sandy has his mind on more interesting alternatives?

🛠 Has mealtime become a battle time so food fussing is entrenched as a habit?

🛠 Is the fussing normal behaviour for that child? If not, then treat it as some irritation somewhere; take it easy, keep up the fluids and keep an eye on their eating behaviour for a while. Maybe substitute a known favourite next mealtime.

🛠 Is there so much anger in the air that the tummy has tightened up too much to eat anything?

🛠 Does fussing or refusal usually result in them getting something they prefer? If this is the case, either settle for what they prefer (and save the fights) or just give little amounts, mixed in with preferred foods.

🛠 Does the child have trouble digesting food or a reflux problem? If this is the case, share the problem with your doctor, friends, family, the clinic sister, and anyone who'll listen. Find some easy options, such as little meals eaten more frequently.

🛠 Does the child just have more sensitive tastebuds? Some foods turn them off, some they just dislike or they hate. If their nutrition is okay, stick to what you know will work and extend the repertoire ever so slowly.

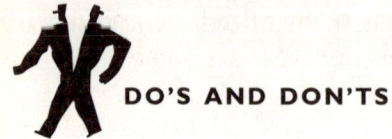

DO'S AND DON'TS

✸ Don't make them eat or punish them for not eating. Forcing kids to eat is likely to make them throw up and it makes mealtime so horrible that everyone ends up hating meals.

✸ Put small healthy snacks where kids can self-serve. It's a technique called 'good grazing', which is ideal for the fussy preschoolers like Sandy. The idea is that he can graze when hungry, his parents know he's getting the goodies and it takes the mania out of meals. What's more, because he's grazing on good food, it means parents can be much more positive about what behaviour they want at the table.
  - Select healthy foods that you know Sandy likes, such as grained bread, cheese, milk, carrot sticks, fruit and eggs.
  - Prepare these so they're self-serve and in finger food form as much as possible.
  - Keep them somewhere consistent so Sandy knows where to look.
  - When the worms get wistful this is where Sandy hunts.
  - At mealtime offer small portions at the table of what everyone else is having, but don't force.
  - If Sandy doesn't want to eat or starts fiddling with his food then don't go chasing him around the room with one bit of egg on a spoon thinking you've won something bigger than Lotto if you land one mouthful.
  - If Sandy won't eat at the table, use reverse psychology. Let him know that that's okay, only 'big people' know how to eat at the table. That way the motivation shifts from getting attention by not eating and forcing the 'catch me if you can' game, to trying to prove he's big!
  - If Sandy leaves (the table, that is) let him do something quiet (not TV); if he can't, then he spends quiet time in his room.

✸ Don't have unhealthy food around so the kids won't be tempted. If good old Gran wants to sweeten them up, let her know your regime and reasons and try to discourage the indulgence, but it's not worth spoiling the relationship over. Just keep 'your' rules in 'your' house.

- Let older kids help prepare the meal so they have more interest in the outcome. Have a rule that whoever cooks has to help in the clean-up and if they don't help then cut out cooking rights or other favours. You could use the Fridge Disk Discipline in the Appendix, (page 351).

- Sometimes young children will eat much better if the food is in little containers that they can open up and finger-pick out.

- Cut up sandwiches for lunch into animals or other interesting shapes using your cake and cookie moulds. Young kids love finger food and prefer things in small bite-size bits.

- Take away all uneaten food without drama. Telling them that they've just wasted another Ethiopian means nothing.

- Sometimes serve the food in different ways, on different plates and in different areas. Kids love novelty and you may rekindle tired tastebuds if you've got the energy to let them have the odd meal in the cubby house, or in a sheeted tent under the table (on a blanket). Maybe let them have a meal outside as a picnic.

- Preferably let preschool kids eat when hungry. They'll learn about mealtimes when they go to school, as they get into the rhythm of eating before, at and after school to create the three-meals-a-day pattern adults prefer.

- Remember that very young children like to feed themselves; it's part of learning to be independent. Just be prepared for the mess with some of the following:
    - newspaper or plastic sheeting under their chairs,
    - untippable or suction-secured bowls,
    - safety drinking cups,
    - and large feeders on the children so the mess they make is easily cleaned up.

- Healthy snacks are good for growing kids and take the edge off their edginess, especially in the afternoon. You can use the time for a bit of a chat and rest-up too if they've been rushing around. Good snacks could include fruit, a slice of toast spread with Vegemite, peanut paste or cream cheese, a cup of soup, a crumpet or a muffin, a bowl of cereal, a sandwich, a glass of milk or a milkshake, a fruit iceblock, etc.

❋ Try to avoid too much of the following:
- salt—young kids' kidneys have trouble with excessive amounts;
- sugar—young kids can eat cereals and custard without lots of sugar or honey;
- fast foods—these usually contain loads of salt, sugar and/or fats.

❋ Water is the best drink for young children. It can be freshened up in the fridge or with a squeeze of lemon juice. Unsweetened fruit juices are good for kids and can be diluted with water if preferred.

❋ Full cream milk (if they have no intolerance to cow's milk) is better for young children than low-fat milk, but the critical thing is the amount of calcium they get. Children 1–7 years need a minimum of 700 mg (at least two cups of milk or the equivalent) per day. Children 8–11 years need approximately 900 mg (three cups of milk or equivalent) per day, and 12–15-year-olds need 1000–1200 mg. (Source: National Health and Medical Research Council)

❋ Young children have very tiny tummies. They're much better with small meals more often than with large meals three times a day. Their appetite often peaks in the late afternoon, so it may be better on everyone to give them something substantial at that time, rather than waiting till late evening when they may be too tired or cranky to handle it.

It's worth remembering that it's not what they eat but what they digest that makes them grow.

❋ Catherine Saxelby, famous author of the *Busy Body Cook Book*, sums it all up with these 10 top tips for fussy eaters.
- Set an unfussy example—especially Dad, as apparently most kids copy Dad's likes and dislikes.
- Serve small amounts.
- Keep mealtime routines regular.
- Don't bribe, because the ice-cream you offer after the broccoli does nothing for their love of broccoli, it just makes them want ice-cream more.

- Don't fill them up on fluids just before a meal or they'll feel full.
- Let them help—kids are more cooperative if they've helped prepare or served the meal.
- Find a substitute. If they hate veges, what about fruit? If they don't drink milk, what about yoghurt or cheese? If they don't like chewing meat, try mince, fish or baked beans.
- Check it out—sometimes there are problems causing the fussy habits that need clearing with the doctor.
- Try again with rejected food (but not the same serving) another time and another way.
- Think about why you're hurrying them. They're not going to die anyhow, so why worry—the less you do the more relaxed their tummies are and the more they'll eat.

Bush Remedies

At three, Kate became fussy and declined most offers of fruit, instead demanding chocolate. It all changed when I invented new names for things—grapes became lollies, as did scoops of watermelon. Chocolate is now a thing of the past.

Using chunks of food (cheese, meat, raw vegetables, fruit, dried fruit) let young kids construct shapes, combinations and kebabs out of whatever appeals or just skewer the food and eat it that way.

For messy eaters, if plastic or newspaper doesn't appeal, get a hungry dog. It works. Janey our corgi would eat every morsel dropped from highchairs. The down side was that Janey put on so much weight she had to go on a diet.

I didn't worry. They eat when they are hungry, and they love fruit so that's what they get.

I encouraged children to eat some of each food and played 'train in the tunnel'.

FUSSY EATERS

'Adam eats nothing,' sobbed his mother. 'I don't know how he's still alive. He won't eat any fruit except apples, and then they must be red ones with the skin peeled. He won't eat any vegetables except potato, and then it must be mashed. He won't eat any meat (he used to tolerate sausages, but now he hates them) and he'll only eat steak if Dad has cut every skerrick of fat off and then cut it into tiny pieces. He won't eat fish or eggs unless they're in pancakes. He won't eat butter unless it's melted on toast, and he won't even eat ice-cream unless it's chocolate. I have come to hate dinnertime so much I now eat at the breakfast bar. It's either that or I do as I did last week and tip it over his head.'

Apparently eight-year-old Adam had been a problem eater for years, but the facts were that he had plenty of energy, he slept okay, and was a bit underweight but no more so than he had been since preschool. The interesting thing was that when he went to Grandma's he couldn't wait to tuck into a roast dinner. Sure he was a fussy eater, but the family was making it worse in three ways.

1. They were making mealtime so miserable that the gastric juices that inspired his hunger were replaced by tight tummies ready for battle.
2. The whole family went along with his anxieties which meant that they hated mealtime so Adam became more fussy and anxious about food.
3. The family had just started a new home office business which meant that the tension lines between home and office had also become blurred.

The family quickly learnt that Adam's fussy eating was more a reflection of family tension than the quality of Mum's cooking. I gave him my diagram of the good food character that had a potato head, spaghetti hair, egg nose, nutty eyes, loaves of bread for arms, apple hands, pea fingers, milk body, steak legs and fish feet. Adam's job was to write down his score for how many different foods on the diagram he had eaten that day. If he ate more than five he won a smiley face. Meanwhile Mum and Dad were to enjoy their own meal, make no special meals just for him and take the pressure off food. Three weeks later his health was good, his weight was much the same and Mum was much less manic. In fact she had noticed that Adam was actually eating more for some reason.

Throwing Up—in the Car!

This was an issue that I hadn't expected, but parents added it to the problems I was surveying because a few claimed that it had caused a faster rise in their blood pressure than anything else the kids had done.

Some kids are keener on this colourful form of oral entertainment than others and you should plan their food/drink intake accordingly. For the kids who do get carsick, keep a wet towel handy, place them near the window, cut back on milk drinks and talk to your chemist about Kwells, Travelcalm or Andrumin Junior tablets (those new ear pads are not for young kids).

Bush Remedies

- Kids being sick in the car makes for a very dangerous distraction and one of the most horrible odours known to mankind. So I got sea bands from the chemist and we travelled 21 hours, with no car-sickness for any of my three children.

- I soothed the child as well as I could until we could pull over. I always had water on board as well as a change of clothes.

- I pulled over as soon as possible. Now I carry an empty ice-cream container everywhere and bicarb soda in the glove box. It honestly takes all the odour out.

- My daughter was always carsick at the beginning of a journey or on a winding road, so now we put her in the front and the problem's solved.

- I put a brown paper bag on her stomach to stop sickness. It is also handy as a sick bag, just in case.

- I just believed in the space dimension, and hope that it will be absorbed into the atmosphere.

🍃 I just kept driving and opened all the windows and cleaned up when we got home. Cleaning up in traffic is more stressful than the odour.

Food Refusal

Some parents insist that their kids live on air. But of course the facts are that little kids tend to take as much as their body needs to survive and all toddlers tend to drop their intake amounts for a while.

CHECK

- If their energy level is okay then chances are you need to do nothing.

- If their energy level is down, if they're listless or can't keep up with other kids, then they need a full medical check-up as there could be many reasons for their refusal.

- If they're just not eating lunch, then that's fairly normal, but do have a word with the teacher about the problem.

- If they're just fussy, see comments in the Fussy Eaters section (page 132).

- If there's lots of stress and pressure on eating then the gastric juices that entice their appetite will disappear and they won't be hungry.

- If there's lots of sadness in their life then they won't feel like eating.

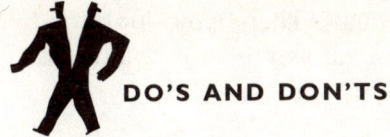
DO'S AND DON'TS

❦ Select from the suggestions in the Fussy Eaters section (page 132).

❦ If you're worried then keep a record for one week of what the kids eat over each day, and you'll probably find that they're actually eating much more than you thought.

❦ Regularly check their milestones for weight and height with the clinic sister and I'm confident that you'll again gain some reassurance.

❦ Check their daily intake against the diet pyramid (eat mostly cereals, breads, vegetables and fruit, eat moderately dairy products and eat less fats and sugars) and you'll probably be surprised that they're not bad dietitians themselves.

Bush Remedies

🍃 I mashed veges and used to put them in fun moulds. It worked! Dinnertime is always fun time for the family to share events of the day. It also helps to have their favourite foods incorporated into meals.

🍃 I didn't push it—the food I mean. It took a lot of patience though.

🍃 I ran to the bedroom and cried, thinking they're going to starve, and then the next night I didn't worry and they ate everything on their plate.

🍃 I put their veges in between bread and butter.

🍃 I used to scream, yell and now have decided that they are like 'goldfish'. They will eat if they're hungry; I've never seen a child willingly starve itself.

- I provide healthy enjoyable food for meals. There is no junk food, no eating between meals, and they can eat as much or as little as they like, with no pressure and no compromises.

- If she didn't want any dinner I would say, 'That's fine,' but she still had to sit at the table with her dinner in front of her. I ignored the fact that she wasn't eating as normal, and she always ended up eating her dinner.

- We let the cat and dog finish the food if he eats 75 per cent of it. But we make sure we stay around while he finishes his meal so he doesn't feed them himself.

- My child just refused to drink out of a cup. Then I found these Mag mugs with four stages—teat, sipper, straw and lip. It works wonders.

- When my child will not eat dinner I have dessert out where they can see it. I will go as far as eating my dessert in front of them.

- *Twin advice*:
  I have twins, but feeding them is four times the problem. When they get to solids, unless you're ambidextrous, one spoon and one bowl is the easiest way (just as long as one doesn't have a cold). Another tip is that two highchairs can often take up too much room; why not try those clip-on chairs once they can support their back.

- I've tried never worrying too much. I was always made to sit there and eat everything and I can still remember being sick at the thought. Just have a huge bowl of fruit and plenty of bread.

Older Kids' Food Refusal

Food refusal or food vomiting is also becoming a bigger problem, not just with adolescents but with some primary school children as well.

WEIGHTY PROBLEMS

Helen has a problem that she shares with lots of other females. She doesn't like the way she looks in a swimsuit. She thinks she's too fat. The difference is that Helen is only six and desperate to go on a diet. 'All my friends' bones stick out, why don't mine?' she wailed to her mum. On the other hand, chubby Sam is so worried about his weight he wears an oversized T-shirt in the pool, playing in the park, to bed—Mum hasn't seen him naked for a year. He's 10!

These are stories from a recent magazine article which also quotes research indicating that 60 per cent of 11-year-old girls and 30 per cent of the boys said they wanted to lose weight. Part of the *kids'* problem is *our* lifestyle. It's faster, more stressful, and when we're stressed we often do one of two things—we either go right off food, or we use it as a soother. Our kids are also desperate for the image that can keep them socially afloat, so looks, clothes and our status symbols are all more urgent than ever. Then they're expected to weave their way through the marketing minefield of what's bad for their body but good for their image. No wonder we're all a bit mixed up and no wonder the kids are feeling the effects.

It is a fact that this generation of children has more eating disorders than ever before (both overweight and underweight) despite a healthier diet, and the problems are appearing earlier than ever before.

CHECKS

You know if Sandy has an eating disorder if he shows up on the following:

* weight loss

* preoccupation with food and weight

* feeling distressed or guilty about eating

- trips to the bathroom after eating
- excessive exercising
- loss of energy
- obsessison with certain clothes as body cover-ups
- hiding food
- abnormal moodiness

DO's AND DON'TS

- Do have healthy eating habits as a family.
- Don't get obsessed with diets. Not only does dieting not have a good success rate (less than 10 per cent) but the kids pick up the anxiety and obsession and react accordingly.
- Don't talk diets for them or in front of them. Research shows that focusing on diets with kids seems to make the problem worse. If you're worried, talk to the doctor and get professional advice from a paediatric dietitian through your local health service.
- If you have a few weighty problems of your own then take the load off your mind without loading it on your body or family with the help of some soul food—that could be meditation, yoga, prayer, psychological counselling, hypnotherapy or whatever food your soul craves.

Overeating and Junk Food

You probably know that one in every five kids is overweight and that a few school canteens are still doing their best to make it one in four. Yet we all know that being fat is not only a health hazard (diet contributes to 60 per cent of deaths in some way), but fat kids are teased, feel bad, and a recent British study shows that kids on a poor diet do more poorly at school and on IQ tests. It's difficult for a kid to feel spick if he has too much span!

CHECKS

- Is your Sandy at risk? You'll know if he:
    - gulps food down with excess gusto and greed,
    - is considered by the doctor to be overweight,
    - sneaks or steals food from home or other lunches,
    - craves food, especially junk food,
    - eats up big on junk food but then can't eat the prepared meal,
    - lives in a home with poor eating examples,
    - gets cranky if people talk about their diet,
    - stores food in his bedroom.

- Is the weight part of a family physique? If so, the kids' shape/weight needs no more attention than the rest of the family's.

- Has the weight suddenly appeared? If they're over 10 years old then this could be part of prepuberty (particularly girls); if not, then it's worth a check-up.

- Are the rest of the family junk food junkies? In this case the only way change will happen is if the whole family gets professional advice and takes the issue on as a team.

- Is Sandy looking for a quick fix to soothe deeper pain—he feels worthless and unliked, he can't keep up, has no friends, has no coordination, is lonely, etc? If this is the case then that's the area to fix, not the food at first.

- Is Sandy a sweet freak? All kids love sweets, but if he's craving sweets, risking life and limb to find hidden sweets or eating sugar by the spoonful then get him checked out by your doctor for diabetes and/or other medical problems.

CHUBBY CHECKERED

'Chubby' was a big lump of a kid who hated his school nickname, even if it fitted better than his clothes. Chubby was a gentle giant who had an old-fashioned Mum who really believed that a healthy boy had a bit of beef on him. Over time, eating became his dominant passion, especially after Dad left home for the dreaded secretary. He had no friends and nothing else to do. It wasn't long before Chubby became known as 'King Kong Bundy', which he hated even more, so he started to skip school, stay at home and ... eat even more.

We talked to Chubby about things he'd really like to do to have fun and then worked out they'd be easier if he felt fitter. Dad agreed to take him horse riding on his access weekends if Chubby rode over to Dad's place on his bike (and even that took some training). Mum agreed that the whole family had to shape up a bit, changed her shopping priorities and joined Weight Watchers with *Chubby* (Charlie). Diets do not have a great success rate and should only be done with dietitian advice but so far, so good. However, it would have been easier, healthier and cheaper if Charlie had never had to throw his weight around in the first place.

Charlie's not alone with this problem. If you have a problem eater, the most important message is to forget the nagging. Stress seems to stimulate the sweet tooth. Let the doctor do the talking about easy diets. The flip side of successful weight management is energy output. Every body is built differently and it's unwise to aim for a 'Baywatch' body. However, no Australian child needs to be a blob. Switch off the TV and get them outside, into games, sport, going messages and if possible let them walk or ride to school. If they complain, well even that's using up even more energy.

 **DO'S AND DON'TS**

✱ Limit the amount of junk food. If they're addicted then cut out junk food from the shopping list altogether.

MOUTH AND EATING PROBLEMS 147

❊ Have plenty of healthy snack food around to take the pressure off meals. Good snacks could include fruit, a slice of toast spread with Vegemite or peanut paste or cream cheese, a cup of soup, crumpets or muffins, a bowl of cereal, a sandwich, a glass of milk or milkshake, a fruit iceblock, carrot sticks, grained bread, etc and get hold of a colourful animated food chart that appeals to the kids.

❊ Set food rules for the family such as only fruit snacks after 5p.m., if you can consistently enforce such a rule.

❊ Get professional advice if:
   ◆ they have an addiction to sweets or chocolates,
   ◆ they're constantly drinking,
   ◆ their appetite changes suddenly,
   ◆ they're stealing food,
   ◆ certain foods seem to make them edgy and irritable.

❊ Don't:
   ◆ believe that chubby means healthy; early fat cells are hard to lose,
   ◆ make too big a fuss over food,
   ◆ use sweets as a bribe (use other treats like play, games, etc),
   ◆ put lots of sweets in their lunch,
   ◆ give them too much pocket money to swallow.

Bush Remedies

🍃 Have no junk food in the house—eat good food or starve.

🍃 Don't give your child junk food, instead encourage a hunger strike—it won't last long in any case.

Biting

Biting is always mentioned as a problem in every seminar I ever give for coping with preschoolers. Remember that young kids have just found their ego, they have the will but they don't know the way to get their will. It's the arrival of brand-new fangs that gives them their first assault weapon in their history, and they're not going to let that go unnoticed. But some kids attack with the venom of a vampire or the jaundice of Jaws! It has to be stopped, and that won't happen with nice little lectures on the proper role of teeth!

CHECKS

* **Has Sandy made the mistake of being between 18 months and three years (give or grab six months)?** If so, then that's brand-new fangs in tandem with a brand-new ego on a power trip. If they're older, then that's one angry kid who hasn't found a better way to work out his anger.

* **Is Sandy 'experimenting'?** He may just be trying it on to test himself out. When this occurs, just use a short sharp 'NO'. It has the same startle effect as a smack without the side effects. Let him know that biting is a no-no because it hurts and then give him some other distractions so he can experiment elsewhere.

* **Is Sandy 'teething'?** If so, offer him something soft and satisfying to chew on that doesn't feel pain (eg frozen bagels, large carrots, teething biscuits or even an old safe dummy or teething ring).

* **Is Sandy a 'frustrated' biter?** Other little kids crowding his freedom can be a major cause.
    * Use the short sharp NO.
    * Give comfort to the victim.
    * Sit the biter on his own for a bit so that he gets no encouragement for an encore and gets the very clear feeling that it's a NO-NO from your hairy eyebrow and sharp tongue.
    * Then let him know that it hurts and is not allowed.
    * If you like you can tell him that skin is not for biting and show

him what is. That means have him practising his new-found skill on something safe (like an old dummy or teething ring, but not food) again and again.
- ◆ Keep him doing biting practice (what we call flooding technique) till you're quite sure he's worked out his anger and doesn't need to do it any more.
- ◆ If he understands time out then use this as an alternative to the Practice mentioned above. You could use this talk time to try and teach him a few words he could use when he's feeling frustrated with another child.

* **Is Sandy a 'threatened' biter?** In other words is he biting in self-defence when he feels under attack? This is more likely to happen when he starts at a centre, in a playgroup, after a move, or after some home stress. If this is the case, use the same techniques as for the frustrated biter.

* **Is Sandy a 'power' biter?** Some kids just want the power and, when they see the dramatic effect biting has, can't wait for a replay. Use the flooding technique mentioned above and again use an old dummy or teething ring to saturate the biting urge. This is much more effective than telling him not to do it or you'll get more because you've reinforced his power and impact. Make sure the biter gets attention when not biting so they learn other ways to win attention.

Check where and who they're biting as that can give you lots of information as to what might be causing the problem. It might be near mealtime, it might be a particular child, it might be just when they're asked to share toys etc.

DO'S AND DON'TS

* Don't bite back. It teaches that biting or hurting is okay if you're big enough and it's a hard lesson to erase once it's learnt. A short sharp NO followed by lots of attention to the victim and no attention to the culprit gets the message across much better.

- ❋ Parents and caregivers need to use common tactics with the biter so the kids get a consistent message.

- ❋ One good preventive measure is to reduce the pace, the pressure, the noise and the general hype or the kids will try to bite their way out.

- ❋ Try to help them find words to let people know how they're feeling. That's the best way to arm them and disarm the biting.

In other words, praise any sharing, shove chewies into gaping gums, show them the world's best toy if they're tangled, and whisk one away if war's looming. They do grow out of it.

ONCE BITTEN

Young Bill and Vince were your typical two-year-olds who played and snatched and pouted. When Vince wouldn't give him a toy, Bill exercised his brand-new teeth on Vince's cheek and bit so hard that the doctor honestly thought a dog had done it. Well the parents shrieked, washed, nursed and cursed while Bill looked on amazed that just one little bite from a boy could bring on a giant shriek from mankind. Anyhow, parents bought Vince the victim a special ice-cream, and do you know what the little mug did? He went straight up to Bill the biter and gave it to him. We often find that abused or scared kids will try to please the abuser like this.

Bill, by the way, is no longer a biter but now he has other problems with his teeth. Apparently he's now refusing to use toothpaste because he reckons none of his teeth are loose enough to need pasting.

Bush Remedies

- When number two bit number one, I gave number two his own arm and told him to bite it if he needed to bite anyone—he didn't.

Restaurant Rebels

I was surprised at how many parents shared my own personal frustration with the behaviour of kids when you take them out for a meal. No matter how 'promise-primed' they are on favourite food, fire engine drinks, a favourite parent to sit next to, what you end up with is something a little different—extra large servings of 'I wasn't kicking', 'I'm bored', 'She flicked food at me first', 'How much longer to wait, Mu-um'. The worst part is that the waiter is determined to prolong your pain to teach you a lesson you'll never forget. So let's share a few ideas for restaurant survival.

CHECKS

- Is the restaurant too formal, too slow, too soft or too quiet for kids?

- Is it one that encourages kids? Does it have things like games, puzzles, an informal atmosphere, kid-style meals (light, informal, finger food, treats or gimmicky food), highchairs, and a baby change room?

- Is the restaurant family-friendly? Is it fast on service, cheap and with seating such that the kids are easy to supervise and talk to?

- Do eating-out meals have a good track record with your clan?

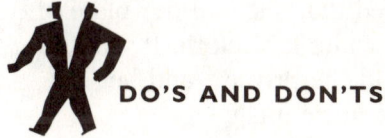
DO'S AND DON'TS

- Don't take the kids! The marriage, the nerves, the hip pocket and even the kids will be better off!

- If you do take the kids, check the deal before the meal. Anything much better than pizza or the 'golden arches' is more whining than dining!

- ✺ Start early—kids tire on a full tum.

- ✺ Clearly state a few house rules as you arrive, such as tablecloths are not serviettes and no soft drinks before eating.

- ✺ Go prepared with boredom beaters like puzzles, pencil games, pizza mat or even a few cards out of Junior Trivial Pursuit.

And if kids get a bit edgy waiting for their dinner, just remind them how long they wait when they go fishing.

More suggestions were made by parents to this problem area than to any other. Maybe that was because every family that has children has feeding difficulties at some stage or maybe it's a reflection of just how frustrating the day-to-day habits of young kids can be.

Maybe we all need to aim at eating practices that take the pressure off eating and focus on an atmosphere that helps everyone's digestion. That means more time to just be together, share and help, and how much they eat will probably look after itself.

Bush Remedies

- I took a little box of crayons and a colouring-in book and that kept them quiet for nearly the whole meal.

- When we went out to a fancy restaurant with our children, who wanted to impress everyone with just how grown-up they were, our older kids were highly embarrassed by our youngest daughter's behaviour. They had a vote and decided that she and her plate of food should move under the starched white tablecloth. It worked well, she liked her little igloo space and the privacy, and her big brothers and sisters maintained their mature image.

Eating Summary

CHILDREN'S EATING HABITS ARE THE CAUSE FOR MUCH MORE CONFLICT THAN THEY DESERVE.

- **E** Every child is a fussy eater, just don't copy them.
- **A** Arrange a few favourites precooked and frozen to take the mayhem out of meals.
- **T** Take time to develop good meal habits and that doesn't happen glued to the TV.
- **I** Involve the kids sometimes in preparing and cooking to promote tastebuds.
- **N** No child dies of starvation these days, so don't force-feed if you want happy meals.
- **G** Grazing food to be eaten when the worms get wistful can take the pressure off meals.

FAMOUS FOOTNOTE

THE PARENTALLY INCORRECT

Kathy Lette

AUTHOR

The caring and sharing nineties has produced a grim new breed—The Parentally Correct.

I'm talking about women who make their own teething rusks. I'm talking about women who wear the kind of cheesecloth smocks through which you could strain tofu. Women who video every nano-second of their child's life for the archives—then immediately view the footage . . . you know, *to bring back memories*.

When not in their role of the Cecille B. de Milles of the videocam, these Stepford mums talk about wanting another baby because they feel cheated by the caesarean they had the first time and want to 'get in touch with the Fertility Goddess within'.

This, to me, is a little like Terry Waite saying he feels cheated by being released before the electrode torture to his testicles.

The Earth Father Fraternity is just as tedious. You know the sort—Porsche-driving progressives about as relevant as a 'Free Nelson Mandela' T-shirt. Sebastian, Orlando or Julian (the progeny of the Parentally Correct address their parents by their Christian names. Way too informal for me. I mean, it's not as though my children and I have known each other all that long) is invariably writing a book about his Fathering Experiences.

These men are Gentlemen Fathers—the type who hold forth at every opportunity about the joys of fatherhood—but farm their kids out at the drop of a small turd.

Earth Fathers call housework 'a highly skilled operation at the interface between culinary and residential management provision and in-home pedagogy'.

Meaning, of course, that he doesn't do any.

Earth Fathers also prefer the word 'companion' to 'wife'. 'It's a gender-inclusive, non-heterosexist substitute for the word spouse.'

Meaning, of course, that he screws around.

Beaming at each other like Christian Scientists, these smug parents whose babies sleep through the night have spent years instructing me on the benefits of cotton wool balls over nappy wipes, professionally fitted shoes over hand-me-downs, homemade food over the canned variety, why breast is best . . .

'You're bottle feeding! That's a shame!' pontificated a complete stranger in a supermarket express queue in Balmain once, the sort of woman who volunteers for medical research in order to save rats and monkeys the discomfort of being used to advance the health of humans.

'Well, he's teething,' I explained guiltily, 'meaning that he's biting my nipple.' Now *there's* a bonding experience. But members of the Earth Mother Mafia breastfeed until the baby has beard stubble.

'Then I hope you're giving him fluoride? *You're not?* Oh well, not to worry. He does have another set of teeth to come and it *might* not affect them . . .'

Which brings me to one of the greatest mysteries of the Universe. *Why do express lanes move so glacially?*

My high point in parental lows came at a dinner party in Glebe one night when I joked that I only hit my kids in self-defence. The other guests shrank away from me as though I had slug larvae coming out of my nose. (That's what I love about the Politically Correct—their low anxiety threshold.)

'Have you thought about therapy?' asked the man opposite—a Tibetan Healing Chanter and trainee psychotherapist. 'Who are you training under?' I wanted to ask him. 'Doctor Seuss?' Earlier, his wife . . . oops, 'companion', after swearing me to secrecy, had confided that they'd just entered their offspring in the cover competition for *Totler*—the baby version of *Tatler*. Legal proof of child abuse in my view.

With my second child about to start school, I now know that years of lectures, kind of Toddler Tutorials, from parents with an Interferiority Complex have proved to be about as useful as, well, as a father in the delivery room.

The only Instruction Manual a new parent needs contains five points.

1) A balanced meal is whatever stays on the spoon en route to baby's mouth.
2) The only way to find missing Lego is to turn off the lights and saunter around in bare feet until you crush your instep.
3) If your partner asks you what you want in bed, the only reply is 'breakfast'.
4) The answer to 'Who's Mamma's lovely baby boy then?' is—your husband. And, most vital of all,
5) *Don't listen to the Parentally Correct.*

CHAPTER SIX

Tongue and Communication Problems

Communication with children is so important, it's so easy but it takes time, and adults are so busy that they may try to hurry their kids' thoughts and efforts to communicate. Give them time to come up with what they want to say.

Sometimes it's hard to find that time at home, so try to take off and go to neutral territory, and just be there, no big plans, no shopping, just be there and make contact and communicate with each other. And then just see what happens next, don't try to plan it all.

Sometimes when Cameron was uptight about something we'd take to the golf course and talk and swing and breathe and just be near each other, and by the end of the course we'd be okay.

BRONWEN DADDO, mother of the famous Daddo brothers

[READ MORE OF THE FAMOUS DADDO FAMILY STORY, INCLUDING TIPS FOR GRANDPARENTS, AT THE END OF THIS CHAPTER.]

Without any doubt the **tongue** is the part of the head that causes so much hurt. It's not just back-answering—although that was rated in the top three problems on every survey—

it's the arguing, swearing, whingeing, lying, teasing, smutty talk and screaming that drive parents berserk. And then there's crying! For children it's their communication, for parents it's their crisis. The pitch and intensity of that cry may be nature's way of guaranteeing attention, but to many mothers it's proof that God is a man! It's that cry that has been the cause of more baby abuse, hitting, hurting and shaking than any other behaviour, so let's address that one first and treat the others in some order of age of onset.

Crying

CHECKS

- Try to get to know the type of cry and what it means. See how clever you can get at picking the message in the mayhem—it's not easy so don't expect too much of yourself but at least it can keep your mind on the job and your emotions in check.

- If the baby has been asleep for three or more hours, chances are it's **hunger**. These cries tend to be rhythmical—a short sharp cry followed by a pause to catch breath, then another cry. Some suck their fingers or fists to show you.

- If it's a sudden, intense, loud and long cry, followed by a long pause, then it may be **pain**. Often the kids will have mouths wide open, trembling chins and feet and hands may be drawn up or tensed up. This is the survival cry that sends protective parents scurrying in to make sure everything's okay.

- If it's a more whiney, nasally cry and the baby is flushed then it may be a **fever** cry from having their shots or some infection.

- If it's a fake, low throaty moan followed by a cry sound or two then more moans then it may just be **boredom**. If so, it will keep going until hopefully Sandy gets the attention or has you firmly in his sights.

- If it's just a howl at the end of a big day, it may just be **letting off steam** and will settle after that's done.

- If it's high-pitched, aggressive, loud and determined it may be a cry of **rage**, maybe not liking his position, his feed being stopped, not getting his way.

- If it's more of a whimper than a cry and it goes on and on, that could signal some **real distress** and should be checked out smartly with the clinic sister, family doctor or after-hours medical service.

- **Check the home tone**. Babies are super sensitive to parents' vibes—if we're angry or lack confidence or rushed then Sandy may become more bothered and protest more.

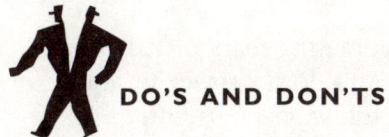

DO'S AND DON'TS

- No matter how long he cries for, how frustrated he is, or how much of a failure a crying baby makes you feel, he will be okay, if you're okay.

- Have a quick look at the Angry Parents' First Aid Guide (see Appendix, page 363), rate your level of anger and follow the instructions.

- Don't strike or shake your baby—a lot of permanent damage can happen by shaking the baby through neck injury and brain damage.

- Remember that crying is a little kid's communication, so if you're not sure the meaning of the cry then here's how to place your bets:
  1st bet—hunger—If so, no juice or dummy will shut them up for long.
  2nd bet—pain from discomfort—Top-and-tail, dress and drain and keep them warm, cosy and comfortable.
  3rd bet—out of sorts—They often just need a cuddle and many will pick up the second they're picked up. They're not spoilt, they just need the contact until their bodies and brains can go it alone a bit better.

4th bet—evening colic—The best that can be said here is that it only lasts a few long weary weeks. It's still not known what precisely causes it although there are some good theories around. Meanwhile, some parents claim success with burping Sandy before and during a feed, others feed in a near upright position, and others say it helps if they use equal parts of water and lemonade to help them pass wind (the child, that is).

5th bet—unknown causes—Try rhythmical sounds or movement or sucking, or anything that makes you feel better and back in control. Here are some ideas for this group:
- walk, rock, dance or bounce Sandy in arms or on a waterbed,
- take Sandy for a long walk in the pusher,
- talk or even sing to the baby—remember, babies are tone-deaf,
- carry Sandy around in a baby carrier close to your body,
- lay Sandy tummy down across your lap or across a warm water bottle and stroke his back.

6th bet—frustration—With toddlers come the tears of frustration. They know what they want but they can't do it or they're not allowed—they've got the will but not the way! Diversion and distraction are still the best tactics for this problem so keep a supply of surprise specials in your car or handbag. See 'Travellers' First Aid Kit for Families' in the Appendix, page 356).

* If nothing works let someone else take Sandy while you take fresh air or put Sandy down safely, close the door and phone anyone you can: a friend, family member, family day care, kids' clinic, Nursing Mothers Association, CAPS, Kids Helpline or Lifeline (see Contact Numbers in Appendix, page 365). **It's better to go on strike than to strike**. No parent is meant to go it alone and to be honest, I worry more about the lonely parent than the lone parent.

* When you get time, read one of the books mentioned in the References (see page 367).
And then as you gaze down with sleep-sapped eyes on their pathetic tear-streaked face, bear in mind Kauffman's immortal words: 'Children are a great comfort in your old age and they help you reach it faster too!'

How do families survive this trial-by-tears torture? Well, as some faithful parent said, 'Until kids get the sense to tell us what's going on, God made them gorgeous to gaze upon'.

CRYING IT OUT

Tania was just five months old, but she wouldn't stop crying. She fed well and gained weight but no-one could enjoy her because she was forever crying and only ever took catnaps. She had plenty of attention from doting parents and grandparents who shared the house at the time but nothing seemed to please her. Finally her parents took her to the paediatrician and then the Tresillian hospital to analyse and stabilise the problem. What they found was that once all the attention was off her, young Tania started sleeping through the night. Because she was being picked up every time she whimpered, little Tania had never had her own space. What she needed was more calm and less stimulation, so she had been crying through sheer frustration. Once the parents got less fussy with her fussing and let her have her space she settled down and hasn't looked back since.

What every child needs is healthy food, healthy cuddles, healthy fun and after that a little bit of healthy space.

Bush Remedies

- When the crying and whingeing was caused by teething I used a cold or frozen carrot, a frozen slice of banana, a chilled dummy or frozen water-filled teething rings. My friend suggested they chew on a dog biscuit—apparently they're safe—but I wasn't game to try. I wanted Fiona and our dog, Janey, to stay friends and not fight over the same food.

- For a crying Sandy confront him with a large mirror so he can see himself and then watch his expression turn to horror.

With our help kids can grow through pain; without our help, they can spend a lifetime burying it.

Whingeing and Boredom

Whingeing was ranked in the top three in every one of my surveys of young kids' problems. But let me tell you about whingeing. It's the first and most successful way kids learn to manipulate their parents. It's brilliant! It takes so little effort and reaps such wonderful returns. They can even whinge while they're watching TV and not miss out on a single murder. Now let me tell you something else about whingeing—it's universal among young kids whose ambitions far exceed their abilities—so they try to leg-rope a parent into helping.

Boredom is generally a cover-up for other things—being tired, not coping, not well, low self-esteem, no friends, etc. Because it puts guilty parents on the back foot, it's used very often to mask problems and unhappiness elsewhere. So, instead of reacting out of guilt for being a poor provider of fun, look a bit further into it and then react.

CHECKS

- If they're just young kids with little communication skill then see it as a communication of boredom, slightly unwell, uncomfortable, hungry, tired or just waiting for the whinge to work and parents to step in and entertain. The timing, style and urgency of the whingeing will give you more of a clue.

- If whingeing is not their 'normal' style, there may be some other irritation making them feel 'off' (eg teething) but a clinic check or medical check would be in order if it continues.

- If the kids are of school age, if it's not their normal style, and the problem isn't medical, then chances are they're in psychological pain somewhere (eg playground problems, not keeping up with schoolwork), particularly if it's occurring before school.

- Is it that they feel they have no friends? If so, see ideas under self-esteem and loneliness in Chapter Seven (page 198).

TONGUE AND COMMUNICATION PROBLEMS

✴ If it's happening at home but not elsewhere then chances are:
  ◆ they've become over-dependent on parents to jump-start their brain and make them happy, or,
  ◆ if home is unhappy then whingeing is the kids expressing what the rest of the house is feeling. If this is the case then their moods may well be a good barometer and good reminder to sort things out where they really count.

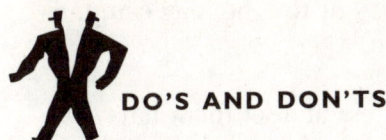

DO'S AND DON'TS

✴ Encourage the kids, from an early age, to make little (but not open) choices on things like cereals, clothes and games.

✴ Don't nag—the *whinge* is *nag*'s little brother. So don't get annoyed about the whingeing and then give in to it because the kids then learn that it works. Even saying 'don't whinge' is pointless because you're not only giving them attention, but you're also highlighting the very thing you don't want.

✴ Praise and reward with hugs and attention some non-whingey pleasant behaviour so the kids come to enjoy the alternatives.

✴ Do a grizzle countdown.
Ist grizzle—cuddle, attention, and check for comfort (dirty daks, thirsty, etc).
2nd grizzle—soothe, turn off noisy irritations like phone calls and vacuum cleaners.
3rd grizzle—treat as tiredness and in need of urgent R & R in their room.
Treating it as tiredness has a two-way advantage. If they're tired they'll get the break that refreshes and if they're not then they get the message that whingeing won't win.

✴ Try to be fair but firm with guidelines and rules so the kids don't develop the idea that they can whinge their way past your guard. For instance, you could have a few little house rules such as:
'If you want me to hear, speak when my ears are clear.' or
'Ask once and I listen, ask twice and the answer's no.'

- Try to encourage kids from an early age to learn to enjoy doing things for themselves so they don't become overdependent. Parents can also empower children by not stepping in every time the kids trot out the 'I'm bored' line. I treat boredom as a springboard to their own creativity, so why intrude? If that fails, then it means their mind is too tired to think and a rest in their room is again in order.

- To beat boredom, beg, borrow or hire other kids at any price. If it's holiday boredom, maybe hire yours out to a holiday camp, a vacation school or sports holiday clinic.

- Generally treat the bored call as tiredness and let them have a break on their bed. This is a good opportunity to use the 'Think Light' (see Appendix, page 355).

- With holiday boredom, water would have to be the best activity for hot weather. As long as they're well protected, the fun and creative potential are infinite. For cooler weather the Play Stations and Nintendos, digital pets, collector's cards, yo-yos, yo-ho diabolos, basketball cards and video games and computer games are all the rage. But I like to see kids a bit more active. Get hold of the Arrow Press publication *What To Do When There's Nothing To Do*, which has ideas arranged in different age groups.

- Check out the 'Boredom Beaters', the 'Children's Interest Inventory' and 'Web Sites' (some useful Internet addresses for kids' games and activities) in the Appendix, page 358, 357 and 359.

- If you happen to have time off then play is a wonderful stress reliever for the child in all of us. Maybe you could jump-start their creativity with something simple like turning an old box into a cubby that they can paint, cut out windows, and fill with dolls and cushions.

- If you'd like to gain a bit more distance think about erecting a small tent up the yard. Maybe they can sleep there overnight with a mate and swat away their boredom.

- If they're into drama then use a box or kitchen bench for a puppet show. They can hide behind the bench and you can be treated to those wonderful impromptu concerts using sock or stick or even shadow puppets.

BORN WHINGER

Ryan was a whinger and was driving his family insane. But kids only whinge if it soothes or if it's successful.

So after a medical all-clear we checked the pattern. We found that whingeing was more likely after school and, as Ryan was the youngest in the class, tears and tiredness could be expected.

But more to the point, Mum and Dad had both come from broken homes and were determined to have a happy home, so any whingeing was met with lots and lots of loving attention.

So from now on any whingeing would be taken as tiredness and Ryan could rest in his room until he felt better. That gave him the time to unwind and took away the attention that he was getting whenever he whinged.

Mum spoke to the teacher to see if he was coping in the playground and classroom or whether he should repeat while he's still young enough to enjoy the difference.

But all young kids love charts, so his parents designed two. One was a 'Time Out Pointer'—just like the Hangman game with six elements (a head, a body, two running legs and two arms). Each whinge added one element, and the last element to be added was one of the arms, which pointed to a sign saying 'Time Out'. If Ryan reached that point and the arm was drawn then that's where he went till the buzzer went.

The other chart had a featureless face and for each happy thing he did Mum added one more smiley feature, with extra Sega time if the final feature, the smiley mouth, was drawn. Like all charts, the idea had to be changed and freshened up after three weeks but it did whittle away the whingeing.

- Another multi-purpose idea is to inspire the kids to create their own movie theatre at home. They can set up a mini theatre, hire a video, make popcorn, make tickets and invite their friends around ... you could even charge a cleaning fee.

- If they like gardening, but lack staying power, then maybe help them make a terrarium using an old aquarium—preferably when the fish are absent—or a plastic drink bottle cut in half; the bottom acts as the bed and the top half can be used as a megaphone when there's mega mayhem.

- If they like reading and writing then some time spent idea hunting in the air-conditioned comfort of the local library will appeal. Alternatively, they could send away for some of the 200+ items in *Free Stuff For Kids*.

Bush Remedies

- I had an activity cupboard where I put things they rarely played with or new things and let them choose one of these.

- When the kids whinge we 'switch off our ears' with a gesture like turning the radio off and we don't turn them back on again until the whingeing has stopped.

Screaming

This is dangerous territory because the scream is pitched well beyond safe noise levels. In other words, it hurts, and parents are in danger of hurting back. Remember that as kids gain voice and the ability to use words, they also gain the ability to misuse voice in ways we don't like but they love. So treat it as a problem of aging—it's just a question as to who does the most aging, the parent or the child.

CHECKS

- Is screaming a family style? Does the family work on the philosophy that the loudest voice contains the most truth? If so, a collective agreement to drop the decibels will work wonders for screaming and sanity.

- Is screaming Sandy's normal style? If so, then retrain using the 'Practice List' (page 354) or other ideas outlined on pages 167–168.

※ If screaming is not Sandy's normal style, then:
- have a quick check on what or who could have triggered it,
- if nothing is obvious, then check body language for pain,
- if Sandy's not in pain then a physical check with your family doctor would be in order.

※ Is it just a scream of frustration, of self-centred toddlers not getting their own way, not being heard, or something they want to do but they don't have the skills to do? If so, just take it easy, but in future, don't fix things when they scream or they'll scream louder and longer next time they're frustrated. Talk quietly, tell them to settle down, leave it a minute or so until after they've settled and then help out. This way they don't associate their scream with your help.

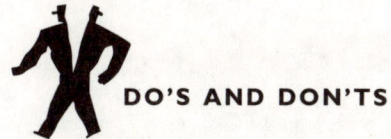

DO'S AND DON'TS

※ Tone down the noise so ears can hear and psyches can survive, and vary your volume for greater interest. **Recent research shows that the lower the voice the more authority it carries.** So, ladies, drop down to a bass and watch the kids' reaction! I bet they listen, not in awe, but in wonder—they'll wonder whether you've lost it altogether.

※ Kids will listen only if they need to, so as of today get into the habit of telling them once and meaning it. They only get the goodies for good hearing and they miss out if they didn't hear.

※ If they never take any notice then they need practice after practice in following your first instruction till they're sure they understand the new rule.

※ It's true that the odd scream can work wonders but if the parent screams all the time the kids won't listen; they'll hear a whisper at 40 paces and not hear a scream at two. Just to prove my point, drop your communications to a whisper and notice the cooperation and attention you get. And remember that sometimes even silence can deliver the loudest message.

❋ Here are some other 'Scream Reduction Strategies'.
- Try sending them outdoors—when the echo changes so will their scream.
- Try a diversion—a soothing cold washer, flicking the light on and off or waiting till they're taking a lungful and saying, 'Daddy's home'. Then head for the door to check and maybe even check down the road a bit.
- If you're shopping, head for a change room or whisper in their ear; but never reward a scream at full peak.
- Generally treat it as overtiredness. You'll be 90 per cent right and besides, a stint on their bed's not a bad idea anyhow.

❋ Remember that a scream is like the ref blowing the whistle to stop play. So have a look around: is there too much action or noise; is Sandy hungry or overtired; or is he looking for attention or kids to play with?

SCREAMING AND SHAKING

God made a mistake or two when he made babies, first there's their screaming—which at 100 decibels sure has to be silenced—and then because he wanted them to learn lots from day dot, their brain is at a very delicate state of growth so any early damage can last long-term. And together with a tired adult whose own brain and eardrum are at bursting point it's a formula for disaster. In their efforts not to hit their kids parents may shake the baby instead and that may be just as damaging. Because their skull is so hard but their brains so soft, and their head control so poor, any shaking means their brain gets catapulted into the skull, causing damage from tearing fragile blood vessels. In fact, four shakes in two seconds can cause brain damage or death, according to Dr Michael Ryan of the Child Protection Unit at the NSW Children's Hospital at Westmead, Sydney.

Just being aware of how vulnerable babies are is a start, as well as being aware of how vulnerable we are as parents when we're tired and testy, lonely or loveless. If you have a new baby then you'll both be safe if you use friends, family and the phone for help. Use your front door for a fast exit outdoors to shake out your anger rather than shaking your baby if things get bad. Kids will cry; it's their communication. Don't make it your crisis.

Fortunately screaming is just a passing phase, it's at its worst when they're too old to cry and too young to swear.

Bush Remedies

- I sit and mentally put up my umbrella so all the 'shit' runs off. I wait until everyone cools down, then I speak quietly and hope for the best.

- I told my fighting sons to go to the opposite ends of the room, then I rang a bell, they had five minutes to yell, scream and say whatever they liked. They couldn't think of anything to scream about after only half a yell.

- If they screamed and yelled or made terrible noises we did the same thing back and they laughed.

A quiet voice and open ear will keep more kids behind shut doors than the loudest curfew.

Car Whingeing

This problem was also rated consistently in the top 20! The whingeing starts with a fight over who sits in the front seat and no matter how you handle it, the smuggest face is the real winner.

Some parents try to prevent the problem with a game like 'I Spy', which goes on forever and only ends when signs of driver dementia appear, after not guessing that 'cow' was the clever answer to something starting with D.

Remember that whingeing and bickering are kids' favourite pastimes and they last until everyone has been screamed at and the winner is then entitled to poke his tongue out at the losers and the game starts all over again.

Another great game is 'I need to wee/poo/throw up'—generally played just as you're overtaking a truck that has held you up for hours, when you're in a traffic jam or within minutes after you've left a loo.

But perhaps the favourite game is 'Are we there yet?' with 'How far to go?' as the flip side. This chorus only ends when the driver loses his cool completely then, after a minute's silence for his lost temper, the game starts again.

CHECKS

- Is it just their way of keeping in tune with the motor? If so, it probably means little more than a pit stop soon.

- Is it belt discomfort? Make sure you have the right harness or seat for little kids as they can not only slip out of the seatbelt but it cuts across their neck and face. (By the way, you can now get soft little furry animal wraparounds to put over seatbelts.)

- Is it general discomfort? Are they hungry, achy, dampish, smellish? If so, nothing short of a solid stop, top-and-tail and freshen up will do.

- Is it frustration and boredom? If so, the ideas below will help.

DO'S AND DON'TS

- Whingeing kids can be a serious road hazard if it causes driver distraction because distraction is the second biggest killer on the roads!
  Anyhow, as the RBT (Random Breath Test) has saved so many lives I thought it was about time we devised the RPT (Ranting Parent Test). It's really an adrenalin rating and can be measured in decibels or wheel grip pressure. Next time you have the family in the car, have a go at scoring your trip on each of the following and see if you're exceeding the safety limit:
   0.01 for each kid not in seat strap, harness or belt;
   0.01 for each kid in hitting distance of another;
   0.01 for each kid with sticky fingers, drippy food, full bladder or feeling sick;

0.01 for each occupant running late;
0.01 for each child without a window;
0.01 if the driver is the only adult in the car.

If your score exceeds .05 the chances are you qualify as a ranting parent and your car load is at risk. This is real road rage!

- For short trips remember the car isn't a home on wheels. It's not well geared for eating, arguing, testing homework, signing late notes or checking hair and teeth. It's the most deadly missile ever invented!

- Strap up *every* time they hit the seat so the kids never get a sniff of freedom, especially as most car accidents happen close to home.

- If you're going to try drinks to douse their whingeing, then use unspillable drinking cups or poppers (some poppers stain badly, however). If eats are allowed, take some healthy finger food. If the kids get carsick, see the tips on page 139. But above all go well armed with a few games, goodies, magazines, talking books, magnetic draughts, pop tapes, etc (see 'Travellers' First Aid Kit for Families' in the Appendix, page 356). But be careful about using books if your children suffer from carsickness.

Bush Remedies

- On long-distance trips I would take four or five plastic bags filled with toys and rotate them along the way.

- I always have books, games or a favourite cassette in the car. They love to sing along with their favourite song, especially if they haven't heard it for a while.

- I got some toys out and shared the back seat with them.

- We settled for our annual holidays at various spots within two hours of home.

- We sing songs, look for coloured cars and numberplates. Be prepared for long trips, organise them to coincide with naps.

- I tried to always have some of their favourite books or toys on hand. When they were very little I tied a stocking from the hook in the back seat of the car and attached various toys and objects.

- Each child/parent picks a different colour. Each time the person spots a car/vehicle in that colour they get a point. Another idea is to make one word from the letters on car numberplates (eg BRD = bird, LKG = looking, UBL = unbelievable).

- I died of stress. I would hug or sing and eventually gave Phenergan and she grew out of it.

- I found a good baby car seat cover with pockets on both sides—toys and food can be put in each pocket for a bit more fun and easier travelling.

- I always took books to keep them amused. *Where's Wally?* is one of their favourites.

- We travelled at night and stopped every three hours. At other times we took plenty of toys.

- We packed each child a bag of goodies that were all identical of pencils, pen, paper, toys, lollies, anything we had. My husband built little pockets into the car for their bags to go in so each child had their own personal spot and a bag of goodies that could take at least two hours to get through.

- Our son is autistic and has lots of problems, but he is a very good traveller, which is just as well, because we live on a one million-acre property in south-west Queensland. We are three hours from the nearest school and five hours from the nearest town. I take lots of tapes and school tapes to be learnt as we're in a distance education program. He learns well in the car; I believe the movement stimulates his brain.

- We played cricket—one run for a car, two for a car and trailer, three for a motor bike and four for a truck. You're out when you pass a hitch-hiker. The kids take turns to see who scores most on a long trip.

Swearing

Swearing is the most powerful tool kids possess after the bite. All swear words have the same ingredients: they are explosive to pronounce, so they ease tension; they torture us on our taboos, such as body parts, sex or religion; they are nice and naughty to say and they attract so much attention. So Sandy goes to preschool, learns a nice little word like 'bum' (or worse), slips it out at home, gets a big reaction and so he says 'bum! bum!'. When that draws even more horror then the 'bums' will multiply.

CHECKS

If Sandy has taken to swearing check for the following things.

- Is swearing a family habit?

- Is Sandy's swearing only uttered after the odd pain or frustration as a way of letting off steam?

- Is it an attention-seeking strategy, ie he can't succeed in the playground or classroom, so he tries to shock others into attention?

- Is it just trying to keep up with the peer group?

- Is it just a function of age? All little kids will take to the odd swear word because it's so easy, so satisfying and so effective in getting attention.

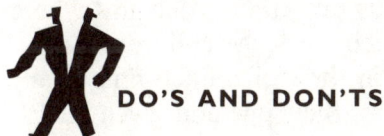
DO'S AND DON'TS

- If you or your partner are swearers then it's probably pointless even trying to stop Sandy. The best you can ask and do is to make sure he knows the time and place where he can swear without getting into trouble or upsetting other adults.

- If it's just to let off steam over something not satisfied by a weak old 'ouch' then don't be too hard. Ignore it at the time; it's hard to tell kids it's a naughty word when they've got murder on their mind. Later on, when the pain settles, is the time to let Sandy know it's a NO-NO and insist that he finds some inoffensive alternatives (such as custard!). But also keep in mind that it's because swear words are powerful, short and just so explosively expressive that little kids of all ages find them very attractive.

- If Sandy's swearing is peer group-provoked then make his time with those kids conditional on him being able to control his tongue.

- If it's not a swearing household then nine out of 10 kids can be fixed with a hairy eyebrow or two.

- Sometimes they need to be 'buzzed' each time they forget with some penalty attached if they forget again (or use the 'Time Out' pointer mentioned in Whingeing and Boredom, page 162).

- But if you've tried to stop Sandy again and again to no effect use the 'Swearing Saturation Strategy'.
    - Instead of saying 'don't swear', 'please don't swear' over and over, use flooding and reverse psychology.
    - Say, 'Silly me, I didn't know how important those words were for you. Just pop off into your room and you can practise them again and again till you've had enough and I'll close the door so no-one can disturb you.' Swearing becomes much less fun on your own, in your own room, with no audience.
    - If they start again, immediately apologise for not giving them enough time and they go back in and practise again.

- Another way used by families trying to rid their family of foul language was to put a pile of 20c coins up on the sideboard where the kids could see it. At the end of each week the children received, as a bonus, any money still in their pile. Each time anyone swore, one coin was taken from their pile and given back to consolidated revenue (viz. Mum).
One desperate dad demanded one piece of silver in the swearing jar for each swear word—money to be sent to deaf kids deprived of foul language! The kids have cottoned on fast—there's not nearly as much swearing but you ought to see their sign language!

TONGUE AND COMMUNICATION PROBLEMS

Of course some parents still insist on washing their mouth out with soap and water. I find that cleans them up inside, but they can get awfully dirty outside.

BLOODY LANGUAGE

Lee-ann writes:

'One morning, after we'd had family over for dinner, my three-year-old came and announced, 'Mum, cause Dad's not here, can I say "bloody" all day?'

'No,' I said, 'bloody is a naughty word.'

'But Uncle Michael says it heaps.'

'Yes,' I said, 'but Uncle Michael shouldn't and I'll be telling him not to from now on.'

I thought I had handled it well, but now, every day, he asks me, 'Mum, you know that really naughty word "bloody"? We aren't allowed to say bloody are we, and Uncle Michael doesn't say bloody any more does he, and no-one else can say bloody, can they?'

Now what do I do?

Lee-ann, read the suggestions opposite and my answer to Karen's letter (see Back-Answering and Arguing on page 176), but don't be too hard on the odd expletive. As Mark Twain said, 'Under certain circumstances, swearing provides a relief denied even to prayer.'

Bush Remedies

- I found the only way was to try and stop swearing myself, and when I did, I pulled myself up in front of the children so they could see that if it's good enough for me to stop, then it's good enough for them too.

- We have a rule, no swearing. If the rule's broken, then the person must apologise and if it happens more than once a day then it means privileges are taken away.

- I just acted really disappointed and told them how bad it sounds coming out of such a beautiful mouth.

- We used fines, till their father realised he was losing more money than the rest of us put together. It stopped him (most of the time) and then the kids stopped doing it too.

- Substitute words like 'truck', 'shoot', 'piffle' and 'custard'.

What's the point of arguing with someone so ignorant they can't even see they're wrong and you're right!

Back-Answering and Arguing

Back-answering was rated in the top five in every survey of parent problems that I undertook.

CHECKS

- **Is it a family style**—everyone back-answers everyone else? If so, then see suggestions below.

- **Is it deflecting a bossy style?** Just for the exercise, see how your family compares to this ordinary old back-answering domestic.
  Parent: 'Go and clean up your room.'
  (**Mistake 1 giving a bossy command**.)
  Child: 'In a minute, when this program finishes.'
  (**Mistake 2 'in a minute' is probably every parent's favourite phrase**.)
  (**Mistake 3 asking kids to do anything when they're glued to the TV is always going to draw a snappy back-answer**.)
  Parent: 'No, now! I asked you three days ago and it's still a pigsty.'
  (**Mistake 4 add an insult**.)
  Child: 'Why don't you ask Dad to clean up the shed? It's worse than my room.'
  (**Mistake 5 getting sidetracked into a slanging match**.)

✴ **Is it just a very effective strategy?** That is, does it wear down or frustrate the opposition to the point that you'd rather give in than give them something more memorable?

✴ **Is it the symptom, rather than the problem?** Are they not making out too well in the school stakes, the friendship stakes, the sport stakes, the child stakes. In other words, do they feel like giant mis-stakes?

✴ **Is it directed only at one child or one parent?** If so, that's where the pain is coming from and that's the one that needs to be addressed.

✴ **Check your style** of communicating as some styles attract more back-answering than others.
   ◆ Style 1—THE FIGHTERS Fighters try to resolve differences of opinion by attacking and outpowering the opposition with a loud voice, violent explosions, interrupting, insulting, nagging, sarcasm, threats and aggressive ultimatums.
   ◆ Style 2—THE FLIGHTERS Flighters try sorting things out by withdrawing—acting super-polite, telling themselves it doesn't matter, getting depressed, going silent, saying things behind people's backs that they can't say to their face, getting sick, anything to avoid anything unpleasant.
   ◆ Style 3—THE FLOW-ERS Flow-ers put their own ego in neutral and latch on to where Sandy's coming from so they actively hear and the brain stays in gear. If we're part of the flow, we can't be the foe so their defences drop and their ears open. After that, creative brainstorming can generally find a way through without anybody 'losing face' and it sets a better lead for Sandy to follow. Don't worry if it fouls up a bit as kids pick up the new tone and that alone halves the anger.

COMMUNICATION INJECTIONS

According to Hugh Mackay in his book *Why Don't People Listen?* the basic problem in many communications with kids is that we're trying to 'inject' our message. We believe that the secret to getting a message through is to inject it through nagging, shouting, insulting or anything to force its passage. But listening doesn't work that way; it can't be forced, it has to be received. According to Mackay, it's not what our message does to the listener, but what the listener does with our message. And that means the message has to be respectful, so they listen; relevant to their lives, so they understand; and reflectful back to them, so *they* have to deal with it.

Just remember that the *grace* of listening is lost if the listener's attention is demanded, not as a favour, but as a right.

DO'S AND DON'TS

✸ Pretend they're a workmate or even friend when you ask them to do something and the respectful tone alone will get rid of 50 per cent of back-answering.

✸ Instead of an order, use a question with a bit of built-in choice so you've made it even harder to back-answer. That'll cut back the back-answer even more.

✸ Quiet determination is the key in the follow-through, so make sure you mean what you say. And *when* you do, make it work:
- not too often or they'll ignore,
- not too loud or they'll switch off,
- not too long or you'll lose them,
- not too insulting or they'll think revenge not remedy.

TONGUE AND COMMUNICATION PROBLEMS

Karen writes:
'I was so sick of being called an f...ing bitch when I'd done nothing more than ask Kyle to turn the TV off and get ready for school, that I got some curry powder and poured it in. But then he swore again, so he got another dose and another, until it was dribbling out the side of his mouth. But last weekend when his cousin was over Kyle dosed him for swearing so now what do I do?'

Karen, that's the problem with hurting kids to punish them, they think revenge not remorse. You have to go in heavier each time you punish them and they're likely to copy. So:
- No morning TV at least until he's ready for school.
- Call the teacher and check how he's going.
- Keep a good tone in the morning with the help of classical or guitar music.
- If he swears again, draw a sad face on the fridge to let him know he has hurt you.
- He gets no privileges, TV, mates, treats or stories until he has made up, either by doing a few jobs for you or doing as he's asked politely for an hour.
- If Dad's around he could give Kyle some practice in doing as he's told over and over again till he gets the message that swearing and back-answering are not in his best interest.

Giving Kyle curry is not the answer. Psychologically it doesn't work, intestinally it works too well; either way it's a mess to clean up.

Communication around the home is all about handling those we love with the same respect we do outsiders.

Bush Remedies

My four-year-old son was being very rude and back-answering so I asked him where he had left his manners. He stopped, thought and then said, 'I think I left them at Jonathon's.'

- I'm afraid I'm not a very patient person when the kids back-answer me. Once I feel the volume rising, I know it's a bad scene with worse to come. What my boys and I worked out was that when I was frustrated I would raise my hands above my head and steadily raise one finger at a time. They knew that meant I was finished arguing and they had 10 seconds to say their piece and then stop, argument over. If they didn't stop, then they got sent to their room or given a job to do.

- I gave one warning and then took privileges away if they persisted.

- I introduced something really ludicrous into the conversation and it seemed to penetrate better than just arguing with them. Then I'd get them to apologise when things had cooled down.

- A lot has to do with the way we speak to kids. As my mother once said, treat kids like dogs and they're bound to bark back their answer.

Lying

Lying rates as the most hated habit of kids. We feel hurt, betrayed, disregarded, disrespected and so very bitter. Part of the answer is knowing why they lie because that could give us the lead to the remedy.

CHECKS

- **Are they lying to avoid pain?** If so, check your style of punishment and concentrate on rewarding courageous truth.

- **Is your style of management overcontrolling**—that is, where the kids must be good all the time? These kids act goody goody and mature to keep adults happy but deep down want to be baddy baddy and very immature. Their good behaviour is an act. Outside overcontrol has left them with inside under control so when the pressure comes off, so does the maturity. What's more, these kids will often laugh after accidents or upsets to others as another way of letting off steam. Naturally, if they get caught out, they will use lies to jump the gap between the real and the ideal.

- **Are they lying to avoid embarrassment?** If so, just watch where and when you ask them for some answers.

- **Are they lying because there's better pay-off in taking the risk**—that is, the laughs they get or the status they've won make lying a small price to pay? If so, look carefully at how and where you handle the lie and try to use reflective style back to them in private. For example, 'Are you scared of losing friends or hurting friends? Is that why you tell me things that aren't true?'

- **Do they have a weak ego?** That is, do they say one thing and then do another and then try to cover up because their ego is not strong enough to blend the two? If so, consult a child or clinical psychologist to help the kids find themselves and believe in themselves so they have some rudder in life.

- **Is it just a factor of age?** According to the book *Why Kids Lie* right and wrong varies with age. Up to the age of four kids see right as getting their own way and their reason to be good as getting rewards and avoiding punishment.
    - At about ages five and six what's right is doing what you're told and your reason for being good is so you won't get into trouble.
    - But it changes for children between six and eight, where lying hits a peak. Doing what's right is doing what they want to do and their reason to be good is simply what's in it for them. So if there's less in it for them if they tell the truth, guess what you'll get?
    - In the eight to 12-year age group, what's right is living up to others' expectations. If you expect more than they feel they can deliver, they'll lie to make up the rest.
    - For older kids let their motive govern your management:
      —if it's attention, take notice of honest efforts;
      —if it's to escape savage punishment or a court martial, handle the penalty quietly and respectfully;
      —if it's fear of disapproval, lift the rate of approvals;
      —if it's to frame others, work on the jealousy and hurt rather than the lie;
      —if it's to protect others, get your information elsewhere.

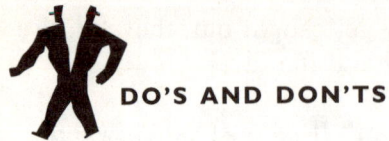

DO'S AND DON'TS

🕺 Look into areas for repeated lies as clues to things they're not handling too well, such as school.

🕺 For kids caught jumping the gap between their real level and parents' ideal level, the clue is to help *them* bridge the gap.
  ◆ Ask their ideas, get their opinions and their decisions on choices.
  ◆ In other words, get them to declare their own truths; if they've made their own bed of truth, it's much harder to lie in it.
  ◆ If it has become a habit that is shaking the family to the foundations then use the habit-busting techniques outlined in more detail in Chapter Three (page 71) and the 'Practice List' technique outlined throughout the book and illustrated in the Appendix, (page 354).
  ◆ If you're not getting good progress within three weeks, get advice from a psychologist; **they've got the couches for people who like to lie**.

🕺 Check your own habits. Some families get quite a buzz out of conning the police, the salesman or taxman, and that's one fantastic breeding ground for little lies. It's just that when our kids do it with less sophistication we get upset. Count the number of white lies, fibs, exaggerations or black lies you use today and then ask yourself whether it's just that the kids are less sophisticated.

🕺 Allow kids a bit of private space. If families are allowed to have a bit of private space in their own bedroom or bathroom without a quiz on everything they do, then they are less likely to lie in order to protect their privacy.

🕺 Work from day dot in building up trust. The more trust you give, the more bonds they feel, and the more bonds they feel, the more it hurts to lie. But all young kids will lie, so don't get too carried away by their feeble young efforts to handle conflicting pressures. To be quite frank, from their point of view, it's nothing personal!

✸ If the trust is broken then the job is to work on ways to rebuild the trust rather than torturing them over the lie. Unless the stakes are high a tortured confession wrecks the trust and gains little. In fact it often turns little lies into high court drama and it can be just as costly.

✸ If you're dealing with a lie, look at eyes and body language for information. Most parents tend to use face cues for honesty, but they're the worst, because the kids are concentrating so hard on the lie that they can look just so sincere. Look for twisting and wringing of hands and feet as they try to release their tension and get to know kids' giveaways like eye aversion, defensive shouting, stretching neck, tightening or licking lips, forced smiles or flushed face.

✸ With chronic, constant or serious lies I try to act quite naive and take them at their word so they carry the consequences. If they say that it was all Larry's fault then respectfully and with a straight face organise to catch up with Larry's mother straightaway to sort things out. As you start carrying it out give them a chance to save face and ask again whether they might have had a teeny bit to do with it. Once you've cracked the ice you often open a floodgate.

✸ Please don't ever label the kids as liars or that's exactly what you'll get; we all live by our labels.

But some kids just have all the answers, don't they. As one 12-year-old said to me, 'Parents are to blame for most of the lying kids do. They insist on asking questions.'

Bush Remedies

🍃 I've found a very effective method for dobbing. After the dobbing has been done, say, 'And what happened before that?' It makes them think of their own role in it all and helps sequence it in better perspective.

🍃 Easy—don't believe anything they say!

Dad had had enough of kids' lies, any more and the culprit would get Tabasco on the tongue! The kids hated the torture but, being typical kids, they loved seeing others suffer so they dobbed in each other mercilessly.

Melanie dobbed in her sister, Leanne, for telling a bad lie. Leanne was seething and said she wanted her sister dead. Dad was sick of this talk so he thought he'd stop that too. 'How about then,' he said to Leanne, 'I spray your sister's plate with some surface cockroach spray and then you're rid of her?'

'Great idea,' said Leanne. 'Then she'll never dob me in again and I'll have the room and her clothes all to myself.'

So while Melanie was out of the room he pretended to spray her plate in the kitchen. Then when Melanie came to the kitchen to get her plate, Dad whispered the plot and told her to pretend she was poisoned after eating her breakfast. Leanne watched silently as Melanie ate and when Melanie coughed and collapsed and writhed on the floor, Leanne just pulled her feet out of the road.

Dad called the game off, horrified that Leanne could let it go so far, but I would imagine you're even more horrified that any family could be so cruel about kids' conflicts. Cruelty might just stop the lie but it makes kids cruel to each other. And do you know the lie that caused the deadly dob? Leanne had said it would rain and it didn't!

Smutty Talk

Sometimes smutty talk is the only way kids have found to attract attention. Sometimes they're copying sleazy role models, sometimes they're mistaking their longing for skin touch with sex touch and sometimes it's just personality. But sex has to rank as one of the most obvious areas for kids to attract our attention by invading our taboos. Just look, for instance, at all the words we use as euphemisms for genitals. The boys' penis is variously called aerial, banana, bird, dingadoo, dinkus, peanut, pickle, thing, wiener, wee-wee and wormie willie. Just recently I've also heard it called 'you know what', pecker and rudie. Girls are taught flower, front, garage, little po-po, monkey, potato and toto! As a psychologist I'm amazed that we insist on such shy substitutes for 'down there'!

CHECKS

See also the checks for swearing on page 173.

* **Is it just a fascination of their age?** All little kids finding out about boy/girl differences will be very tuned in to sex talk.

* **Is it a way of attracting attention because they know adults react immediately?** If so, maybe use some habit-busting or flooding techniques referred to in this chapter (eg page 174).

* **Has it suddenly started and it's not in keeping with their character?** If so, see ideas below.

* **Is it a family favourite style of humour?** If so, then either grin and wear it or work out with them what's grown-up talk and what's kid talk. This tactic doesn't usually work very well, I should add, because kids tend to copy.

* **Is it just trying to keep up with the peer group?** If so, see ideas below.

DO'S AND DON'TS

* If you suspect that there's some unhealthy sex play/activity going on do the 'Body Check'.
   ◆ Start with a little chat and be up-front about the fact that they're saying a lot of body words now.
   ◆ See if they would like to ask you anything about their body: how it works, sex differences, even anything recently that may have happened to theirs in case there's something that's on their mind.
   ◆ If they talk about something bad that has happened to someone they know or they don't want to go to Uncle Paedophile's place any more or some kid makes them do bad things then phone the local Child Sexual Assault team (see Contact Numbers on page 365) and ask their advice.

- ◆ If your little chat finds nothing then that's wonderful. At least it has the double-edged advantage that smutty talk will be met not by punishment or lectures, but by information, so they're armed with information rather than smirking away their smut.

- ❋ If you think it's being peer prodded then here are a few steps you can take.
    - ◆ As soon as possible, enthusiastically invite Sandy's friends over to play.
    - ◆ Wait for the first infringement and call them inside.
    - ◆ Without any fear or embarrassment, tell them what your standards are and offer to explain any words to them privately if they would like to know, but that those words are private, not public.
    - ◆ If they infringe again, tell them in front of the others what the word means. Kids don't like that type of embarrassment in front of their friends.

- ❋ Check that you have plenty of factual information around in age-appropriate books about sex so they don't have to let fantasy overtake the facts. The choice on such books is now enormous but one of the best for this purpose and this age group is Gill Mullinar's book, *Not Just Four Letter Words*.

- ❋ Make sure that kids feel free to talk about any issue with you so they don't have to take it out of the mainstream and into the gutter. Research clearly shows that children who are given good information are less likely to engage in smutty talk or premature sex.

- ❋ Make sure that the kids are getting plenty of skin contact (hugs, cuddles, stroking, even pet play if they're not cuddly) so they don't have excess skin hunger which is so easy to mistake for sex hunger.

Bush Remedies

- Talk straight, use proper names, lower your voice, don't judge, and discuss the meaning of what they've said or done.

SMUTTY SMITTY

Ten-year-old Smitty had a dirty mind and a dirty mouth. The teachers called him 'Smutty Smitty'. He was obsessed with sex; every comment had a double meaning, his drawings were lewd and he switched in to any comment or any TV show that suggested sex. Recently, when he was clowning around in class and the teacher told him to leave the room, he had to have the last word: 'I was only just drawing her tits: Is there something wrong with that?' The same day he dropped his daks to giggling girls and was suspended.

Despite what you'd think, he was not from a bad home at all. Mum and Dad were just as concerned as you or I would be. He had a few learning problems so he may have been trying to win back a bit of pride and attention, and he also had a bit of ADHD and like a lot of these kids he tends to shoot from the lip. So we had to set up a few steps to de-smut Smitty.

- First we had to have his Ritalin dosage adjusted, as it was way too low to impede any impulse.
- He got on really well with Dad, so Dad decided to take over any school problems. He temporarily stopped any overtime and gave more time to being there, getting Smitty back into sport and to monitor any reduction in TV time if he couldn't break a bad habit.
- The teacher changed Smitty's seating and his work expectation so he didn't need to attract attention by sexy sensationalism.
- But the main move was for Mum and Dad to meet *every* snigger and snide comment with information, taking as much time as it needed till it was more fact than fun. They got those see-through Body Books with diagrams and drawings and explanations so he could learn what he was giggling about.

So far so good, but sex has always got a giggle and befuddled the best of us. As Plato said: 'There is no greater or keener pleasure than that of bodily love and none which is more irrational.'

Teasing

Teasing is a common problem that can also become quite a serious problem for many kids who can get very distressed, even suicidal, in adolescence if they can't handle it.

CHECK

- **Is it just normal banter between kids?** For many boys, teasing and nicknames are part of declaring mateship.

- **Is it fairly evenly balanced?** That is, are the two kids concerned giving as much as they're getting? If so, then they're enjoying it more than they let on so don't get sucked in to a solution that neither really wants.

- **Is goody-two-shoes' cry of 'Sandy, stop teasing me!' just loud enough for Mum to hear?** If so, don't take sides, they're both in it in their own way. All that's needed are some clear rules to handle kids' conflicts.

- **Is there a particular pattern to it?**
  - If it's always **before or after school**, but less at weekends, then some sense of pressure or not coping at school may be making them lay off their frustration.
  - If it's always **teasing the same child** then it may be because they feel threatened by that child or, the very reverse, they may sense some domination and power over that child so they use every opportunity to exercise power that they probably don't have anywhere else in their lives. The pattern will tell you where the pain is coming from.

- **Is it just a nuisance way of beating boredom?** If so, use the 'Think Light' boredom-beating tactics outlined in the Appendix, page 355.

DO'S AND DON'TS

✤ Remember that from the age of three, kids know how to get in and out of bickering and teasing, if they want to.

✤ It may be that they've just developed a habit that they feel is innocent—even if the victim doesn't quite feel the same—so you need to make them habit busters. That means using something like the one, two, three re-offences and they're struck out, into time out, till they can work out what they will do differently when they come out. If they're showing good form at breaking the habit then that can lead to privileges.

✤ If Sandy's secretly smirking then that's where I use the 'Practice' idea.
  ◆ Tell Sandy you didn't realise it was so hard so give him some practice at setting up a different and less annoying habit.
  ◆ For instance, if he can't walk past his sister without teasing or annoying, then have him practise walking past and not annoying.
  ◆ Practise this again and again, till you both feel he's got the hang of it.
  ◆ Practise even more if he slips up again.
In other words make the whole problem reflective on him and his solutions rather than being caught in the middle.

✤ If it's destructive teasing and not just banter, do the following:
  ◆ Call the kids together (maybe during a favourite TV show so it contains a sense of urgency to be resolved).
  ◆ Ask them what it is that's going wrong between them.
  ◆ Get both versions and ask them both what they'd like to happen or change.
To assist here you may want to use something like the 'Mike' technique.

GAMES

THE MIKE

- Get a piece of cardboard and cut out the shape of the old butter paddle or kid's beach spade.
- Write on it 'The Mike' (or draw a shape that looks like a microphone).
- Hang up 'The Mike' on a hook somewhere handy in the kitchen.
- When there's an argument, tell the kids that if they can't sort it out by the time you count to three, they can use 'The Mike'.
- If it goes on, grab 'The Mike', call them both together and make them sit down at the table, either side of you.
- Ask them who wants to use 'The Mike' first. Because it's a microphone that means they only have to talk softly.
- As the first one speaks and gets their point of view out, the other listens and cannot interrupt until the first one has finished.
- When the first kid has finished, the second must sum up what was said.
- If everyone's happy that the point was heard then roles are swapped—the second has 'The Mike' and the first one has to listen and repeat their message.
- Because they've both had their say and both been heard, it's usually easy to sort out and to find alternatives to teasing.
- Encourage them to be open and honest as it may involve a bit more mike time if they're not.
- Work out what each wants, how it's going to happen and let them know you'll be reviewing it at the same (inconvenient) time the next night.
- Follow up each night for at least a week so they get the message that you mean business.
- After one week see if they're ready to handle it alone and follow up a week later when everyone can comment on how it's working and if not what now needs to be changed.

✼ For kids who are the *victim*, who keep getting teased, it's very important that they learn tactics that empower them to beat it. These have been outlined in my previous book, *Coping with the Family*. Don't just ask them to walk away and ignore it, that isn't enough help for victims.

The technique I use often is my 'Teasing Tossing Tactic'.

GAMES

TEASING TOSSING TACTIC

- ◆ I get the kids to tell me all the hurtful things they're hearing,
- ◆ Then I hit them with the lot and ask them to count out loud every time I've used a word that's trying to hurt. By the way, the most common teasers (in order) relate to being overweight (fat, fatty, fatso, dumpling, fatstuff, tank), then to being underweight (skinny, beanpole, skin and bone, lamp post, legs eleven, bag o' bones, skinny cow, match stick, anorexic) to intelligence (dumb, idiot, stupid, lamebrain, cretin, brainless, useless, dork, peabrain) to other aspects of physical appearance (Ginger Meggs, shorty, stumpy, icepole, four-eyes, train tracks, pigtails, paleface, flappy, big nose, big ears) and then to aspects of personality (sissy, whinger, crybaby, old chook, Rudolph, hyper, Betty beachball, fairy, goody-two-shoes, boggie bommer, liar, cheat, strawhead, dog).
- ◆ Then I do it again but this time they count under their breath.
- ◆ When they can count accurately, no matter how hurtful the words thrown at them, then they're ready to beat the bully.
- ◆ I get them to count how many they get the next day and put it on the kitchen calendar.
- ◆ I promise that if they can keep their mind on the count, not the content, then it won't upset them and the teasing score will go down and down and within two weeks will have more than halved if they can play it straight this way.

✼ The big goal is to shift them from being the victim to being the victor. Kids get teased not because of what they can't do or haven't got but simply because of the way they react.

Silly Talk and Showing Off

This problem is a habit that really bugs parents so here are some ideas.

CHECKS

- **Is it part of an Attention Deficit Disorder (ADHD) syndrome?** If this is the case suggestions in Chapter Three for ADHD (page 85) will be useful. Remember that many ADHD kids have trouble inhibiting responses, sitting still, staying quiet, etc. Those with the hyperactivity dimension of ADHD have excess body tension to release. It's not primarily for attention or annoying people (although they enjoy that too) but rather it will be at random times, often when no-one is around. **Its goal is not attention attracting but tension relieving**.

- **Is it part of an Attention Demanding Disorder syndrome?** If this is the case then it will be done when there *is* an audience as the goal is attention attracting not tension relieving. See suggestions under Attention Demanding Disorder in Chapter Three (page 72). Remember that the best way to manage attention seeking is to give attention to behaviour you like, and isolate them away from attention for behaviour you don't. That forces a shift in their game plan.

- **Is it an immature way to release tension when they are embarrassed or overexcited** (eg visitors asking them questions, going somewhere exciting, getting ready for a big event)? If this is the case, see suggestions below.

DO'S AND DON'TS

- If it's an immature way of relieving embarrassment, then quietly show or practise the behaviours you'd prefer. That way you're redirecting their outlet rather than trying to block one.

※ For the most part treat silly talk as a habit. Management then means:
- making the kids aware that it's bothering people,
- asking them if they're aware that they're doing it,
- working out a signal to remind them (eg call their name, then when they're looking at you, sign a zip action across your mouth to remind them to zip up their mouth),
- use the one, two, three, strike out rule after that for breaches, or if not sending them into time out, then some other penalty for forgetting the rule (eg doing jobs).

※ One way that can work is to train Sandy on a 'Noise Nobbler' counter action:

GAMES

NOISE NOBBLER

- When he starts clicking or making silly noises get him to do an alternative Noise Nobbler blocking action (eg putting something safe in his mouth between his teeth such as a mouthguard, a leaf or a piece of laminated cardboard).
- Get him to start the habit, then do the Noise Nobbler blocking action.
- Repeat this sequence four or five times till he's sure he knows what to do next time he starts.
- When he starts the noise, give him the signal to nobble his noise, and this he does till he's sure he has it under control.
- If it resumes do more practice with the Noise Nobbler, as much as is necessary and at a time that doesn't particularly suit him, so he's keen to improve.

Communication Skills Summary

C Communicate calmly, concisely and clearly.
O One direction at a time.
M Modify your language to suit their age.
M Market your message rather than inject.
U Understand where the kids are coming from, get down to their level and you'll halve your arguments.
N Nurture their trust in your communications. Backhanded or sarcastic comments destroy the faith children are developing in talking.
I 'I' language is much more effective than 'you' communication, which tends to make people defensive.
C Call a stop action if interchange is out of control and apply the 20-minute rule of no contact, ask for feedback on the impact of what you said, reflect, revise and check.
A Avoid distractions. When talking to kids make sure you have their full attention.
T Take time to communicate and tell stories, lots of them, so they love to share words, thoughts and feelings.
E Encourage good communication habits by your lead; listening, not interrupting, respecting others' feelings, and taking turns.

FAMOUS FOOTNOTE
A DISTANCED MUM

Bronwen Daddo

MOTHER OF THE FAMOUS DADDO BROTHERS

I miss my boys. We have five children and my busy husband is often away a lot of the time. But we've always been very close. The kids are still very close and constantly talk, think about or visit each other, even though we're very scattered. The kids have always been very special and important to me. They're the centre of my life.

I've always enjoyed being their mother, but no time is really easy. Being a parent is hard work but also so rewarding. Certainly when Jamie had his accident at age 18 it was hard on the whole family. He wasn't looking, he walked onto the road, was hit by a car, in hospital for three months, in rehab. for 12, and has been in a wheelchair ever since.

Times when the kids have been separated from us have been hard too, so it's nice they all care enough to stay in touch. As children grow they move away to their own space and their own mistakes. We give that freedom. If we do it right they won't even know permission was given.

As a parent one of the principles I've tried to follow is to let children grow as they will. Lead them to water, allow them to drink, but don't question how they drink, just be the listener and share the excitement.

Perhaps for our family, maybe for every family, the hardest part is to learn to say 'goodbye' as happily as we say 'hello'! The greeting we give never equals the parting. As they travel we hope in our hearts their paths will often cross over. Distance, time and commitments can all block this. But though the meetings become distanced, our love stays the same.

But, you know what I think is the real issue; not how we cope with the hard times but how do we create the good times!

My mum taught me some wonderful lessons; when the kids were sick, I remember Mum said to just put cool gentle hands on the forehead. Sickness will pass and the joy of clean sheets, flowers and a jug of lemonade will make you feel better. That advice has always stayed with me and I've always operated on that rule. If any of the kids had a temperature, then it was always 24 hours in bed and get pampered.

I've always believed that boundaries are necessary, but they're there to explore. Starting with the playpen, these boundaries are good, because they help the kids feel secure in their own space. When they're ready, they can push up and the boundaries become a tool in growth. Then they need fences to offer security, but then later they're ready to climb those and go beyond to the wider world. It's a process of breaking boundaries for new discoveries.

But you've always got to be prepared to make exceptions. Sometimes I'd allow Lachlan or Cameron a day off school when they were feeling off and we'd just spend special time together. Sometimes when Cameron was uptight about something we'd take to the golf course and talk and swing and breathe and just be near each other, and by the end of the course we'd be okay.

Communication with children is so important, it's so easy but it takes time, and adults are so busy that they may try to hurry their kids' thoughts and efforts to communicate. Give them time to come up with what they want to say.

Sometimes it's hard to find that time at home, so try to take off and go to neutral territory, and just be there, no big plans, no shopping, just be there and make contact and communicate with each other. And then just see what happens next, don't try to plan it all.

I'm now a grandmother—here are a few ideas I've picked up so far to stay in touch with grandchildren you don't see every day.

- ◆ Young children don't really get a great buzz just answering Grandma's questions, so instead, tell a story. They'll listen and together you share.
- ◆ Another way to stay in contact with them is to send a little present. They call back with the joy of having received your sharing.
- ◆ Send a throwaway camera to be returned—you do the developing and the photos are great!

Communication is the key, but to work it well takes time and effort, it won't just happen.

CHAPTER SEVEN

Heart and Relationship Problems

Our children ... need us to love them whoever they turn out to be, whatever path they follow, whether or not they validate our life-choices. The important thing is to love them as the individual human spirits they are, grit our teeth through the bad patches and to be there when they need us. As they most certainly will.

SUZANNE CHICK, author
[READ MORE OF SUZANNE'S SENSITIVE STYLE AT THE END OF THIS CHAPTER.]

Humans are social animals! So, if relationships aren't working, then for most kids that means life isn't working, and that means they'll be real animals! If they're hurting, you can bet their nearest and dearest will be hurting too. The **heart** is Sandy's engine—his motor, his motivator—and if it's struggling, through low self-esteem, feeling lonely, hurt pride, rejection, jealousy, disappointment or lost love, then Sandy's in sad shape.

But let me share a radical idea. I believe it's a good idea for our kids to have a struggle or two or a setback or three in their lives, to toughen them up enough to survive the knockbacks later in life. No well-balanced parent I've ever met has had the good life handed to them on a plate. They've had to work through low times, loneliness, disappointment, failure and rejection. They've had to learn to dig deep and find that inner strength that we don't even look for if life is too easy. Some kids, including those who become very depressed or suicidal, expect that others will solve their problems for them. They have no coping mechanisms or experience. So, when a girlfriend rejects them, this is hurt like they've never felt before and their psyche can't solve it.

So we need to help kids solve problems of the heart, not do the solving for them.

Self-Esteem

Self-esteem is probably the biggest issue in the book! Armed with good self-esteem kids can cope with life; without it they can't. It's as simple as that! The grades they get, the jobs they get, the relationships they make, the mates they make, all reflect self-esteem. If kids have low self-esteem they can be impossible to manage, and no threats you make, no punishments you deliver, no privileges you remove, make the slightest difference.

Let me position its importance this way; 60 per cent of kids are born by accident and too many die by accident. If, in between those two, the kids don't get the stamp of approval from others, then why hang around?

Self-esteem is a term that's been bandied about so much I prefer to think of it as self-worth. That feeling of worth is not helped by empty praise or just being told they're good. It's a feeling they get because they know they're liked by others and someone somewhere has said to them, 'Good on you, Sandy, I'm glad you're here. I'm glad you're on my team.' That's the best feeling in the world for kids. It's a feeling that starts at home and has to be continued at school.

CHECKS

- Firstly do a symptom checklist.
    - Do they make friends easily?
    - Are they active and happy in their play and interactions with others most of the time?

- Are they happy with the way they look?
- Can they make decisions easily?
- Do they have energy in the morning?
- Are they interested in new things and taking initiative?
- Are they confident in tackling day-to-day tasks?

If they're failing on a few of these then they'll be feeling they're failing life's fitness test.

✻ Check that your head and heart are giving them the same message—not empty praise, but real sense of worth. That feeling can be very confused by:
  - parents telling them they're valued but never finding time to be with them;
  - parents wanting kids to talk and share but never finding down time to listen;
  - parents wanting kids to be happy but never finding time to share a laugh;
  - parents wanting kids to enjoy and do well at reading but never finding time to share stories and books with them.

✻ Check that you're meeting their needs rather than their wants. Their wants are for the weeps-as-she-wees-as-she-walks dolls, transformers, roller blades, designer labels, etc. Their needs are for security, self-esteem, love, fun, friends, family, trust, encouragement and respect. These things have no price tag.

✻ Check that you're giving them that feeling of security through strong leadership, unqualified love and clear rules, *not* from overprotection and indulgence!

✻ Check whether you've found their talents so they believe they have something of worth to offer. Especially for those with disabilities, by far the biggest priority is to find what they're best at and then find groups or sports to match. That's not always easy but **a talent on the go can save an ego**.

✻ Check that your management is focusing on success, not failures. If you're trying to do repair work here's how to do it.

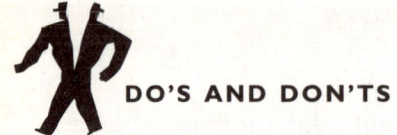
DO'S AND DON'TS

✸ Find what they love doing. The things you can see from their eyes and face that really give them a lift. Follow those up, no mattter how obscure their interest.
  ◆ Use the 'Children's Interest Inventory' in the Appendix, page 357 for starters and really think hard about any talents they have.
  ◆ Get their reaction on a few and their suggestions.
  ◆ If they're obscure or uncommon interests then phone Community Information Services for a local contact.
  ◆ If their self-esteem is so low they can't even make the effort, and if you have some good 'contacts' around town, see if you can orchestrate a 'surprise' phone call or visit. If parents suggest anything it's probably doomed to rejection but if the offer comes from outside, it tells them that they really are wanted.
  ◆ If school is a problem then a word with the teacher about ways to lift their status or success rate will work wonders.

✸ Focus on success, even though they want to focus on failure. One way to shift that focus is a technique called 'Reframing'. It is designed to get kids to see their problems differently. For instance, if Sandy feels that everyone hates him:
  ◆ start by challenging the fact that *all* the kids feel that way,
  ◆ see if he can identify any that don't hate him and which ones speak to him and what their friends might like about him (eg being kind, doesn't cheat, shares games, doesn't try to go first all the time) then work out ways he can get the kids to see these talents and watch the reaction he gets.
  ◆ That night talk about the tactics he used, how it went and what he'll do the next day to build bridges to friendship.

✸ Challenge them to identify habits they have that might not go over well. Then see if they're ready to do some habit busting, work out what different behaviour they'll try to do instead and report back the next night on how it went.

✸ **Teach positive self-talk skills** if your Sandy is using negatives on himself—'I'm stupid', 'I'm ugly', 'nobody likes me'.

HEART AND RELATIONSHIP PROBLEMS

- Some use challenges such as, 'Am I stupid or is the person picking on me stupid?' or 'What if they do think I'm an idiot, so is Bart Simpson, and see how many people love him?'
- Some parents help the kids to compile positive self talk phrases that give the child a lift back to the lighter side of life.
- Some parents play a game of cutting out each of these features and letting the kids put them in order of ones that most apply to them down to the ones that least apply.

GAMES

THIS IS ME

- I HAVE LOTS OF FRIENDS
- I KNOW HOW TO MAKE MONEY
- I AM GOOD ENOUGH TO BE ME
- PEOPLE LIKE ME
- MY PARENTS ARE PROUD OF ME
- I LOOK AFTER MY BODY
- MY PARENTS LOVE ME
- I AM KIND TO ANIMALS
- I HAVE A SMART MIND
- I AM KIND AND CARING
- I CAN FORGIVE PEOPLE
- I AM PRETTY HEALTHY
- I CAN TAKE CARE OF MYSELF
- I AM GOOD AT SPORT
- I ACCEPT MYSELF AS I AM
- I AM A GOOD AND LOYAL FRIEND

My extras:

✻ Do find areas where they can achieve at school even if they're not brilliant at schoolwork—art, sport, kindness, craft, projects, computers, board cleaner-upperer. Kids need endorsement that they have something to offer before they can feel good about themselves.

✻ Have a success sharing time every night so everyone can talk about one success or good thing that happened that day and maybe one problem they successfully solved.

PROBLEM WINNERS

How does your family go about solving its problems? Some pretend they don't have any; some, like me, go for the quick solution and back onto the happy stuff. Some live as if life is just one big problem on the way to the grave and others opt for something to pop, sniff, drink or jab to take the pain and the problem away.

But let me tell you about Jaclyn, a lady who has had her share of problems. Her husband had an alcohol problem and walked in front of a bus and then her son was electrocuted. So she struggled with three boys, a hijacked heart, a massive mortgage and life was too much.

At one of her lowest points, one of her kids said, 'Why don't we each see what problems we can solve today?' It was just an innocent comment but it turned her life around. Instead of avoiding problems and living in fear, they confronted them. Each morning over a hurried breakfast the family would rattle off what problems they expected that day and then in the evening they'd talk about how they solved them or whether they didn't end up happening at all. In other words, they accepted that problems were part of life; you can't and shouldn't avoid them, but the secret is to find the ways to solve them, and tell others who might need to know.

So there you go, swap a problem. It's always easier to solve someone else's!

✻ Keep a scrapbook for each of the kids with all awards, memorabilia and anything else that makes them feel good.

✻ Think about doing a tape recording of things Sandy likes or does well to be played when he's feeling down. Or if Sandy can read, use the 'Magic Macaroni Tin' (see page 34).

✻ Talk to Sandy about which animal he really likes, then help him to adopt the positive traits about that animal.

- Talk to his teacher about things that can be done at school to boost his feelings of worth. For example, younger children can take a turn in the middle of the classroom to be bombarded with positive statements (things other kids like or respect about each other). With older kids it's often less embarrassing if they write them out and hand them across to the child in focus.

Bush Remedies

- We focused on the clever things she could do at an early age, looked through photo albums and talked about the kinds of things that were happening in our family around the time that the photos were taken.

- Physical affection is very important even if you don't feel like it. Really listen 'actively' and offer to go with them to get support such as with a counsellor or to set up an important person as a sounding board.

Often the difference between a good and a bad school day is five minutes of our time.

Lonely Kids

Few experiences hurt kids as much as loneliness or rejection. Some kids are lonely because they're so withdrawn there's nothing to hang a friendship on or they have some little quirk that irks other kids. Others fail to win friends because they just don't have important friend-making skills, such as making eye contact, praising others, giving ground in conversations or even an open friendly body posture. Others may have copied or inherited a loner style of a parent. For whatever reason the problem of the lonely 'loser' is so common we can all relate to it.

Here's how to tell if it's just their quiet, self-contained style or if it's a problem.

CHECKS

- Check whether they're stealing or borrowing money to buy a friend.

- Check whether they're spending their time alone in the outdoor play area, the playground or in the school library.

- When you ask them for the names of their friends, see whether they can nominate several, easily and enthusiastically, or whether they mumble, or mention different kids each time.

- Ask yourself how often they receive any phone calls from friends or invitations to go/stay over or go to parties.

- Check whether they're being bossy boots in their peer play—if they are, you can bet that they have few friends.

- Check whether they're saying, repeatedly, that they have no friends.

- Check with the teacher if it's seen as a problem at school. It could be that the cry of lonely is just a ploy to get more attention.

- Check whether they are fit and well enough to keep up. If they're not then the other kids will pass them by because kids' friendship is all about doing things together. If someone can't join in, then it's hard to be their friend.

DO'S AND DON'TS

- Don't take over. Don't lecture. We've all had to weather some tough times and we're the better for it.

- Really listen to what Sandy's on about and then reflect back what you think he's feeling rather than blaming, lecturing or focusing on the content.

HEART AND RELATIONSHIP PROBLEMS

❋ Now help him problem-solve a few ways out of his loneliness. What could he do to get kids playing with him? Does he want to be popular? What do popular kids do to attract friends? What are the things he's good at that he'd like to play with others? How can he make others aware of his talents? Use the Ugly Duckling story to reposition or reframe the problem to one that is much more manageable.

The bird was lonely because he was different. Because he was different, sometimes others laughed at him and he thought being different meant being worse, being unlikeable. But when he found out what he was good at and found others just like him then he found that he was not ugly or lonely any more, he was a beautiful swan. The mistake he made was to try and swim in the wrong pool.

❋ Let him weigh up the ideas and select those he wants to try.

❋ If things are going okay, then do some fine tuning; if not, then together share the problem with the teacher. Teachers have many books that work on social skills, eg *Friendly Kids, Friendly Classrooms* by Helen McGrath. If teachers are aware that there's a problem they can make many subtle class bonding activities that can shift the social dynamics:
- seating Sandy near another lonely soul or sitting him near someone nice who will draw Sandy into a group;
- organising for Sandy to select a mate to take a message around;
- stacking the groupings for project work so Sandy's talents and acceptance are maximised;
- having a 'This is Your Life' day for each kid where everyone has to say what they like about each other, so they get to know more about each other;
- role play and explore how it feels to be a left-out kid and what we can do when we feel it or see it;
- go on excursions and camps so the kids get to know each other and feel they belong together.

❋ If the kids seem happy in their own company then that's a different issue. Some kids just like more time alone. As long as they know how to mix, share and have fun with other kids then they don't have a problem at all. However, all kids like sharing their interests so maybe you could hunt down a club or group that picks up on his interest in for instance, cars or computers.

Some find friend making harder than others but in time I think we all come to learn that the biggest ingredient in making friends is simply to be one!

Friendships Summary

F Find their strengths.
R Reassure them that everyone is looking for friends.
I Instil your confidence in their ability to find a friend.
E Encourage positive attempts to make friends.
N Never take over, buy friends or publicise their problem.
D Discourage excuses and encourage action to meet kids.
S Share your own similar experiences and what you did.
H Have a talk to teacher to work on class self-esteem.
I Invite family friends with same-aged kids around.
P Praise any success.
S Stop any home hindrances (eg overprotection).

Bush Remedies

- I just made sure I was there as a friend until they developed their own.

- I reassured them that they are still loved at home.

- Believe it or not, we found one of the best ways to handle rejection by his peers was to agree with them, make a joke out of it, say he was a horrible child and not to bother us again this year. We'd all end up laughing together and it took the edge off their hurt.

- I cuddled them and told them I loved them and told them it was others who were missing out on being their friend.

- We shared the hurt as I could all too well remember how it felt when it happened to me as a child.

> Andrew was a nice kid but he just couldn't make friends. No matter how understanding his parents were, he hated them, hated the world and wanted to die as he was a social reject.
>
> Once kids get to school, no matter how kind parents have been, if they can't get the approval of the pack, the nod of the mob, then they're losers, they know it and so their eyes drop and then the other kids know it too.
>
> In a great book for teachers, *Friendly Kids, Friendly Classrooms*, Helen McGrath outlines the things that are turn-offs for other kids: playing alone; hits or punches; bossing others; looking sad; never saying much; getting into fights; thinking no-one likes them; saying mean things; being a poor loser; not joining in; getting teased; not sharing; not playing by the rules; and not being good at sport.
>
> Notice how some turn-offs are not for being bad but just *feeling* bad. If children are to weather the social storm they need to know they are likeable, they need to know how to give as well as take, and they need to know how to play because it's the players who attract friends.
>
> Andrew has left home now, left school and gone up to Townsville in search of a place where people might never know he was a loser. Missing money and Dad will probably see him home again soon, but it sure proved to me that probably the best legacy any of us can leave our kids is the ability to make friends.

- My daughter went through a period when she kept saying that whenever she saw another child, they either frowned or pulled a face at her. I found this disturbing, so I paid more attention and noticed that what she'd do when she saw another child was just to keep staring at that child until the child probably wondered why she was staring and would frown at her. I said, 'Perhaps if you smile at them then they'll smile back. It usually works for me.' She soon found she got lots of smiles and I felt I'd shown her the way.

- I gave them love and reassurance and tried to find a friend, even if it was an old lady.

- My son has ADD and is not too clever at making friends. What we do now is invite one friend over at a time and make it a special event—a new-release video, make your own pizza, set up the Lego. Playing with younger kids is something ADD children often like; I just watch to see that size didn't bully.

◆ *Twin Advice:*
With twins it is important that they be treated as individuals. If you always treat them as 'the twins' how are they going to react when only one gets invited to a birthday party or one receives an award from school? Don't always dress them alike, especially if they are identical; it makes it too difficult for others, especially teachers and other children, to see them as two separate people.

◆ We put your questions to the congregation at our local church youth group and they suggested the following ideas for lonely kids:
- draw or write a story
- pretend to be a popular person and act that way
- phone a friend
- talk to someone
- go shopping
- smile at someone
- watch TV and eat chocolate
- even when you're feeling really lonely, it's good to know that God is always with you

If kids don't know how to make friends, the group suggested these ideas:
- try to find a common interest
- try to see life through the other person's eyes
- share junk food
- talk to them as if you already know them

Kids who feel like the white elephants in the family often end up as the black sheep.

Bossing

Bossy kids are often bothered kids! It's this anxiety that's making them try to take control.

# CHECKS

If your Sandy is a bossy boots then check him out on the following.

✣ Is it that he's used to being the boss in the house and expects outsiders to do as they're told just as the insiders have done?

✣ Is his bossing coming from a fear that other kids don't like him, so he panics and tries to exert control to reduce the panic?

✣ Is it just that he's an insecure kid who needs order? He can't stand messy games or messy people that lack his order, so he tries to force it on them.

✣ Is it that Sandy is threatened by one particular kid so he tries to dominate proceedings to keep that child away from the action and away from his friends?

✣ Is it a style that's being copied from bossy parents? No boss likes to be bossed, so the home scene is set for major confrontations—'personality clashes', I think it's quaintly called. This is the style that breeds horrible homes, especially when the kids turn into teenagers!

Whatever the reason, bossing is no fun for anyone, not even the boss, so we have to shift the game plan.

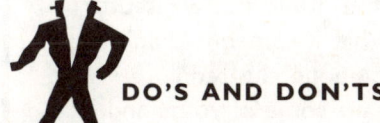# DO'S AND DON'TS

✣ Have a critical inlook before a bossy outlook and ask yourself whether the kids are bad kids or good apprentices. If they're just copying you then use some of the suggestions in Chapter Six (page 176).

✣ If it's just their style, maybe have a close look at how they're mixing and see if you can help them find better habits to fix the bossy one. In particular, are they good at the following social skills?
- asking
- joining in
- being kind
- waiting
- complimenting
- taking turns

- handling disagreement
- handling kids who don't play well or lack skills
- laughing and enjoying themselves
- using their imagination
- keeping up with the game, etc

Alert the teacher to help build those social skills that you both feel are spoiling things for Sandy.

✱ If it's just their style and they're school age then maybe play the alternative to 'Show and Tell' called 'Look and Listen'.

GAMES

LOOK AND LISTEN

- Get them to talk about which kids *they* like and why they like them.
- Ask them about the way their friends play and handle problems in games—'Do they boss?' or 'Do they tell others what to do?'
- What do they do when they're sick of a game, or when kids mess it up, etc? If they're not sure get them to look and listen the next day and come back and share their secret.
- Then see if they would like kids to like them. What can they do that would help other kids to like them? How would they play? With whose games? What if the other kids wanted to play a game that they don't like? What if someone didn't play the game the right way? What if someone cheated?
- Once you have their ideas, then share some of yours and let them select which they want to try.
- Use board games or cards to practise sharing, losing, winning, letting others go first and let them practise the techniques you develop.
- Give them practice with:
  —walking away if they're upset;
  —saying 'I don't want to play this any more' without getting angry;
  —suggesting another game;
  —inviting kids to play their game.

In other words, give them the skills to do what they want to do. I know it takes time, but it's nowhere near the time that patching up fights or supervising school-suspended kids takes!

✷ When friends are coming around, warn your kids that any bossing will bring you in as referee. If it surfaces, ask the assembled group how they think it could all work better and then together work out a few rules so it's more fun for everyone.

MAKING A ROD FOR YOUR OWN BACK

Noeline writes:
'What have I done wrong? I have two children, the girl is fine, but nine-year-old Rodney's so rude to me I just can't stand it. He says we don't love him, but we give him everything, take him everywhere, and it's never enough. I hardly ever ask him to do anything around the house, but he treats me like dirt. He just bosses me and his sister all day. It's only when I cry that he says sorry. He's no trouble for his father, but my trouble is that father is rarely around. What do I do?'

Noeline, change happens inside out. Start respecting yourself and you'll force change in others.

Maybe start by using the Fridge Disk Discipline game in the Appendix, page 351 In Rodney's case, make up a flip disk, red one side, green the other. If he's bossy, the disk flips to red and he has to spend the next hour doing and saying nice things for you before he gets the green light on any privileges, and mean it. If he won't cooperate, then don't stew on it; just let Dad know that Rodney needs help in cooperating and speaking pleasantly. Then the two of you give Rod practice over a few little domestic duties that night. If Dad's too busy then tell him from me that he's making a rod for his own back unless he fronts up, firms up and backs up in a real hurry. During my time working with kids I've learnt a few home truths.

- ◆ Homes are not democracies.
- ◆ Parents who disagree about discipline will have children who misbehave.
- ◆ Effective discipline is as much a part of love as hugs and kisses.

Jealousy

You've heard the old saying: where there is no jealousy, there is no love. I think the author was the same desperate parent who thought up 'it's only wind', 'he's just teething' and 'it's just a stage'. It's certainly hard to see much love in the gouging, biting, hitting and pinching kids invest in their new sibling. And the pain doesn't stop with the new baby either, as the rest of the family has to cope with older kids trying to be young again: they'll bung on the baby talk, become nappy happy again or beg to be fed. Jealous preschoolers often show a top tantrum by day and a flash flood by night. Jealous school-age kids might get the big ache to top, tum or tail so they can skip school. It all seems so silly, but it's very genuine and very common. It's not due to lack of attention, it's a devastating loss of bio-rhythm, of security and of top spot in the pecking order.

CHECKS

I'm not sure what you call the victim and perpetrator of jealousy—jealousee and jealouser, I suppose. Whatever you call them, they're hard to handle.

- Is there a parent's pet child? If so, the others are likely to see the pet as depriving them of all the goodies so they develop a pet hate.

- Did the 'jealouser' have rights or privileges taken away with the arrival of the one they're jealous of?

- Did the 'jealouser' have a role in preparing for the new arrival?

- Is the 'jealousee' close in age to the offender? Jealousy is more common if kids are close in age, or the same sex. There's more competition.

- Do family and/or friends make a fuss over the 'jealousee', making the 'jealouser' worse?

- Is the 'jealousee' more popular, have more friends, etc?

✸ Is the so-called victim subtly trying to sideline the 'jealouser' away from the parents' good books? It will come as no surprise to you if I say that kids can be devious.

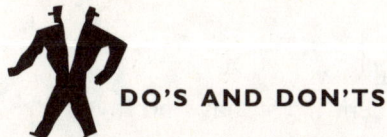
DO'S AND DON'TS

Let's say Sandy is the problem, really cruel to his younger sister and taking delight when she cries.

✸ Don't ask him to be nice to her—that's like asking Arafat and Netenyahu to be mates.

✸ Make sure that you find one-to-one time for each of the kids.
- In that time treat Sandy as the older one and special helper.
- Talk about ways you and he can find special time for each other because you both love it so much.
- Talk about things that bug him about the younger one and together work out ways you want it managed—your role and his role.
- Use signals to let him know to break off contact for a while if he's back to old habits.
- Use your next one-to-one time (eg bedtime) to check how you both went and what new tactics are needed for the next day.
- If Sandy is aged four or more, then use charts to record new big boy skills.
- Every time his little sister does something nice it can go on his chart, so he starts to think she's not all bad.
- Maybe when she goes to town with Mum, she buys Sandy a present and vice versa.

✸ Help each child find their own niche in life so they don't have to be jealous of anyone else's. Try for different friends, hobbies or sports.

✸ Respect each kid's uniqueness and make them feel second to nobody in your heart and in their own mind. If you don't like one particular child then you can bet they know it. Spend time getting to know each other.

- ❋ Show them healthy ways to get over hurt pride.

- ❋ Help them to find a level-headed soul mate they can unload on so it's not brewing up a storm. Grandparents are often very good for this, better than many realise.

- ❋ In summary, here's how to reduce jealousy.
    - ◆ You'll reduce the fights by 20 per cent if you have no favourites in your heart or head.
    - ◆ You'll drop another 20 per cent if there are no other domestics around to copy.
    - ◆ Lop off another 20 per cent by giving them some special treat when they've actually been nice to each other, when the younger one has left games and property alone and when the older one has been 'big' about it all.
    - ◆ Lop another 10 per cent if you don't let them use fights as their only way to get your attention.
    - ◆ Lop another 10 per cent if your punishments make you a worse enemy than each other.
    - ◆ And lop another 10 per cent if you give each one a little private time, draw no comparisons and encourage separate interests and friends.

That makes 90 per cent. The rest you just grin and bear in the sure knowledge that all too soon they'll be grown up and you'll be deafened by the peace they've left behind.

Bush Remedies

Twin Advice:
Twins can be very jealous of each other. Sharing is one of their greatest problems and too often they get shared presents. If two siblings are fighting then you have the advantage of one having a little more maturity, which you can often appeal to in bringing about a solution. When they are the same age this is not possible. Time out in separate rooms can be useful as can be putting them into separate bedrooms.

JAUNDICED JEALOUSY

Paul was so jealous of his brother, David, that he'd sabotage his games, parties and friends, would refuse to eat off the same plate or use the same cutlery, would refuse to sit next to him in the car, and if they were at the table together he'd put a box up in between them so he wouldn't have to look at David. In fact, if he passed David in the passageway, Paul would hold his breath. He'd even timed how long Mum took saying good night to David to make sure he got the same.

Paul had had Mum all to himself for four years before David turned up and he hated the loss of top spot. What's more, because no-one understood why he was behaving so badly, Dad and Dave had teamed up and were as thick as thieves, so Paul felt David had taken away both his parents. He wanted David dead.

We managed to get the hate blurted out, and Dad made a point of starting karate with Paul. That worked really well for them as David wasn't allowed (nor did he care) to do it. The other thing that changed was that their house was broken into, they were both scared witless and, for the first time in their lives, they started to need each other a bit more for moral support.

So there you go, if the kids hate each other, find someone else they both hate more and you may even get an alliance. As some character said, 'organised hatred, that's unity!'

- Children are very jealous of the time they spend with you. They have a big thing about being fair and although *they* rarely are, they like everyone else to be. Setting a time limit on the oven timer for toy change time and giving them special times that they could have certain things taught them something about sharing.

- I used a colour code for our kids. Their own toys and possessions were always in that colour or with that colour sticker.

- I had a rule that their arguing hurt my ears and if they wanted to argue with each other they had to sing it. Arguments were not the same when put to music.

Selfishness

It's a fact that the more stressed and anxious we are, the more selfish is our behaviour. When we're struggling to survive, there's no room for anyone else. Some kids just seem born with that insecure streak that makes them act selfishly for fear of missing out, while others just copy. It's really an anxiety problem which they temporarily relieve by being first, having first go, sitting in the front seat, being the favourite, being the centre of attention, using up all the hot water, hogging the bathroom or TV and always organising everybody else. The problem is that it works, because others give way. The anxiety is temporarily reduced and so it becomes embedded as a style that is very hard to shift.

CHECKS

- **Does everyone in the family have the 'me first' philosophy?** If so, it's probably going to be hard to change because everyone will expect everyone else to do the changing!

- **Is it part of a bossy personality?** If so see page 208.

- **Are they being selfish because they feel they're fighting for their psychological survival?** If it's anxiety-driven, then see suggestions in Chapter Three (page 71).

- **Has the selfishness been taught?** Have parents and siblings been so *selfless* that Sandy has never learnt the give side of the 'give and take' principle? This can often be the case if parents are so grateful for Sandy's survival for some reason.

- **Is it a function of age?** Remember that toddlers have just found their ego, the world is theirs and what they want is theirs—there is no other way they can look at it. If they are two to four years old, expect some selfishness, encourage every bit of sharing you see, and gently sort out the ego clashes quietly, fairly and firmly.

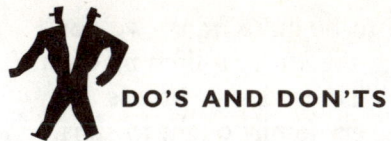
DO'S AND DON'TS

✼ With young kids try the following:
- ◆ Your own genuine acceptance of them may let them learn to rebuild the trust that may have been lost at birth, or that is part of a super-threatened personality.
- ◆ Maybe even play some games to build trust, such as leading them blindfolded around the house then reverse roles, or blindfold them again and get them to fall backwards into your waiting arms.
- ◆ Work on getting the balance back in your own life so you don't lose your balance over the kids (see page 26).
- ◆ Do lots of role play (as Mum, Dad, Grandma, sister, teacher, etc) so they learn other points of view.
- ◆ If they've acted selfishly, signal or tell them to sit on the 'Think Chair'. If they're over four, you may be able to get them to see how it would feel from the other kid's point of view. If they're younger than that, tell them what you want and make them do some sharing with the kid they offended so they learn how to make up and win friends.
- ◆ Let them take some responsibility, such as helping look after the family pet. That way they feel needed and important.

✼ With school-age children try the following.
- ◆ Find something that they're really good at. If you can't then use the 'Children's Interest Inventory' in the Appendix, page 357, to jump start the search. Once they feel they're okay and that others accept them then they will both need and want to change their behaviour to keep the nod of the mob and to stay in the game.
- ◆ Use the trust games and the reflective ideas mentioned for younger children, but remember these will only work if the kids want to change or can see that they need to.

✼ Teachers can help a lot through linking kids together in so many and varied ways that build up social skills. This includes doing class activities that help them understand the impact of their behaviour on others. Camps and excursions are excellent ways to teach kids vital social skills such as sharing, taking turns, helping each other, etc.

Changing selfishness is hard work. But to be quite frank, we don't really have an option or we're committing the kid to a lifetime of hurt and rejection. As Eleanor Roosevelt said: 'The giving of love is an education in itself.' Maybe that's where every family ought to start.

WENDY SYNDROME

Without wishing to be rude let me ask if you are a Wendy? This particular Wendy had had a tough childhood and was convinced she was a total failure. Her two boys were so bossy and selfish that they'd do nothing for her at all. And her once-charming husband who courted her with flowers now taunts her with failure. Wendy couldn't risk the kids not liking her or her husband leaving, so if the kids got upset when she asked them to do something then she'd back off, apologise, take all the blame and beg their forgiveness. No boundaries were being taught so the kids did the same at school and were loathed by all and sundry. In fact, they even looked loathed. Finally Welfare was called in after a bashing incident and Wendy realised that trying to buy love could cost her all she did love. Wendy was referred for help and started with the simple decision that she had the right to respect. This step was helped, she said, by reading a book called *Born to Please*.

- She told her husband he was either 'in' or 'out' and 'in' meant right in, helping not judging.
- She joined a 'Trust Your Inner Self' course and then an assertiveness course.
- Part of the recovery was to search for the hero in herself, and to search her history right back to BC (before children) to find the soul savers from her past.
- Then, with another lost soul she met at the course, Wendy started to write down all the things she did right that day and she and this friend would then trade triumphs to rebuild self-respect and confidence.

There was no magic Wendy wand. All it took was determination, persistence and *very* small steps to success. As she gains more self-respect, the kids have changed and flowers have reappeared on Dad's repertoire. Wendy had finally learnt that trying to buy their love almost cost her a family.

Bush Remedies

- I prepare for going-out visits before we go by telling my daughter what behaviour I expect so she doesn't act selfishly. I remind her that people are always happy to welcome back well-behaved children and so good behaviour is likely to lead to more invitations.

- We have adopted new rules—we lead by example!

Kids appear to be born naturally knowing how to be happy. It takes good teaching and good example to show them how to make others happy.

Cuddle-shy

Have you ever noticed that some of your most bad-tempered and explosive kids are those that find it hard to hug? They will squirm, move away or stiffen as if you've just put fresh nail polish on their neurones. The lack of contact means their bodies suffer from skin hunger which means they behave like a coiled spring or they lack the warmth and intimacy that comes from touch. As grown-ups, they may constantly search for sex at any price to earth their emotional electricity. I find a lot of delinquents can't accept a hug but will push and wrestle and slap each other, partly in play, and partly to get the contact they crave but haven't had.

CHECKS

- **Is the hugless style part of a family style?** It's up to everybody to find a way to make contact. The fact is that not only does hugging and touching earth the kids and make them feel less stressed, but research has clearly shown that the haemoglobin in the blood significantly increases when we're touched and hugged. And it's the haemoglobin that is so important for so many things, including the vital job of carrying the oxygen around the body to the brain and heart. No wonder unhugged kids look edgy and irritable.

🕺 **Is it just that Sandy was born with that style**—that arches on contact, is irritated by touch, etc?

🕺 **Has there been some body trauma, abuse or fear** that has increased body defensiveness and made kids recoil from touch?

DO'S AND DON'TS

🕺 If you're not a hugger or toucher then work away at the little you can comfortably handle and try building it up slowly with the help of something soothing like music, a bath, hair brushing or massage, till you're more in the mood to make cosy contact with others.

🕺 For kids who are 'hug-shy', again try things such as a bath, hair brushing, cuddly pets, back stroking, shoulder squeezing, holding hands, neck rubs and messy mud play. Even dropping the tension in the home can help.

🕺 Experiment on your style and their reaction to see what feels right.

🕺 As they grow older, be ready for changes in the way they like to be hugged, and the intensity and frequency of it. For instance, once girls reach the privacy age at about 10, their skin contact will be much more defensive, particularly from males. Kisses will probably be steadily deflected from lips to the symbolic peck on the cheek. Some boys tend to recoil from touch as they mature, but don't too readily put off all touch just because they're 'cuddle-shy'.

🕺 For both boys and girls, find the when, where, how and who possibilities for any skin contact.

When—I find kids are often easier to cuddle before bed, after being in water, when they're having a laugh, in front of TV, listening to some music, after having their hair done or after their back has been rubbed.

Where—Some kids will accept no more than a ruffle of their hair, a hand on the shoulder, someone sitting beside them on the lounge or stroking their brow.

How—Some like the cheek touch, the sideways hug, the full-on hug, the back massage or the neck rub. I find that most kids have a soft spot on their spine somewhere that responds more to stroking than other parts, but for some kids even finding that one spot is hard work.

Who—some will take hugs from Mum, a few less from Dad and some love Grandma's hugs. Some growing boys find them hard to handle, so talk to the kids. It actually makes for a great bit of communication and fun for the kids to talk about or role play the styles of the adult huggers and kissers in their little lives—which ones squeeze their cheeks, which hug too hard, which embarrass them a bit, etc. If there's a problem in the way they feel about some contact from some adult (eg cuddling them like little kids as they reach puberty) then explain that to the innocent offender, without hurting precious pride.

- If they don't like human contact then substitute playing with pets; at least that way they're still getting skin contact. Research shows that people who only have cuddly pets tend to be happier and in better health than people who have nothing or no-one to cuddle.

- Use their imagination as a way to reduce skin defensiveness.
  - For example, some parents who had been abusing their young kids were taught how to do the 'Weather Report Massage' on their kids' back (see page 44) when the kids were crying so it made the babies feel better and turned bad touch to good touch.
  - Sometimes I'll invoke older kids' imagination by getting them to shut their eyes, pretend that they are somewhere different (eg walking through the bush) and judging what they're going through by the type of touch—tall grass on the legs, branches flicking their arm, finger-tip touch on their head for rain, etc.
  - Maybe play a 'Guess Where?' game. You carry out the different type of touch (representing grass, bush, bed, etc and the kids have to guess where they are by the type of touch). Then reverse the role. You can follow up the ideas in Point 5 above with a 'Guess who?' game; they deliver and you guess who or vice versa.

TOUCH START

Just how important touch can be to us has never been more dramatically demonstrated than with the recent research on premmie babies. Dr Tiffany Field compared premmies who'd had a few minutes stroking for the first 10 days with those who hadn't and the results were remarkable. The massaged babies gained 47 per cent more weight, were more alert, interacted better and stayed in hospital on average six days less than the others.

But it doesn't stop there. Kids who are stroked and cuddled and have lots of face-to-face contact with their parents do tend to be better adjusted later on.

Make your relationship with baby a touching business. Stroke downwards and outwards, talk to them, sing to them, watch how their eyes follow you, how they try to copy expressions, how they turn to sounds and how they react to being picked up. In other words, let your fingers do the talking so that kids of every age can feel the love and grow up believing that life is a touching business.

Bush Remedies

- I found, for kids who didn't like to be touched, I would use what I called butterfly kisses. This was just touching their skin with my eyelash and they would really love that and laugh.

A hug each day keeps this doctor away.

As Princess Di said, 'There's a potential hugger in every family.'

Self-Esteem Summary

THE KEY TO SUCCESSFUL MANAGEMENT OF RELATIONSHIPS IS SELF-ESTEEM.

- **S** Start young.
- **E** Encourage children's talents, focus on their strengths.
- **L** Link them up with others with similar talents.
- **F** Find a way through (accept or cover) their weaknesses.
- **-**
- **E** Environmental manipulation (eg contacts).
- **S** Share your own experiences and how you conquer self-doubt.
- **T** Take time to touch and cuddle.
- **E** Elevate your own life beyond the kids' problems.
- **E** Encourage kids to take responsibility (pets, younger siblings, etc).
- **M** Make contact with teachers and work as a team.

FAMOUS FOOTNOTE
AN ADOPTED MUM

Suzanne Chick

AUTHOR

Mothers are a big theme in my life. I am a mother and I have two mothers. I also have two fathers and numerous siblings. But the only ones I've ever met are the ones I'm not related to. I am adopted, you see. Families don't necessarily come in neatly packaged lots. Adoption is one of many issues that cloud the white-picket-fence picture of the family.

Daughters are another big theme in my life. I am a daughter and I have three daughters. As an adopted daughter my genes pulled me one way and my upbringing pulled me the other. My life's struggle has been to find out who I am.

Who are our children? When I first fell pregnant I dreamt about the perfect baby girl. When Gina, our eldest daughter, was born and I looked down on her little face with its button nose squished up between its innocent light-dazzled eyes, there was no question in my mind of her identity. She was mine. By the time our second daughter, Danielle, was born, twelve months later, I knew differently. Then, before Gina was three and before Danielle was two, our third daughter, Kristin, arrived. All three girls had very strong and very separate identities. Already they were themselves.

Parents 'bring children up', 'raise them' and 'rear them'. The sense is of physical, mental and moral growth—upwards ever upwards. In my pregnant perfect-child dreamings I imagined Doug and I could protect and guide our children smoothly so that their delicate feet hardly touched the rocky mountain path that leads to the adult world. What a misconception! Sometimes all we could do was to stumble up that road beside them, all of us stubbing our toes on every boulder. But eventually we did get them there. Then, having raised them, reared them, brought them up and got them there, we had to face the hardest part. That mountain was a launching pad to life and there we had to show our unconditional love for our children by letting them go to make their own choices and their own mistakes. To be whoever they were.

Whatever the values of your particular family, it is more than likely that one or more of your children will take positions you disagree with. Dislike. Detest.

It can hurt. It can be a struggle to maintain your love and support. But our children are not our clones, our possessions or our trophies to be worn like bright membership badges of our group in society. If there is one lesson being an adopted daughter has taught me, it is that our genetic blueprint is a large part of our identity. What comes from outside acts on that blueprint but can't rub it out. Our children must find their own way to their own identity—we can't impose it on them.

Achieving identity needs practice. If we give our children the chance to make choices—mistaken choices even—while we're still around to help pick up the pieces, and if we don't panic, there is a chance that our children will turn full circle. But they may not. They need us to love them whoever they turn out to be, whatever path they follow, whether or not they validate our life-choices. The important thing is to love them as the individual human spirits they are, grit our teeth through the bad patches and to be there when they need us. As they most certainly will.

Gina, in her late twenties now, calls her father and me her trampoline. Picture her. There she is, off and flying. When she needs to come down to earth she knows she can bounce off us and soar again. Sometimes it hurts a bit to be a trampoline. Your neck gets cricked and your eyes water a little looking into the sun for the glittering form of your offspring—and you worry, did she make *her* wingfeather wax heatproof like *I told* her?

CHAPTER EIGHT

Hand and Aggression Problems

Sometimes, when I am the person handing out the punishment in the house, I am met with comments like, 'I wish you were away on tour', or 'Mum would let me do this'. This is really hard to deal with because there is a part of you that actually believes that you are not wanted. Whatever the reason, you just have to deal with it the best way you can. Usually, I just keep very calm, I don't let the anger show, and I say something like 'Well, I'm not on tour, so you'll just have to do it', or 'I'm not Mum, and either way, a rule is a rule.' It's not a very clever answer to the problem, but again, it is a controlled response with no inappropriate or violent response.

GREG 'WIGGLES' PAGE, children's entertainer
[READ MORE OF A WIGGLES WAY OF HANDLING THEIR OWN KIDS AT THE END OF THIS CHAPTER.]

Most parents see aggression as naughtiness, more often it's emptiness.

Why do we hit kids for hitting? Maybe it's instinct, but it does seem silly because we're actually teaching them to do the very thing we don't want them to do. And what effect does it really have anyhow? Whatever the reason, the figures for abuse have risen by 20 per cent over the past 10 years, at a time when many countries are outlawing physical punishment. Now there's a contrast.

As a kid I remember that I hated going to Sunday school and would give my little brother, Warwick, a hard time on the way. One Sunday a neighbour came out of his house and shouted at me, 'Look, son, I've been watching you laying into your brother every Sunday. If you do that once more I'm going to kick you in your tail till your nose bleeds!' The thought of being kicked that hard really frightened me and I never forgot that lesson and I never again hit my brother... anywhere near old Jack. But I did hit him after I passed old Jack, because it didn't change my feelings.

That's the problem with hitting kids for being bad; they still feel bad, probably worse, and it doesn't alter their feelings, it just alters the location for the attack. How can we get kids to stop hitting kids when they're frustrated if we hit them when we're frustrated? What's more, the research consistently shows that hitting kids for aggression tends to increase their aggression rather than decrease it.

Most little kids hit out because they have the will, but only know one way to get there. Generally it declines with age or at least shifts from muscle to mouth. Most aggressive kids are poor eaters and sleepers, impulsive, irritable, moody, slow to adapt to anything new and not good at communicating their feelings. With a load like that, who wouldn't be aggressive!

The hand is the problem part for this type of aggression so I've linked them together in this chapter. In my surveys, parents nominated the following aggression problems:
- fighting siblings
- fighting at school
- bullying
- destroying things
- setting fires
- stealing
- and pulling hair

Aggression

Some kids appear born with a more aggressive streak, some have it thrust upon them from adult height and some are hitting out their hurt.

But one very good reason so many kids hit out is that it works!

Research suggests that up to 80 per cent of aggressive acts are successful, so why wouldn't they keep doing it? The problem is that there are some side effects that make this cure worse than the problem. The answer is to get to the problem early.

CHECKS

If your little Sandy's aggressive then do some checking out.

- Check for **medical causes**. There can be little irritations in the brain, especially if the aggression is out of the blue and he doesn't know much about it afterwards. Some parents and experts also believe that certain chemicals in the bloodstream can make kids feel restless and angry; chemicals in foods such as cola, sauce, sugar, and preservatives, colourings, flavourings and yeast have often been named as culprits.

- Check for **marital causes**. If parents are at war, even if it's a Mexican stand-off, Sandy will soak up the scene and act out accordingly.

- Check for **attitudinal causes**. If Sandy is seen as the enemy and surrender is the tactic then aggression is obviously the answer.

- Check for **environmental causes**. If there's a lot of aggression going on around Sandy then you can bet he'll copy; TV, violent videos, aggressive mates and aggressive parents can all be triggers. If so, cut out violent videos or TV, cut back the pace, give him a bit more space, link him up with some rough-and-tumble outdoor sport and play up the caring, sharing, cuddling side indoors. On the other hand, if there's something going on in their little world that he's not coping with (bullies, teacher trouble, divorce, etc) then the frustration–aggression double act will certainly operate.

- Check for **management causes**. If the family's method of management of behaviour problems is violent then kids will copy. It's as simple as that and as powerful as that.

DO'S AND DON'TS

※ Aggression management needs a system that works immediately, not just one that is good in theory. Here's one idea that you can use or modify to suit.

1. Work out together with the offending offspring (let's blame Sandy again) what things stir him, what body signals he feels (angry, red, sweaty, confused, etc) and what he could do to keep his brain in charge of his hands to 'beat the biff'.
2. Then work out with Sandy what signs show that his aggression is starting to get out of control (eg arguing, voice volume increasing, etc).
3. Then set up a signal you can use to let him know that he needs to cool it. Maybe talk about what you do when you feel aggressive (if you don't know, then you've just found one reason why Sandy has a problem!).
4. Often I'll use the 'Traffic Light' system as the management, communication and signal system.
   - When he starts to get agitated, tell him that things are getting a bit RED. If that's not a strong enough warning, tell him he's heading for a STOP LIGHT.
   - If he can't cool it then he's told that he has hit the red light and can go and use his 'Think Light' for some ideas (eg play with dog, watch TV, play on computer, help Mum, set the table, read a book) on how to change his act to something more acceptable (see Appendix, page 355).
5. These ideas of good things he could do should be developed *with* Sandy, not *for* him. This yellow or think light is also meant for him to take stock, so suggest that while he's thinking about something better to do, to also think about what's bugging him and come and talk about it when he's ready.
6. When this hot-headed little Sandy has cooled off and thought of an idea, then he can ask to come out and do it. You may or may not give him the green light to do so depending on what he wants, whether you're ready for him to give it a go, or whether you feel that there's still too much anger in the air for it to be safe yet.

7. If, God bless him, Sandy comes out and he is still carrying on then it's back to his room to consult his yellow light and come up with a stronger or better idea that will work.
8. Use the time when he's doing his yellow light activity, or after it, to talk about why he got into trouble, what was bugging him, what he will do next time he feels that way and even what he feels you could do next time to help him handle it.
9. Reach some sort of forward plan for the future. If it's happened before then write the plan down and get Sandy's trembling little hand to sign on the dotted line as an indication to you both that you mean business.
10. If he breaks the plan, then tell him to take time out to give it much more thought. This time he does not get the yellow light choices until it has been sorted out.
11. If it's not improving, despite promises and apologies, then consult a child or clinical psychologist.
12. When you ask him to go and think in his room, make sure it's not done with excess anger or he either won't go or he'll wreck the room when he does.

❋ If he won't go to his room then this is serious, as it could cause damage to everyone. Look up Time Out Refusal (page 298).

Try concentrating on their good points and you'll get much better behaviour. As the proverb says, faults are too thick where love is too thin.

Bush Remedies

- I had a punching bag and they put drawings on it of whoever had made them angry: usually it was teachers, sometimes a kid at school and sometimes it was Dad. I never saw my picture up there, but I'll bet they were tempted.

- An idea I picked up at playgroup for aggressive preschoolers was to put one on each side of a sliding glass door, spray both sides with window cleaner and then give both angry kids a cloth. By the time the glass is dry, they're both over it and usually laughing at each other.

MAT THE BRAT

Mat was a little thug. He was only eight but he was in more fights than Kostya Tszyu and he fought as dirty as Mike Tyson. Dad was proud of Mat's fights, but if he hit at home he got thumped or belted with a rubber hose. Dad thought he was disciplining Mat, but discipline means to teach, so the only learning Mat was picking up was to thump your way into power, which he did. I shared with Mat's Dad three other well-accepted tactics.

The first is **Preventive**. Plan what happens where so there's less conflict and work out rules *with* your kids so *they own them*. But remember that much of what children learn is 'caught' rather than 'taught'.

The second way to stop aggression is **supportive**. Picking the danger signs, removing the source of conflict and moving quickly with a special time out or zipping mouth signal might stop the aggro in its tracks.

The third way is **corrective**. It doesn't have to be nasty, but it does have to be firm.

1. Stop the behaviour.
2. Ask them what they are doing.
3. Then ask, 'Is it against the rules?' Don't accept excuses.
4. Then say, 'What did we agree were the consequences for breaking that rule?' Carry them out, as non-aggressively and matter-of-factly as possible.
5. Then ask, 'What will work better next time?' Help them think of alternatives and a plan to carry them out.

This works well if you can keep your cool, but then again if you lose it a little, just remember that Jesus was the only one who was perfect and he was too wise to have kids anyhow.

Anger and Bad Temper

It's dangerous to treat the symptom and ignore the cause. If we can clean up the cause, it's easier on everybody.

But misplaced anger can be bad news. Researchers claim that 60 per cent of homicides are the tombstones of temper and anger out of control. We also know that some of the great mass murderers like Charles Manson and Adolf Hitler were incredibly angry kids (both were victims of child abuse too).

According to Alice Miller in *The Drama of Being a Child*, the real killer is not the anger, but the failure to deal with the *feelings* surrounding that anger. Alice Miller claims that *Adolf Hitler never denied that he had been beaten. What he denied was that these beatings were painful. And by totally falsifying his feelings, he would become a mass murderer.*

There are three ways to handle anger. You can *muzzle* it (ie send the pain inside), you can *muscle* it (ie send it outside onto someone else) or you can learn to *manage* it. The muscle style is so dangerous it gets headlines every day. The muzzle style is just as dangerous but it destroys inside rather than outside. Below are some ideas to manage anger. Part of the problem is that our society doesn't accept anger as a legitimate emotion with the result that 'nice' people try very hard not to ever be angry.

CHECKS

* We all feel anger. Check around and see which style each of your family members use.

* Regardless of the style, try to find the triggers. From my experience, the top ones include:
    * rejection, painfully deep, hurtful feelings of being unloved;
    * frustration, something Sandy wants desperately to do and just can't;
    * embarrassment, especially for kids with lots of pride;
    * confusion, to the point that they can't cope with the mental chaos (eg asked to pick which parent to love and live with);
    * jealousy, based on the fear of loss or abandonment;

- ◆ grieving, over the loss of someone or something that's much loved;
- ◆ defeat, for high-achieving or high-expectation kids, being beaten is a sign that they've failed, or that the other kid cheated!

✸ Check that there's no chemical cause (from particular foods) or neurological cause (from some brain irritation).

✸ Check that it's not being copied as a way of coping with frustration.

✸ Check whether the style is being reinforced. For instance, if it's acted *out*, does Sandy end up getting his own way? If it's acted *in*, are parents telling Sandy how good he was to just let his little brother bop him with his truck without getting angry?

DO'S AND DON'TS

✸ First start with a change of attitude. Anger is okay, it's how it's handled that is the real issue.

✸ Often taking control of anger means taking control of fear—fear of losing a friend, a place in the team, respect in other kids' eyes, respect of parents, self-respect, etc. By facing these fears we can help Sandy learn to harness the anger.

✸ At some time when it's one-to-one with your angry child, talk about your deepest fears and the effects those fears have on you. Encourage Sandy to share with you his fears. Just getting these up and out does a lot of good.

✸ Facing the beast in ourselves—this means being game to admit and identify our 'nasty' side without feeling threatened by it. With kids you might be game enough to make it a game.
  - ◆ First they pick an animal or soft toy that has all their good points—kind, loving, nice eyes, playful, etc.
  - ◆ Then they might pick an animal or toy that has a few bits of their nasty side—jealous, angry, easily upset, etc.

- ◆ The goal is to encourage the good side and learn how to harness the nasty side so it doesn't take control, then work out ways to do just that.

✻ Try 'reframing' anger, not as uncontrolled anger, but as above-average levels of sensitivity. This is how to reframe the problem:
- ◆ I tell Sandy that what he has is a wonderful God-given gift of being super-sensitive and that gift will in the future save many lives because he can tell who is down, angry, sad, who likes whom, etc, as soon as he walks into a group.
- ◆ If we can cherish and nurture the sensitive side, and learn tactics to handle the down side, the side that gets hurt so easily, then he will be a formidable force for good in the world.
- ◆ Then we work out ways to think and act that don't hurt him or anyone else.

✻ Sometimes kids and adults need to face and share hurts from the past. Some parental ones you may not want to share with the kids, in which case get the help of a psychologist or a hypnotherapist to get them up and out so they don't go on doing damage and dictating the angry outlets.

Most kids are more able than adults to share their hurt if it has happened at school age and if they feel someone loves them enough to want to listen.

✻ Learning to talk about feelings without muzzle or muscle is the art we're all trying to develop. This means saying things we need to say the way we want to say, with clear and easy 'I' statements rather than attacking 'you' statements. Practise these with the kids—'I don't like it when you do' ... 'It makes me feel ...', etc. (See also suggestions in Chapter Six, page 157.)

✻ Help them find healthy outlets for angry energy: football, bike riding, karate, basketball bouncing or pounding up and down on the trampoline.

✻ If they're too angry and the problem is too urgent then find some outlet around the house that helps release but hurts no-one: trampoline, pillow, drawing, punching bag, or the 'squeeze ball'. Again, we'll try it out on Sandy.

GAMES

MIND MUSCLE MANAGEMENT

- The squeeze ball is any little ball that kids can squeeze and put in their pocket (eg squash ball or foam ball).
- The idea is that when Sandy's angry, he squeezes the ball and keeps squeezing until the muscle in his arm gets tired, which means that his mind muscle has won the day! (Boys often like this challenge, especially if you can give big cheers when their mind muscle has won.)
- If he doesn't have a ball with him at the time of the angry feeling then he squeezes his fist really tight, again till the arm muscle gets tired.
- If the way out of their anger is to leave the scene quietly, then I use the squeeze for the anger and the little coloured spot on the squash ball as the button. That button brings over the 'bat shield' (or whatever) which means other kids' taunts just bounce off as Sandy drives the Batmobile slowly away from what was making him angry.

✻ In dealing with angry kids our goal must be to teach, not a desire to punish. Contrary to popular opinion, punishment is not the most effective way to communicate to children what we expect of them. One of the best answers to angry kids is something as simple as holding them in your arms to encircle them so they feel more secure, and at the same time you earth their anger and destress their little systems.

Anger is part of our make-up, but it's a tragic truth that often the results of unharnessed anger are much more serious than the causes.

TEMPER TOSSING

Young David had a foul temper and so did his dad, Mark. Father Mark burnt most of his out doing the wages and organising the workers in the supermarket he ran. David acted it out at school; he was noisy, pushy, sensitive, easily hurt and would explode if things didn't go his way. Mum had had enough of Dad and the school felt the same way about David.

As fate would have it the kids had a scripture lesson about David and the nasty giant Goliath and David decided that he had found his answer. He drew up a chart to see if he could beat the giant Goliath of a temper that had been beating him hollow. He carried a smooth lucky stone in his pocket to soothe him when he was angry and to remind him of the stone David needed to ground Goliath.

David has done well and now Mum says she only has to whisper Goliath and he regains the edge on his anger.

The lucky stone is now on the sideboard and *anyone* blowing their stack, including Dad, is handed the stone, which they must clutch till their mood soothes. Apparently the embarrassment to Dad in being handed this stone has been so effective that Mum told his staff. So now they've given their boss a huge lead fishing sinker as a substitute, and as a fun reminder of the lead weight he had been in their lives for so long. Mark is not amused but he is much milder.

Bush Remedies

All kids need to learn how to handle anger, you can't just pretend it's not there. I'd allow my kids to run around outside till they'd exhausted the temper monster. My friend had a batch of playdough which the kids could whack, chop, punch or whatever. That never worked for me, but another idea that did was to capitalise on their new-found ability to count and get them to count to five, or when they were a bit older to 10, in a loud angry voice.

Fighting (Sibling Rivalry)

Sibling rivalry is the quaint name we give to the act of brothers and/or sisters trying to kill each other. It was rated by parents in the top five problems on every survey—normal functional families being driven around the bend by the endless barrage of 'I hate her', 'Mum, he's hitting me', 'She hit me first', 'I wish you hadn't been born', etc.

The first 16 years are the worst, especially if they're the same sex, close in age or in hitting distance. All that changes with age is the sophistication of their weaponry—toddlers use the bite, preschoolers use the extremities like foot and fist, primary kids rely on the hand either to punch, poke or pinch, and high school kids rely on the face ... the huff, puff, glare, stare or, worse still, tongue torture.

The good news is that we're heading for 1.7 kids per family and it's going to be hard to fight with a .7! I've tackled this one in *Coping with the Family* but I have a couple of new tactics I'd like to share.

CHECKS

* **Is it worse when parents are around?** This means that they're jostling for position and you're best not to take sides.

* **Is it jealousy-based?** You'd be better off getting to the bottom of the jealousy rather than smacking the bottom of the kids.

* **Is it just the normal bicker and banter**, which is the healthiest way kids learn how to cope with life?

* **Does it have a pattern?** For example, is it always in front of TV, always just after school, always at the table, always in the car ... or probably *all* the ways I've just mentioned? If you can pick where, when and with who, then there's your line of attack.

* **Is it environmental?** If there's lots of fighting and anger around then the kids' fights are just acting out the mood of the house. If this is the case then check back to the Balanced Management in Chapter One (page 26).

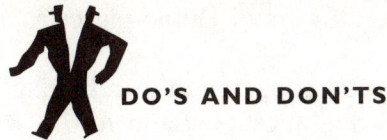
DO'S AND DON'TS

❋ Make sure the behaviour code is clear and that the kids have had their say in the rules that are set up; it's hard to be disobedient to yourself and break your own rules.

❋ Praise any good efforts at resolving conflict without resorting to warfare.

❋ One good way to record improvement is to use charts with kids aged four years to about 10 or 11 (see examples in Appendix, page 349). For kids fighting, the 'Cooperation Chart' could be used this way:

GAMES

COOPERATION CHART

◆ Each child chooses his own colour to record success.
◆ Every time he does something which is 'family friendly' then his spot (texta or sticker) goes on the step.
◆ When each of the kids has their spot on that step then the family moves forward to the next step.
◆ The fact that each colour has to be on each step means the sibs work hard to encourage family-friendly behaviour from the others, rather than trying to put them down or outperform them. That is, it becomes *cooperation*, not *competition*.

❋ Another version involves a glass jar with red and green Lego pieces. If any child does something kind to another then a green piece goes in, and if both are kind then two go in. If they do something nasty then a red piece goes in. If the greens outnumber the reds by dinnertime, then kids get ice-cream or some treat. If not, then parents get treated to some extra help from the misery makers. It keeps it fun and the consequences are good for parents either way.

- ✼ As an easier alternative, I often use two towers of Duplo pieces as my 'Good Kids Gauge'.
  - ◆ The family chooses one colour for good cooperation or resolving conflicts without hurting each other and another colour for fights not called off after one warning.
  - ◆ Mum or Dad put a Duplo piece on the friendly pile or the sad pile after each 'incident' and the kids can see during the day which pile is winning. It's the same principle as the Lego jar, but it's much easier for kids to calculate how they're going.

- ✼ When an argument is on, give the kids one warning only, tell them to cool it or take it outside. If there's no truce then kids can be asked and taught to 'freeze', ie everyone comes to a dead stop. If they can't or take too long to freeze, then freezing goes on the Practice List (see Appendix, page 354) and they have to get it right before they get privileges. Freezing allows sanity to seep back in quietly. **It's better to have kids thaw than sore.**

- ✼ With endless arguments sit the kids down at the table and let one tell his problem first with no interruptions. The other doesn't get his say till he has been able to summarise what his sibling has said and then roles are reversed. It's much easier to settle arguments when they've actually heard each other. This is using the 'Mike' technique demonstrated in Chapter Six (page 190).

- ✼ Here are the 10 steps for fight management.
  - ◆ Step 1—Try to ignore the little bickering if you can; it's just kids jostling for status.
  - ◆ Step 2—Unless it's desperate, don't even try to keep them apart or the anger will simmer.
  - ◆ Step 3—Try not to blame one or the other. Most times children can avoid arguments if they want to.
  - ◆ Step 4—Confirm your rules or better still, get the kids to help design them.
  - ◆ Step 5—Calm them down so tempers settle. That won't happen if you're screaming at them.
  - ◆ Step 6—Summarise the disagreement as *you* see it, because when kids are upset they can't think clearly.
  - ◆ Step 7—Ask them to come up with a solution, because it's *their* problem not yours.

- Step 8—If they can't find an answer, suggest a few, but don't let the kids loose till the solution has been agreed.
- Step 9—Whatever the solution make sure they stick to it.
- Step 10—Praise them for carrying it through.

I know one mum who, quite seriously, if the kids won't try to stop fighting, quickly sorts it out by sitting one kid on the front step and one on the back, so she can refer to them as her step children till they make up.

Bush Remedies

- My tips for fighting kids have been learnt over 18 years and six kids.
  - Don't allow one child to dish out the ice-cream for another.
  - Do have just one child and keep him isolated.
  - Don't allow kids near each other unless they're asleep.
  - When you see two children talking send one to their room because a fight will soon follow if you don't.
  - When all else fails don't worry, that's kids.

- I just locked myself in the bathroom with a good book.

- When our second daughter arrived, I said to her in front of the other one, how lucky she was to have such a great loving sister. I believe this really helped; they've been great mates all their lives.

- I just sent them to their room and told them not to come out until they could behave.

- Don't fight, don't even think about arguing with them. You only hype them up and it's not worth it. Settle the problem when the kids are not angry.

- I separated them and asked them how the other child would be feeling.

- This may not sound sensible, but if they started fighting I'd have a play fight with my husband. They hated that. If they were out of control I got them to do deep breathing and so did I.

- Retreat! Then in the privacy of your room think of positive ways to get rid of the offending child, such as flying him to the Arizona desert, dumping him in the middle of it and flying home as fast as you can. Sometimes in these situations you have to think creatively.

- I found I could stop lots of fights over toys by simply saying, when you're finished your brother can have it. That wasn't as threatening and although they may have played on that little bit longer, it seemed to take the sting out of their arguments.

- Just remember that fighting often stops if there's no audience. Get on with some outdoor work or use the time to catch up on a bit of that book you've been longing to get back into. That way the kids' fights have a little light edge to them.

- I had two rules: no hitting each other, and if conflict couldn't be resolved then everyone was punished—eg TV was switched off.

- If the boys were fighting we just sent them to their room to get rid of their 'sillies'. One time I peeped in to see what my youngest son was doing and he was in there doing a tribal dance to get rid of his sillies.

- We gave them time out, writing lines on something positive. Instead of writing: 'I must not be naughty', we would get them to write: 'I am a well-behaved kid.'

Destructive Kids

Destructive kids are just angry kids acting it out on property rather than people. Some do both.

CHECKS

- Do the marital, medical, environmental, nutritional and management checks referred to in Anger and Bad Temper (page 233).

✺ Is the damage to their own property, or to someone else's? If it's their own then the motive may be to self-hurt (muscle their anger in). If it's always the property of others then that may tell you where or who is the pain. It could be jealousy or it could be that they've substituted property for person because they're scared to hit or they're trying to send a message to that person. Sometimes the message is: 'I'd like to play with you more, I like you and that's why I'm not hitting you, but I'll destroy your toys so you take notice of me.'

✺ Is it just a short fuse that doesn't give them time for all the tactics we'd hope they'd use?

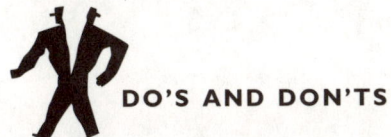

DO'S AND DON'TS

If your Sandy has a short fuse then here are some restraining orders.

✺ If he's preschool age, hold him from behind with your arms grabbing the same side hand. Take that hand across to the other side of his body so your arms hold him like a cross-over seatbelt. Kneel on the floor, turn your head to one side so you can't get head butted, hold firmly and talk softly until the rage has subsided, even if he says to let go. If he's school age, try the up-front hug instead of from behind.

✺ If he's too strong to be held then take him by the hand and hurry outdoors and keep walking. A change of scene usually changes his act.

✺ Take any breakable or precious objects out of his room beforehand and send him there for some cooling-off time or put him in a safe room or time out spot where he can do no damage.

✺ After it's over, talk about what made him angry and what he'll have to do to make sure it doesn't get that bad again (eg coming to tell you when he's upset, removing possible stirrers such as TV or sugary cereals or whatever you feel could be the trigger). If he doesn't know what's stirring him then you take your pick of likely culprits, preferably ones he'd rather you didn't remove so he's keener to beat the problem.

🌟 Make sure that he pays back for any damage done, either in pocket money saved or in jobs or favours he does until you feel he has paid his dues. This ask is fair dinkum and not just a timid token gesture that he quickly forgets. But hitting, grounding or yelling at Sandy will not work as it doesn't get to the bottom of the problem, it's not logically connected to the issue and it allows him to shift the focus from *his* problem to *your* management problem.

🌟 If it shows no sign of improvement then get help from a child or clinical psychologist.

BRUNO THE BRUISER

If you reckon your kid's a bit aggressive then let me introduce Bruno. Five-year-old Bruno turned up at his new school, banged the door open, called the teacher a f...ing b...., knocked anything upright horizontal, threw playdough in the fish tank, upended a table on the teacher's foot and broke her toe. When the teacher hobbled after him, trying to cuddle him quietly, she got bitten for her trouble. The police took him home and on the way bought him a settling popper. 'What's this shit?' said Bruno. 'Give me a beer any time.'

Mum and Dad were both sort of home, both sort of with it and both were unemployed. Dad blamed the cops and Mum blamed her mother for not letting her adopt Bruno out at birth.

That was six months ago, and Bruno is now in foster care. But what do we do with cases like this? Maybe child care should be a compulsory course in high schools, maybe parent training courses could be compulsory for those receiving the supporting parents allowance and maybe nurses could go around visiting every young child to make sure that the parents are getting the support and training they need before they turn anguish to anger. Maybe NAPCAN's 'Good Beginnings' program will get families off to a good start in Australia! But let's get our priorities right; if our children are our future then let's give them a future by prioritising family support services, because the cost to us all in the long term is astronomical if we don't.

Bush Remedies

- One child in my preschool group is fairly destructive and I used the time out corner consistently. He knew the consequences and when he destroyed another child's building, I looked at him and he said, 'I know, I'm going'. It settled down after we talked to Mum and Dad who felt it was coming from the fact that the family was just too busy to find much cuddly time for each other.

- We had a rule that they had to pay for property damage. Even though some of my son's friends were also implicated, every day of the holidays Steven had to do jobs to get money to pay back. It worked.

- If property is destroyed the privilege to use it is lost. The property has to be replaced or repaired and paid for by the child.

Competitive Kids

Competition is what makes free enterprise anything but free! It is basic to the way Western countries do business so, if it's part of a healthy psychological system, then it probably spells success. But in overdose it's not only hard for parents to handle, it's very hard for the competitive kids to live with! Every day in every way their ego's on the line and that's stressful. Many of the tactics for handling anger apply here (see page 233). Competitive kids are kids who are highly threatened, so you're better to focus on that rather than wasting your time telling them not to be so competitive. But here are some specific extras.

CHECKS

- Check why they're feeling so threatened.
    - Is there a brighter or more favoured sibling?
    - Is it a general insecurity?
    - Is it a fear of failure?

- Is it a high self-expectation?
- Are there high parent expectations to be the best?
- Are they trying to win approval, etc?

If you can identify the source then that's where to start.

DO'S AND DON'TS

※ Do expect that this trait is there for a long, long time—it's not likely to shift because to drop their guard is a threat in itself.

※ Meanwhile make every effort to get them into activities and sports where brothers or sisters don't go and where they learn to take defeat without seeing it as life-threatening.

※ Teach them some relaxation ideas that appeal to them (see ideas in Chapter Two page 31).

※ Talk to the teacher and change the reward system for this particular child, so that there's no big deal made over winning, getting everything right or beating somebody, but there is plenty of encouragement, awards, stickers, etc for handling being beaten, not worrying if work was not finished, putting in effort, etc.

※ Get them into activities that don't challenge their ego all the time, that are not competitive, that appeal to them and that give them some peace on earth—art, rock collecting, craft, pet care, ballet, bushwalking, reading, etc.

※ Teach them some face-saving tactics to use if they're old enough to admit that they have a problem. Sometimes it might be as simple as reading their own body signals and walking away.

※ Try 'Stirrer Monster' making.

GAMES

STIRRER MONSTER

- Get Sandy (this kid sure has plenty of problems, doesn't he) to help create his own stirrer monster and talk about what the monster says—'you're no good', 'look, you've failed again', 'other kids are going to laugh at you now', 'now the whole world knows how stupid you are', etc.
- Then we make up an image of what this monster looks like—colour of hair, eyes, skin, teeth, size, etc. Kids like this because they can identify with their own self-talk.
- By making it a problem out there (ie by creating a physical monster) not something in his head, Sandy will find it easier to tackle. He competes with *it* rather than himself.
- So, when he feels under attack and the same old negative messages start seeping through, he knows it's the stirrer monster and he works out ways to beat him.
- This could be squeezing the squeeze ball, or having some soft foam ball in his room with the monster drawn on it that he can kick, hurl or squeeze till he feels he has beaten it.

Bush Remedies

My daughter was always so competitive that it spoilt any game we were playing or any time she had friends over because she always had to win and she would become so aggressive if she didn't. I think it was because she had a bright, breezy younger sister. Nothing seemed to work until we got her into netball, which her sister hated. I think she not only found something she was really good at but the other girls taught her how to cope with being beaten. It's still the love of her life and she's now playing representative netball.

NASTY NATHAN

How's this for one crazy kid: if anyone teased him, laughed at him or if he couldn't win at something, this kid would scream, race around the room swiping everything off the shelves onto the floor, rip up his books and hit kids over the head with chairs. If anyone tried to stop him they'd get a kick in the shins or a head butt for their trouble. This was Nathan and he was just as bad at home. He had nice parents who had tried everything, but as soon as he was into any competitive situation he went way over the top.

Aggressive kids like Nathan need a medical check for brain irritation, a dietary check for chemical irritation, a parent check for aggression imitation and a consequences check to see whether Nathan's aggression was successful. In Nathan's case, part of the strategy was to create a pretend habit monster that kept taking control of his life and making him go crazy. Nathan and I drew it how it looked, Nathan told me about when it attacked and how it felt and then we worked out ways to stay in control, like a special tree to sit under when he was angry or a squeeze sponge ball to hurl. We even practised teasing like the kids did or telling him off like the teacher did to prove he could take it. Any wins went on his chart and any big losses we blamed something convenient like ice-cream or TV till he had a few crazy-free days.

Nathan is getting better because he has found more reasons to win than to explode. As the desk diary says, temper is rarely without a reason but rarely with a good one.

Bullies

Much has been written about bullies and bullying and by now every school should have its own policy on bullying. If it hasn't, suggest it develop one, not just to keep up with the Joneses, but because we now know that many kids are seriously scared and scarred by bullies. It's one factor nominated as an issue behind the alarming increase in youth suicide.

CHECKS

A Norwegian study found there were four factors that helped build the bully.

* **Insufficient time from parents.** Are you giving kids enough of your time and real interest? The study found lack of time and interest from parents in the early years was probably the most important factor.

* **Personality.** Is the bullying part of an aggressive personality? The study identified this as a major factor in bullying. If this is the problem see suggestions for Aggression (page 228).

* **Tolerance of aggression.** Are you a little too tolerant of aggressive behaviour in the home? The study found that many parents were subtly encouraging or tolerating bullying in some way.

* **Violent Management.** Are you hitting your kids as punishment? The study also identified this as a common factor in the bullying. By the way, that study also found that 60 per cent of untreated bullies went on to have at least one serious criminal conviction.

DO'S AND DON'TS

* Norway is reporting good success with a return to insistence by parents and teachers on decent behaviour, which is then backed up with non-physical punishments. These could be just depriving them of privileges like TV, sport, videos, transport, pocket money or whatever you have control over. Another common tactic is to get the bully to pay back the victim in time or money.

  The message has to be that aggression does not pay. Programs in Australia and the USA are offering some hope for a shift in bullying, with the following techniques:
  ◆ channelling kids into areas of achievement and physical challenge, such as sport, bushwalking, abseiling, etc;

- programs that teach kids skills in conflict resolution;
- programs where the bully actually works with young kids or animals;
- programs where the bully is buddied up to a popular high-flier in the school to copy their style and to gain contact with good kids.

✱ But **victims** need to learn some tactics too (see also 'Teasing Tossing Tactics' on page 191). Good strategies include the following.

- Examining **their own behaviour** to make sure that they ooze confidence and don't cower like a victim or stir other kids.
- Controlling **their own fear** so they're not easily intimidated. This can be done, for instance, by counting the number of times the bully tries to upset them in word or deed, with the goal that by *counting* rather than *reacting* the daily score will go down because the taunt is being wasted.
- **Telling someone in authority** and not being put off by bullies' threats to 'get' them if they dob. Bullying is a form of assault.
- **Calling the bully's bluff** by telling him why they think he is bothering them.
- **Exposing the jugular**—this is acknowledging that the bully could beat them in a fight and, in so doing, it takes the combat incentive away.
- **Networking**—finding someone older and respected by the bully to act as friend and protector, but not as a bodyguard.
- **Depriving the bully of opportunity**—for instance, if the bully is taking their lunch money, bring lunch from home with no money.
- **Reducing points of contact**—playing and going to places where they know the bully does not hang out.
- **Making friends**—many bullies are unhappy and offering friendship can sometimes be a way to settle the problem.

✱ Some schools discuss case studies of bullies in class to work out why it's happening (revenge, sadness, copying, loneliness, status seeking, jealousy, etc) and what should be done about it.

SCHOOL BULLY BEATING

If you're worried about schoolyard bullies then you'll be interested to learn that most bullies are victims turned vicious. The good news is that schools are starting to stop the rot. I've just heard about a Tasmanian school that canvassed the kids as to what rights they would like to have at school. The kids' top requests were not to be made fun of, to expect people to be kind, not to be made sad, not to be scared of teachers, to have friends, not to be scared to come to school and to be safe.

That seems reasonable, but now the kids want to take it further to make sure it happens. Any reported violations are brought to the attention of the elected student magistrate who might issue an 'out of court' caution. For repeat offences the culprits are brought before the court, asked why they reoffended, how they intend to make restitution, and then the court recommends to the teachers the penalties that the court has agreed on.

Getting all the kids involved means that the 80 per cent of kids who have just been bystanders can no longer stand by and see their own rules being flaunted. The kids are keen, the staff are keen, and it will be interesting to see how parents react to their bullyboys being hauled in front of the court. It should be quite revealing, because most bullies I've ever met have felt like victims themselves and are hurting back.

The problem with parents is that they blame their kids' problems on everything except heredity.

Bush Remedies

- When my son started bullying other kids in his class at school they put him in a class with bigger kids and he was meek as a lamb. Then he had to earn the right to be back with kids his own age. It's not a problem now.

Stealing

Stealing ranks way up near the top of behaviours that destroy trust and confidence in families. But the facts are a bit more friendly—most young kids will steal because they're all egomaniacs—that is, what they see they own. Ninety-five per cent get the message by the age of six or seven when they understand adult rules about what you can and can't take. But be careful, kids copy. They may learn, for instance, that it's okay to take things from work or say nothing if shopping change is in your favour, but not okay if it's personal or if you're caught.

CHECKS

- **Is it just a part of the aging process?** If so, a good firm talk, a huge hairy eyebrow and a low voice will probably do the job.

- **Is it the case that they're taking with their hands what's missing from their hearts?** If so, it's the heart problem that needs the attention, not the stealing.

- **Is the stealing always from the one person?** That doesn't mean that that person is not loving them enough. It could be that it's easier access to their money, their punishment is less severe or it's the only money around.

- **Do they have ADHD?** Often I find that some impulsive kids with ADHD have little impulse control. While all kids might be tempted to take money, they have the brakes to stop themselves and think of the consequences (anger, pain, disappointment, hurt feelings, etc) but ADHD kids have trouble thinking of consequences. They do first and think much later, but the good news is that their cover-up is generally transparent. They're not bad kids. There was no malice in what they did, just thoughtlessness. The down side for ADHD stealers (who aren't the norm, I should add) is that they're just as likely to do it again, despite promises, for the very reason they did it the first time.

✴ **Is it stealing to steal friends?** That is, they think that if they had the money, they'd win respect and friends.

✴ **Have a close look at what the clever kleptos are doing with the money.** That will tell you a lot as to where the problem is and what needs attention.

DO'S AND DON'TS

✴ Expect it in young kids and whatever you do don't label them as little thieves or they'll become big ones.

✴ For preschoolers, praise *any* sharing and returning.

✴ If they're in big school, practise the big-world rules about giving, buying, owning and the big 'hands off' rules too.

✴ Try to avoid the court martial—if kids are cornered they tend to fabricate a defence that makes it much harder for truth to surface.

✴ With primary kids treat it as a habit that they can break. Work out tactics to do it, and when they're ready leave planted money around so they can prove their strength. One mum put the loose change in a jar and the kids could take that as long as they recorded when and how much—she said it took all the sting out of her son's stealing.

✴ Many older kids steal to keep up with the group so work hard on a Pocket Money deal (see Appendix, page 360) and exploiting skills so status is given rather than taken. Kids over eight years of age understand money well enough to earn pocket money and learn how to save. Even if they blow it on rubbish at first, when they find they don't have money for what they need, they'll adjust their game.

STEALING—FRAME-UP VERSUS REFRAME

Young Paul came into the clinic with a bottom lip low enough to trip over. He had been stealing and Dad and Mum were convinced he was a budding burglar. They had hit him, hounded him, hauled him off to the police station in their fury and were worried that they had bred a 'klepto' as they called it (in front of him).

In Paul's case he was convinced he was beyond help so it had to be handled differently. We used a technique called 'reframing'. The conversation went something like this:

'Oh,' I said, 'so you steal from shops, do you?'

'No, I've never taken anything from shops.'

'Well, you must steal from your mates.'

'No, I'd be dead if I did that.'

'Okay, it must be Dad.'

'No, I don't.'

'Well, if you don't steal from shops or friends or Dad, you must have more mind muscle than you think. So where is it letting you down? Where did you take things that didn't belong to you?'

So it emerged that loose cash and Mum's purse were his curse, but by reframing it and pinpointing the problem, Paul was able to see and feel that he had the strength and focus to beat it. So Mum deliberately left money out and around for a week and Paul had to walk past it each day for a week. Then he was put in charge of milk money, then given a body belt to do a bit of spot shopping for the family and in charge of returning the change too. In other words, his fascination for money was turned to family advantage. If you have a stealer, instead of framing him, try reframing the problem. You've got nothing to lose except a big bottom lip.

Bush Remedies

I took my son and made him give back the money he had stolen from a child and then took him to the police station for a shock. He hasn't stolen since.

✏️ My friend had a daughter who was stealing, so she arranged for a policeman she knew to come to the home and threaten to lock her up. She hasn't stolen and it's one year since then.

Aggression Summary

AGGRESSION IS PROBABLY THE HARDEST PROBLEM FOR PARENTS TO HANDLE WITHOUT AGGRESSION. BUT HERE'S A SUMMARY OF STEPS FROM ALL THAT HAS BEEN SAID ABOVE.

A Assess the cause—frustration, parents, food, habit, etc.
G Give them very fast time out so no-one needs to get hurt.
G Give them the green light to come out when they've worked out what's bugging them.
R Reflect back to them, once they've cooled down, why it's not on.
E Extract their ideas on what they're going to do about it; if they don't know then you tell them what you think will be done.
S Set a good example by managing behaviour problems in a non-violent way.
S Select the best ideas, write them down and practise them even when they're not angry so they know what to do.
I Use 'I' language rather than 'you ... ' when making your deals so they're not defensive.
O Find outlets for their agggression that don't hurt or offend (sport, punching bag, foam ball, etc).
N Never give in to aggression or you'll get more of it.

FAMOUS FOOTNOTE
A SNAG DAD

Greg 'Wiggles' Page
CHILDREN'S ENTERTAINER

I have two children, a boy, Blaine, who is seven years old, and a girl, Madison, who is seven months old. Being a Wiggles means being away from home a lot, and in turn, being away from my family. This puts a great deal of stress on the relationships within my family at various times. My wife Michelle finds it hard to cope when I am away, on her own with two children, and when I get home Blaine wants me to spend time with him that I can't. Even when I am at home, we still may be performing during the day, having meetings, recording, filming or just looking after general business issues. Quite often when I put Blaine to bed at night he will ask me if I will be home the following afternoon when he gets home from school. If the answer is yes then he asks, 'Will you have time to play with me?' If I know that I have a lot on and I can't move things around then I will be honest with him and explain why I can't. But if I can put off doing some work, then I will make time to spend with Blaine, which I know he will appreciate.

I need to manage my time so that when I am home, I can make myself available to help with Madison—whether it is bathing, feeding, changing nappies, washing or making bottles—as well as time for Blaine. I have to try to put these things first and spend time with Blaine, playing games that we both enjoy together, and then do my work later at night, after he has gone to bed, or while he watches a video.

This does not leave a lot of time for me to spend with Michelle. Once the children are in bed, there are still many menial household chores to do, as well as whatever business work must be done. By the time this is usually all finished it is 10.00–10.30p.m., and we usually just go to bed, exhausted after a long and hectic day. When I do happen to have a day off then Michelle usually marks it in my diary as a day for us to spend together. It pays to be good at juggling time and managing yourself, so as to create time where you can escape for a while.

Another problem caused by lifestyle is that whenever I do get home I like to spend time at home and not go out. This, of course, is the opposite to what

Michelle wants, because she wants to break away from the same old boring routine. Again, it is a juggling act to keep everybody happy.

Like all parents we face the same issues of dealing with children's behaviour. For me, this is where my early childhood teaching course was invaluable. One thing that we learnt was that you always set boundaries and never let the boundaries be broken. In other words, in our house if a rule is made, it is made for a reason, and should not be broken. The idea behind this theory is that if the rules or guidelines are broken, then the child thinks that the rules or guidelines have no meaning and will keep on breaking or bending the rules. In our house, punishment is usually being banned for an afternoon from playing the computer, the Nintendo game, or watching any videos or TV. We actually very rarely send Blaine to his room, unless we get really frustrated with him, and it is usually the ultimate punishment.

And of course, with punishment often comes the obligatory 'you all hate me'. Again, teacher training has helped me here. We were taught to never say anything negative about the person, because if there is a problem it is usually the *behaviour* which is the problem not the person. And it's true! I mean, how many parents hate their children when they punish them? Certainly not me. When Blaine says 'You all hate me', I usually reply something along the lines of, 'No, I don't hate you, I love you, but I don't like your behaviour and that's why I'm punishing you.' I find this is a much less stressful way of dealing with problems than getting all hot under the collar and letting off steam in an inappropriate way.

Sometimes, when I am the person handing out the punishment in the house, I am met with comments like, 'I wish you were away on tour', or 'Mum would let me do this'. This is really hard to deal with because there is a part of you that actually believes that you are not wanted. Whatever the reason, you just have to deal with it the best way you can. Usually, I just keep very calm, I don't let the anger show, and I say something like, 'Well, I'm not on tour, so you'll just have to do it', or 'I'm not Mum, and either way, a rule is a rule'. It's not a very clever answer to the problem, but again, it is a controlled response.

CHAPTER NINE

'Down There' and Immaturity Problems

My mum taught me a lot. One thing she taught me, which I use often when I'm feeling down, is to read tea leaves. That sounds silly, but just reading the tea leaves made me think of something good that's ahead. It's just fun but it gives me a little lift knowing things aren't all bad.

JEANNIE LITTLE, entertainer
[MORE OF JEANNIE LITTLE'S FASCINATING FAMILY STORY AT THE END OF THIS CHAPTER.]

If only little kids weren't so, well, immature. If only they could sleep through the night, communicate other than by crying, eat sensibly, wait, be less selfish, dress themselves, be less demanding and control themselves 'down there'. However, if they did, I suppose there'd be no human race; we'd have been wiped off the earth ages ago because we didn't have the learning ability to adapt to a changing world.

But their immaturity sure is a problem. In many ways the pace of life poses the danger of taking parents further away from kids. When that happens we start to lose, not only our confidence, but also any idea on what to expect of kids as they grow up. Here are a few of the normal hiccoughs in kids' development that cause more anxiety than they should, simply because we're trying to grow them too fast.

- It is normal for **babies** to have screaming evening fits of colic—It is not parent failure.
- It is normal for **eight–18-month-olds** to have sleeping problems and to scream when separated from parents. It's not being naughty, it's normal separation anxiety.
- It is normal for **two-year-olds** to say 'no' to everything and throw a tantrum to show you their ego has landed.
- It is normal for **two- and three-year-olds** not to be able to share—the world is theirs, their ego has landed and asking them to share is like asking a politician to be bashful.
- It is normal for **three-year-olds** to still wet their bed at night and for many to have some quaint hang-ups about how and where they do their poos. It takes time, sphincter muscle control and confidence, which is just beginning.
- It is normal for **four-year-olds** to be know-alls. They have reached an important milestone, they see everything so clearly, in their own way, and they're boss of the preschool. Just remember little children do not know that they do not know!
- It is normal for **five-year-olds** and over to show some imaginary fears and be scared of school, shadows, ghosts (and soap). They're at an age where fact and fantasy sit scarily and potently side by side in their thinking.
- It is normal for **six- to nine-year-olds** to emerge as the greatest liars since we were their age. Truth telling takes time, example, courage and encouragement.
- It is normal for **eight-year-olds** to act awfully independent. They are too old to be kids and too young to know they still are.
- It is normal for **prepubertal kids** to become body conscious (in looks, if not in cleanliness) and to giggle at smutty jokes. It's part of the growing self-consciousness about their bodies.
- It is normal for **11- and 12-year-olds** to become a bit too big for their boots. Remember that they're now the big fish in the small primary pool.
- It is normal for **13-year-olds** to want to act out behaviour like the older kids. Older kids, not adults, are now their reference group.
- And it's normal for horrible teenagers to go on and become parents, and normal for parents at times to wish they weren't!

Poo Refusal

For many families, the first adult communication after coming home from work is not, 'Have you had a good day?' or anything uplifting. It's often, 'Has he done any?' It seems that the more uptight their world becomes the more uptight our kids become and then their poos pay the penalty.

Some families appear to develop a 'faecal attraction' and will smack, scream, plead, give medals, confine to barracks, and spend every waking hour thinking, breathing, watching, listening and even sniffing for excrement.

All little kids will seize up at times. Quite a lot become poo-proud, and others become poo-protective, hiding under tables, squatting in corners and only doing it in nappies. Some, who have had a hurtful blockage or lots of pressure from parents to 'perform', become very anxious about letting go of excreta and then the overreaction of parents cements the problem for some time.

But, for what it's worth, I have no high school kids in the clinic with sneeky poo problems!

CHECKS

* **Is it just that their little systems are taking time to adjust?** Remember, there is no set age for kids to get into a good toileting routine. Some do it easily, while others take years.

* **Is it because of some pain from the past, parental pressure to perform or is it a fear of letting go part of their persona?** Again give it time. Toilet training shouldn't even be thought about till they're at least 18 months old. If *you're* uptight then so will be their excreta.

* **Is it just that the family lacks routines and so their little systems have not learnt to adjust?** Give plenty of fluids, maybe have a five-minute toilet/potty sit after each meal where you have a chat with him while he's there and give him little reminders to have a grunt and go, etc. To be quite honest, little kids often don't know why they're there, so it's only after the glee you show when they drop a

stool that they get to know the game. You could use toilet time as the only time and place they can listen to talking books if you like.

- **Check their motions—take one deep breath first!** If they're a good consistency then their system's working fine, but if they're too hard, too soft or a strange colour then check with the clinic sister.

- **Check your management style.** Toilet training is one area where strongarm tactics don't work. Encourage them to sit, talk about how big they're getting, how they'll soon be able to do big poos like daddy and any other motion motivators you can muster to keep them there. If they hop off and poo 30 seconds later, don't get angry. Just talk about how they're getting closer and closer and soon they'll be able to do them in the potty.

- **If you see 'the squat' or they suddenly go quiet or ruddy** then maybe you can whip them on so they get the idea where you want their donations. But if you're going potty over the potty then chances are you're too angry, too early and the kids couldn't poo if you paid them.

DO'S AND DON'TS

- The idea is to start when the kid seems to be ready, somewhere between one and three years, but 20 months is about average. Don't start to toilet train if you feel you're going to get angry while they're on their Ls.

- Check with the clinic sister or your family doctor for reassurance and ideas if you're worried. These might include increasing warm drinks, fibre, cereals, dried fruits or prunes, fluids and water drinks with a drop or two of lemon, while decreasing milk products, apples, bananas and rice.

- Have a regular time to sit (eg 30 minutes after a meal).

- Dress them in easy-to-undress gear.

❋ Once they get the idea and want to be independent, teach them good routines, such as wiping from front to back (particularly for girls) and washing their hands. Supply attractive towels and soap to encourage them.

❋ Expect kids to become more babyish at times of stress or illness or even for no apparent reason.

❋ If they're scared to let go at all, then that's one uptight kid and one uptight family!
   ♦ At first, go with where they're comfortable (that could be in nappies, squatting, under the table, etc).
   ♦ Then turn the issue into something imaginative. Some parents talk about food, that their body doesn't need, aching to get out. I'll sometimes use the 'Poo Exhaust System'.

GAMES

POO EXHAUST SYSTEM

♦ I refer to their body as a car, so this is their exhaust system and we need to fire off spent fuel so their body can go faster. They all agree that their bodies do run faster after offloading excreta, so this image is not hard for them to accept.
♦ Then we'll work out ways to improve performance, such as going each morning before preschool so they'll be able to run faster and eating good food to make for fast strong bodies, etc.

Did you hear the joke about the gynaecologist who wanted a break and became an apprentice mechanic? He got 150/100 for his last assignment: 50 for pulling the engine apart, 50 for putting it back together again and an extra 50 marks for doing it all through the exhaust pipe!

✹ With kids who will only defecate into nappies, I'll let them do that on the potty and then reward it when they can do it into lighter pants (with nappy liner) or trainers. For kids who are really scared to let go on the toilet, I'll keep the nappy there so they don't have to let the stool drop and then gradually loosen the nappy each day until they are in fact dropping. Sometimes I'll even eventually use an old pair of Dad's daks to drop into! Some parents will wait for summer so it's easier to manage. Others will not let kids do 'big' things like staying up, playing at friends if they still need 'little' nappies.

✹ The main idea of toilet training is to wait for the magic moment, 'Carpe Diem' or should we say 'Carpe Excreta', and praise any successful deliveries.

Here's a fairly standard 'Carpe Excreta' potty program.

GAMES

CARPE EXCRETA

- First, buy a potty and put it in the bathroom (but if Sandy likes using the big toilet with inset seat then that's fine).
- Then give it a name. One parent bought an elephant motifed potty, called it 'Baa-baa', which is easy to say and use, and the kids' job was to feed and water the elephant.
- Next, make a sit on the potty part of the morning routine. If he has a regular time or regular ruddy look on his predonation dial, try and catch the motion by quickly putting him on the potty at that time.
- To increase the visits you can make it the 'daytime story spot', and increase the fruit-flavoured drinks as they tend to stimulate the kidneys faster.
- The next step is to get Sandy confident enough to tell you when he has done something. When he knows what goes where then he's ready to go solo without trainer pants or nappies.

Mistakes will happen, but remember that you're living in 'L' times and there is no manual. Teaching kids toilet training is one of those arts that simply has to be learnt from the bottom up.

Bush Remedies

When my daughter is scared to do poos because she thinks it might hurt, I sit with her and hold her hand and she seems to like to squeeze that for reassurance.

Sneaky Poos and Soiling

CHECK

- **Are they having pain from impacted faeces?** If this is the case, see your doctor as it may require some gentle laxative (eg Parachoc).

- **Check where it's happening.** Is it happening only when they're out, at preschool, playgroup, after certain foods, when they're busy playing or when they're scared, etc?

- **Check what's being deposited.**
  - If it's just streaks or scuds then it may be just poor wiping.
  - If it's watery then it may be some softer matter escaping around impacted faeces.
  - If the whole cake is being deposited, check if they know they've done anything and if they could feel it coming.
  - If they **don't** then all the more reason to set up a regular time so that they don't have to read the signs.
  - If they **do know** but were too busy then the routine of after meals is still the best answer. Generally it's the impacted problem that causes 'sneaky poos'; the blockage seems to extend the anal sphincter so that little bits can leak out and it also

seems to desensitise the nerves around the anus so the kids can't feel when they have let something leak. Again the answer is a good clean-out and a diet that includes fibre and liquids.

DO'S AND DON'TS

❋ With little kids, see the mistakes as normal and just encourage them when they have used the potty, etc. You might be able to use the 'Poo Exhaust System' (see page 263).

❋ If Sandy is a slightly older kid, here's a 'Sneaky Poos' program. (Every psychologist seems to have their own version of this—I wonder what that says about psychologists?)

Bush Remedies

My son used to soil his pants at preschool so we always took along a spare pair. At home I tried to make light of it and said, 'Not to worry, accidents do happen,' but I got him to take his pants to the laundry. He grew out of the problem as he grew older but one good outcome was that all my kids now say, 'Don't worry, it was just an accident,' if something goes wrong, and they're very forgiving of themselves and each other.

GAMES

SNEAKY POOS

- Talk about all the good things Sandy can do so his view of the world isn't restricted to his anus.
- Talk about the sneaky poos so it has an element of fun, makes the problem visible and concrete (so to speak) and so it's more manageable.
- See when it happens, how often and how he has tried to beat the Sneaky Poos Monster before, etc.
- Then use the concept of the Sneaky Poos Monster, more politely called the SP Monster.
- Work out what the monster looks like, when he attacks, and how we'll outsmart him.
- The plan of attack will include lots of fibre, fruit (other than apple or banana), warm drinks, and a regular time to go each day without fail (preferably 30 minutes after a meal) for a five-minute sit, even if he doesn't need to go.
- Sometimes the routine of a half-hour alarm, set as Sandy obligingly and lovingly carries plates back to the sink (you've got to be joking, I hear you cry), will be the reminder everyone needs.
- As for bed pooing, get kids aged over four to help clean out their pants—no shouting or anger, they just help rinse their pants out. It's not meant as a punishment, but it's their download so they can help unload. It also seems to motivate them to try hard to read telltail/tale signs and to get to the toilet.
- If the problem persists then they may get some mild laxative help through the family doctor.
- If little effort is being shown then chances are it's part of a bigger psychological or medical problem and specialist help should be sought.

Apparently some families do go overboard with associating poos and germs. A teacher was telling me that a bad speller in her class wrote that they weren't allowed to come to the table until they had washed their faeces.

> Young three-year-old Jamie, just wouldn't let go. He'd eat, drink and hang on till he either got a nappy or trainers on and he felt safe, or until he literally dropped the lot anywhere. Watson, his dad, had tried different potties, inset seats, bribes, sitting him on the potty in front of TV, listening to stories in the loo, tying him up against a tree just like their dog, but nothing worked. Even at day care he would hang on till he got home.
>
> We decided on a two-pronged attack; the first involved what we call shaping behaviour: putting the trainers on him when he was bursting, but only when he had run to the bathroom. The next phase was that he had to agree to sit on the potty to get his trainers, and then to keep using looser pants till he had Dad's daks, so he literally had to let it drop. Once he was able to let it go then we could try free falling.
>
> The other approach for wees was to paint a clown face on a ping pong ball and see if he could wipe the grin off its face. And I've told the parents to take the family focus off the faeces or he'd be too uptight to download.
>
> So far he's at least unloading in trainers in the bathroom, but Watson's desperately hoping the cure will come before his daks have to be dirtied. He's amazed at the progress but I assured him the problem was just alimentary, my dear Watson.

Just remember that adult explosions often end up in little fallouts.

Bed Wetting

Very few children have a bed wetting problem, it's their parents that have the problem with their wetting. In every survey bed wetting was rated as the most common problem in this section.

CHECKS

Let's check the facts on bed wetting.
🏃 **Are you expecting too much too soon?**
Fact 1: All little kids will wet their bed at night till they have developed sufficient sphincter muscle power to stop it.

'DOWN THERE' AND IMMATURITY PROBLEMS 269

🐾 **Are you expecting dry nights because big brother or sister or big parent was dry by their age?**
Fact 2: Kids vary at the age at which they manage dry beds. Some are dry from age one, but one in three is still bed wetting at age three, one in five is still wetting at age five, and by age 10 there is still about one child in each class wetting (and dead scared the other 29 will find out). By the time they're teenagers wet beds are no longer a problem (wet dreams maybe).

🐾 **Have you checked with your own parents and inlaws on your own wetting record?**
Fact 3: The age at which children achieve night-time control is often similar to the age that one of their parents gained control when they were children.

🐾 **Are you overanxious because you're worried that wet beds might reflect emotionally disturbed kids?**
Fact 4: Bed wetting is not a sign of emotional disturbance (or of kidney problems), unless the child has gained total control and relapsed again or unless the wetting is accompanied by other signs of distress or abuse.

🐾 **Have you established a good night routine so their bladder and brain get the message as to what's wanted, where and when?**
Fact 5: Good night routines including late toilet stop appear to assist, late drinks (especially with caffeine) and the midnight march do not.

🐾 **Are you expecting the bed wetting to stop with no relapses?**
Fact 6: Bed wetting never stops overnight, so to speak; the improvement is generally patchy and improvement must be measured over a month rather than over a week.

🐾 **Are you aware that at times of high stress children are likely to regress and wet more?**
Fact 7: At times of stress children may recommence bed wetting but usually it self-settles as things settle.

🐾 **Have you made the mistake of taking their wet beds personally because they don't wet away from home?**
Fact 8: Children are less likely to wet in unfamiliar beds, probably because the strange surroundings may mean they don't sleep quite so soundly.

✣ **Have they been dry and started wetting again for no known reason?** If so it could be some kidney infection or it could be symptomatic of more serious things. If it doesn't settle quickly, get advice from a paediatrician.

DO'S AND DON'TS

✣ Generally the best management is no fuss. Have some waterproof undersheet to prevent mattress moisture, get school-age kids to help strip, wash and remake their beds, and let time do the rest. But there are three other tried and true techniques.

✣ **Retention:** This method can be used with children who are old enough to feel embarrassed. The whole idea is that you build up daytime muscle for night-time action; children let you know when they want to go during the day, then they have a glass of water, hold on till they're 'busting' and you record how long they held on. Their job is to try and beat their old record.

✣ **Medication:** Some doctors will prescribe medication (eg Tofranil). This may be handy to help the kids through a camp or some embarrassing stint away from home, but it rarely cures the problem by itself and children often revert to wetting once the medication is stopped.

✣ **Bell Pad System:** The most popular technique for children from about the age of six is the bell pad system. This is not the Dry Sleeper with wires attached to night gear. It has a sensitised pad, which goes under the bottom sheet and is connected to an alarm system which is triggered when the pad is wet. This alarm wakes the child, and, over time, their clever little brain realises that the alarm follows the bladder muscle relaxing so (in most cases) it wakes the child as the muscles start to relax and before they wet. In some deep sleepers they still don't wake and parents have to shake and wake and so the learning is slower but it generally works. (See Janet Hall's useful little book *How You can be Boss of the Bladder* for further bed wetting advice.)

BLADDER TAP

'My four-and-a-half-year-old, Jenny, was a recurrent bed wetter and I must admit, it distressed both her and me. One day, when Jenny asked me why she kept wetting the bed, I explained that whenever she had a drink the liquid travelled down from her mouth into her stomach and then into a special bag called a bladder. When the bag was too full it wanted to let the wee out whether she was awake or not. So we decided to put a tap on this bag that she could turn on and off and we practised this on the toilet.

The result is that we still have the occasional accident, but find that we can laugh more about it, saying the bag must have got a hole in it or the tap needs a new washer because it's leaking.'

Not every mum is as understanding. I heard of one mum who noticed the wet bed and disgustedly said, 'Oh, and where have we wet this time?' The kid looked around and said, 'I don't know, Mum, but there's the deep end.'

Bush Remedies

- My daughter used to wet the bed any time anything exciting was coming up. We found if we kept her bedtime routines steady and drew up a chart to record any dry nights then she would really cooperate and make sure she went to the toilet before bed, etc. It's working well at the moment.

- We just took things calmly knowing that one day he would grow out of it and one day he did!

- Make a fuss about dry beds but don't punish wet beds. I had a daughter who wet day and night. At 13 years of age a specialist found that she had no ligaments to hold her bladder in place.

- If they wet their bed we get them to help clean up and remake the bed.

◆ *Twin advice:*
It's so easy to take this one personally, but don't. Try not to get angry with them or think that they are doing it on purpose. Check there is no physiological reason for this. Star charts or the 'bell and pads' sometimes work, otherwise just make sure they know they have responsibilities to put the wet bedding, etc in the laundry and remake their own bed. Most important of all, make sure they know you love them, bed wetting and all.

Sex Play and Talk

Sex is one of those three-letter words that attracts everything from four letters to French letters. Kids learn by asking, exploring and copying. And kids will explore. Sometimes it will be in the guise of 'mothers and fathers', sometimes as 'nurses and doctors', or the more up-market version, 'paramedic and patient'. The good news is the aim is not sex so there's no need to call in Welfare or feel you've reared a sex maniac. (See also suggestions in the Smutty Talk section, page 184.)

CHECKS

- If it's just giggle, giggle, 'show me yours, I'll show you mine' type behaviour then that's kids getting to know which sex they are and what differences there are between boys and girls. Two to three is the age at which they start working this out. I can't help but think of the story of a kinder boy and girl coming out of their first sex education lesson. The little boy turns to the girl and says, 'Are you the opposite sex or am I?'

- If it's just grabbing at each other then that too is normal play, particularly for boys. Just a quiet talk about who's allowed to touch who and where will probably be all that's needed. It could be that you may have to start a habit-busting chart. Maybe even some counter move; if they start pulling at each other then they may have to keep their hands to themselves, say, in their pockets. On second thoughts, not in their pockets, on their head till they reckon they'll be able to remember.

DO'S AND DON'TS

❧ If it's just normal play then clear up your rules. Don't allow closed doors, teach good touch and bad touch and see if things settle. Try not to build shame into it. We want kids to feel good about their bodies.

❧ If Sandy has been penis sucking, fingering, penetrating or any other adult activity, then chances are he has been learning bad habits from someone. Contact the local sexual assault counsellor for advice. Meanwhile:
- Don't assume the worst.
- Just have a chat to the other parent.
- Each parent should then separately sit and cuddle their child for close trusting contact.
- Don't put words in Sandy's mouth as little kids are very suggestible. Get advice on what to say or say something like, 'Let's talk about what you were doing in your game. Where did you learn to do that?'
- If he remembers then ask who showed/asked him. But make no suggestions.
- If he's too embarrassed to talk, maybe you could ask him to show you on a doll.
- Compare notes with the other parent.
- If you get shrugs and giggles then maybe just make contact with your local sexual assault unit (in the phone book) for reassurance.
- If either child nominates some adult or child as the culprit, then please, no accusations, again talk to your local sexual assault counsellor first.

❧ Make sure you have plenty of close, comfy contact so the kids don't have to use sex play to get cuddles and maybe keep their play out in the open.

❧ Sometimes with little boys who keep pulling at each other, I might do some 'flooding'. I suggest that I know they like to pull at their penis, but it's private. So they're welcome to go into their room and pull theirs as much as they like where no-one else has to see them.

✣ Another way they learn about sex is by reading and watching, and that can either tantalise, traumatise or terrify them. If they catch you out making love then talk about lovemaking as a sharing of love between married couples, adults or whatever your values are. Just don't be too apologetic. The other day I was told of a couple who were caught out by their 10-year-old son who was finally prepared to forgive them only on the understanding that they promised to have a baby!

CONDOM CHAOS

It had to happen. The big TV campaign condoning condoms with slick slogans like, 'If it's not on, it's not on' and 'If you love then glove', fell into the flapping ears of a few innocent kids. Recently, one Melbourne mum told me she had been taxiing the kids home from school when suddenly her son asked what a condom was. Not wanting to avoid sex talk she said, 'It's sort of like a balloon.'

So then he asked if he could have one. She said, 'No, they are just for adults.'

'Why,' he said. 'Are they really hard to blow up?'

'No,' a now-nervous mum replied, 'they're balloons that adults wear when they're in love.'

This was apparently too much for the kid who replied, 'Well, where do you wear yours?' By this stage one mumbly mum suggested it was only men who wore them so dad had better explain.

But you have to wonder whether our gimmicky messages are really understood even by some adults. In China their contraception campaign failed miserably because the ads discreetly showed men putting the condoms on their finger and apparently that's exactly what the men did.

Bush Remedies

- Say there's a time and place for this—here isn't, but the bedroom is!

- Explain that they are private parts of their body and explain that private means nobody touches them except them.

- When my third son was two, he wanted to know whether he was a boy or girl, so I told him he was a boy because he had a penis. Next he wanted to know whether his friend Courtney was a boy or a girl and I told him she was a girl because she had a vagina. He was so disappointed. 'Ohh, that's not fair. I want a gina like Courtney!'

- Talk straight, use proper names, lower your voice, don't make judgements, and discuss the meaning of what they've said or done.

- My three-year-old was watching as I was bathing his new baby sister. 'How come she's got two bottoms?' he innocently asked. 'She doesn't,' I said. 'She just doesn't have a rudie like you do.' 'Why not?' he asked. 'Because she's a girl,' I replied. 'Well how can she do wees then,' he asked. 'Girls do wees through a hole, not through a rudie,' I replied. 'Well show me how you do wees then,' asked my amazed son. I wasn't in the mood to give my son a sex education lesson so I said 'some time' but I'm wondering now what I should have said and why I was so embarrassed.

- 'What do girls have where boys have a penis?' my two-and-a-half-year-old asked. I didn't want to call it 'fanny' or anything so I said vagina, which he pronounces 'gyneena' which sounds more like a Japanese car and has offended nobody.

- Barbies became a behind-closed-doors game. We talked about privacy and special touching like bathing, cuddling and tenderness between people. We told them that if any touching doesn't seem normal, like what we do at home, to tell us.

- My son had a bath with his baby sister for the first time and because she didn't have a penis he said, 'Mummy, Christina is broken!'

My son came home and said that a kid at school had kicked him in the nuts! I tutted and spluttered a bit and said, 'Now come on, son, that's not the word we use, is it?' To which, honest to God, he replied, 'That's all right for you grown-ups, but I can't say tentacles.'

Bad Habits

Everyone has different ideas on what they would call a bad habit. Nuns might call it an ill-fitting garment, psychologists might call it an ill-fitting psyche, parents might call it by an ill-fitting phrase or two, as they watch the nose picking, hair pulling, thumbsucking and nailbiting of their little loved ones.

CHECKS

- If they're preschoolers, remember that all of us develop some little habit that relieves tension, retrieves order and that soothes uptight systems. Most grow up and out of them at school with their self-image at stake. Some habits, like thumbsucking, can do damage if it's not beaten by permanent-teeth time.

- If they're preschoolers then don't assume you're causing the problem. Habits and rituals are very satisfying parts of life.

- If the habit has not been there before and then suddenly develops, chances are that they're copying. Catch these ones early, set up some habit-busting tactics (see page 54) and you'll probably see them disappear as fast as they came. If you start punishing them or drawing excess attention to them then you'll just get more because they'll have more stress to relieve.

- If they're seven or eight years old then that's the time most kids are ready to tackle old habits from the past. You may be able to divert, find substitutes, use foils or counter moves before then, but many have to wait to this age to *resolve*. At this age they have the ego, the brain and the social awareness to stimulate their desire and ability to kick the habit.

✻ If the habit is part of other more general problems then don't worry about them. Tackle the big ones and then little habits will tend to self-sort over time.

✻ If the habit's getting worse, chances are so is your management. The more attention you give it, the more need there is for it.

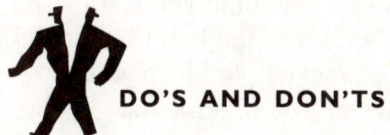 **DO'S AND DON'TS**

✻ With little kids, the idea is to build into your day tension unwinders such as stroking, cuddling, easy routines, relaxation or classical music, and cut back the pace. If the habit has already taken hold, try some easy way to make it harder to do, such as a cap for a hair puller, full overalls for the masturbator, and a mitten for the nailbiter. Don't shout or smack or they'll need the habit more.

✻ With school-age children, give them some alternative such as a necklace for the twiddler, or a reminder such as Bansuk for the thumbsucker.

✻ Applaud habit-busting efforts and treat habit repeats as a sign of tiredness needing bed rest.

✻ If there is still no breakthrough then reverse out. Instead of asking them to stop it, you can try 'flooding'.
  ◆ Instead of saying 'don't', go the opposite way and say 'do'. For instance, if they suck their thumb, have their finger up their nose or hand down their pants, then just say something like, 'I didn't realise you liked doing that so much. Pop off to your room and keep doing it for as long as you like and don't come out till you've had enough.'
  ◆ Once they're in their own room with no audience, no TV and no fun, the kids soon get sick of it and are keen to get out.

- If they start again just apologise for not giving them enough time to practise and send them back to their room.

This exhausting technique works well on most immature habits, and can also be used for swearing, spitting, poking or hitting. They keep doing it at a spot that suits you (eg have a hitting or poking spot on an outside wall).

* For older kids with bad habits, the technique is a little more choice-based.
  - I'll first get them to indicate whether they do want to break the habit. Generally, the older they get, the more embarrassed they become and the keener they are to do something about it.
  - Work out with them some secret signal that the habit has struck again (eg wiggle your finger for nose pickers, hold up your thumb for thumbsuckers, and whatever you like for the masturbators).
  - Then use the 'three strikes and you're out' method, which means if they forget three times then they're in time out for a while.
  - A variation on this, which I sometimes use with tics too, is to have them start and stop the habit, again and again and as often as necessary, so it comes under conscious control.

But habits are strange creatures, aren't they? And the silly part of it all is that so often the strength of the habit is in direct proportion to its absurdity. Below are some hints for three of the more common habits that require special mention: masturbation, thumbsucking and nailbiting.

Managing kids' masturbation is often just trying to find ways to checkmate their mate check.

Masturbation

Little kids' masturbation is probably universal. As some cynic said, masturbating is the only way you can be sure of making love to someone who really loves you.

DO'S AND DON'TS

✸ **For baby or toddler masturbation:**
- See it as normal as they rub on floor, against furniture and against legs. Shift their hand or body if it's offending you or making your visitors jealous.
- If it's very strong and persistent masturbation then it could be there's some irritation, not just in the vagina or penis but elsewhere in their system. Sometimes they can use masturbation as a way of regaining rhythm, pleasure, security (like rocking in a way) when other things are hurting, irritating or confusing them.
- Get them checked out by your family doctor or paediatrician.
- Sometimes you can decrease the habit by the clothes you have them wear or the padding you give them, so they seek satisfaction in more socially acceptable ways.

✸ **For slightly older kids:**
- Remember that touching or rubbing genitals is very common in one- to six-year-olds. In one survey, 85 per cent of kindergarten teachers said it was happening in their class (I assume by the children).
- It's more common at sleeptime, so if you like, just gently move their hands away and give them a cuddly toy to hold.
- Some kids masturbate when they're bored so try distracting them.
- Treat it as a habit and that means tactics such as flooding (see pages 174 and 280) or 'Buzz Busted'. Buzz busted means you just 'buzz' them each time you see that they've gone back to the old habit. If they get caught three times that might mean time on their bed because they're tired, or it might mean practising a counter move, over and over.
- As for younger children you can decrease the chances with overalls, padding or gloving if it's worrying you that much.
- If it's frantically persistent or intense for more than two weeks then it could be a sign that there's something worrying or irritating their little system, so get them off to the doctor.

✸ **With older kids** treat it as a habit that's just not on in public, and work out tactics to remind them when they've forgotten.

Thumbsucking

Despite the thumbs down to thumbsucking, some 10 per cent of six to 12-year-olds are still going strong, often mixing it with a soft or silky bit of material shoved up between nose and mouth to remind them of the good old days.

Dentists don't seem to worry about it before permanent teeth are in place but do warn that after that, constant sucking can change the shape of the premaxilla bone and cause 'buck teeth' and *cost* big bucks in braces.

DO'S AND DON'TS

* With young kids you might substitute those Nuk dummies that draw the teeth back not forward.

* With school-age kids see if they want to try a night glove, a plaster or something like Bansuk to help them beat the habit.

* But if they don't want to beat it, flood it. Instead of nagging them not to, go the other way and insist they keep sucking their thumb because they like it so much and not to take their thumb out till they're sure they've had enough. Make sure that nothing else passes their lips till they agree to try and kick the habit.

And aren't kids proud when they finally kick the digit-dunking habit? I still savour my Mum's comment as some louts shot past our car and gave us the digit salute, 'Never mind, son, they're just showing us they don't need to suck them any more.'

Bush Remedies

* My son sucked his thumb when he was stressed at school. I forced him to stop so he sucked his jumper instead.

- I just told my daughter she would be thumbless by the time she was five. That was enough.

- My friend's son used to suck his thumb until one day his thumb got slammed in the door and he never sucked it again (maybe other parents have found less dramatic ways).

- Don't worry about it if they are only first teeth.

- Make your child wear cotton gloves to bed. With this method, it only took one month for my children to break the habit, day and night.

- Our problem was not thumbs but dummies. I just made a little hole in the dummy and it gradually got bigger and lost its shape and taste appeal.

- My three-year-old daughter couldn't separate from her dummies and because we had a pharmacy she knew that she could always get more. So one day we had an 'undummy party' outside the shop. With much pomp and ceremony, and all the kids watching and witnessing, we had cake, ice-cream and lemonade as the 'last' dummy was dropped into the bin.

Nailbiting

Many years ago some psychologists got together and asked their leader, Sigmund, for some sign that they were sane and everyone else was mad. As Freud held up his hands to calm the crowd he noticed his nails were intact so nailbiting was declared an emotional disgrace.

Certainly, more highly strung people do often nibble nails, but for many kids it's simply a habit left over from the hand-to-mouth stage. Some pull out naturally, but others will only try when they start to feel embarrassed about their stumps.

DO'S AND DON'TS

※ If the kid just needs little reminders then Bansuk, a bandaid, Stop and Grow or some other chemist compound could be enough.

※ Some parents use a chart with each day divided into six sessions and they put up a gold star for each successful session. At first one star a day might earn the reward, then you can up the ante till there's got to be six gold stars for each session.

※ Lately I've been asking older kids if they're greenies and, if they are, we begin our campaign to save their nails. We pick on the easiest one first and I offer $1 per nail.

Bush Remedies

🍃 I told my son that he'd cause his nails to be deformed so, every day with every nail, where I couldn't see white nail, he would have to paint them with Bansuck which he also had to pay for.

🍃 One Mum is offering her boys $1 for each flea they catch between their nails ... and behead.

🍃 I tried to convince my daughter that her nails would become ingrown and look horrible as an adult, but that didn't make any difference. So every night for each nail that had no clear nail showing, I used the nailfile and scoured around near the top to keep it free. She hated it so much that she was happy to use plaster and Stop and Grow to help her break the habit. It's no longer a problem. Now I've got to work out a way to stop her fiddling with her hair.

Immaturity Summary

IT'S UNFORTUNATE IN THIS FAST, FURIOUS WORLD WE'RE IN THAT CHILDREN ARE BORN SO IMMATURE AND USELESS. BUT THAT'S THE FACT AND THAT'S WHAT GIVES THEM THE ADAPTABILITY TO BECOME GREAT ADULTS LATER ON. BUT IT TAKES TIME, MEGA TIME.

- **I** Infants learn best through sense and feel, cuddles and kisses, smiles not smacks.
- **M** Mistakes are part of learning, for both new kids and new parents, so don't be too hard.
- **M** Manage stressful times by playing with kids and with life, as often as you can.
- **A** Applaud their 'growing big' successes, and you'll get more of them.
- **T** Take your time in growing good kids; you can't fast forward childhood.
- **U** Understand their little hangups, just don't copy them.
- **R** Routines are an important way to develop good habits and security in kids.
- **E** Environmental support (other parents, playgroup etc) is vital to deal with growing pains.

FAMOUS FOOTNOTE

PARENTING AN ONLY CHILD

Jeannie Little

ENTERTAINER

I think being there for your kids is what it's all about. I know I stayed on the *Midday* show too long, but it meant I could drop Katie off and be back waiting to pick her up after school and that meant a lot to both of us. Kids have to have someone to come home to, to give them a feeling of security. Sometimes I'd have to stay up till 3a.m. preparing, writing or rehearsing, but I wanted to be there for her. In a way she has never been just the child in our family, she has always just been part of us and still is.

There have been lots of hard parts, but one I know I'll always remember was when I was told I had cancer and I had to have an operation. The specialist said that when I woke up he'd have either good news or bad news for me. The first thing I remember after the operation was Katie's little school hat bending over my bed and she said, 'Mum, you're going to live after all'. I then sank back into sleep but I'll never forget that moment. In fact it changed my life; I realised that Katie and Barry were all that mattered and other things in my life would have to fit around them and I've tried to keep those values ever since.

One of the values we believe is very important is honesty. I always told Katie to be honest, even if she has murdered someone or if she is on drugs. So of course when Katie had her first big love affair she came and told us everything and we went into a flap; our daughter sleeping with someone, what could happen, why is she doing it, have we let her down so much she needs someone else already, etc. So we went to a counsellor, who gently told us we were living in the past.

Anyhow, I know Barry felt enormous hurt and distance from Katie at this time, but we've come to terms with the fact that we matter more to each other than any problem could ever pose. In fact, Barry says that it's only in the last year, when he was able to accept this part of Katie's growing up, that she was able to come to him and give him a cuddle and that made him feel very special.

We've had some very hard financial times, but if you've got your health and you've got each other then you can survive the rest. Sometimes we could only afford to eat mince and sausages but we got by and were able to have a good laugh about it later. As long as you love each other and can talk it out then things will work out.

My mum was married to a man who used alcohol too much and it was a miserable life for us all. She asked her parents if she could come back and live there because it wasn't working out and they said, 'No, you've made your bed, now lie on it.' I think that was so heartless, I don't understand it. Later on when she had had enough, she packed up all seven of us kids and moved into a little weatherboard house. We were all really happy there even though we were dreadfully poor. Mum started her own business and helped my brothers get started in a wrought iron business. But they all did very well and I'll always admire my mum's courage. She didn't just complain or just sit back and take it, she got up and did something to make things better. Not everyone can have two ideal parents, but if you can have one wonderful parent as I did, then that's enough; don't complain, get out and have a go.

My mum taught me a lot. One thing she taught me, which I use often when I'm feeling down, is to read tea leaves. That sounds silly, but just reading the tea leaves made me think of something good that's ahead. It's just fun but it gives me a little lift knowing things aren't all bad.

CHAPTER TEN

Foot and Cooperation Problems

> *I think you have to talk a lot about sharing responsibilities. We've made choices and we're always working to help the choices work. We do a fairly regular stocktake. For example, it would be easier to have someone come in and clean our house but we don't do that. We made a choice. I don't want my daughter to grow up thinking that someone else will take responsibility for things that she should do, so we have a constant review of who's doing what around the house and if it's working.*
>
> **CHERYL KERNOT**, politician
> [READ MORE OF CHERYL KERNOT'S COOPERATIVE PARENTING STYLE AT THE END OF THIS CHAPTER.]

Which area, overall, do you think parents nominated in the survey as the biggest problem? Well, so many of them named kids who won't do ..., won't go ..., that is, problems of obedience and getting mobile. I decided that the foot was the problem part and cooperation was the problem issue.

It seems that kids are just not doing as they're told any more! That's the only conclusion I can come to after looking at the survey results:

doesn't accept no (highest ranked problem), back-answers (third), doesn't listen (fourth), won't hurry (ninth) and won't do jobs (tenth).

But before you take the jump, let me tell you there's a very good reason for this disobedience. In a recent survey done by a leading women's magazine it was revealed that 'over two-thirds of the parents think they are losing their right to discipline and control their children'. But, just a little further on in that survey was the fascinating finding that over 80 per cent of the parents agreed that it was a good thing that kids are able to think for themselves these days. Put these two together and you'll see why kids are more disobedient—how can we get them to be blindly obedient if we want them to think for themselves! And how can we get kids to accept our discipline, to be our disciples, if we haven't got a clue where we're heading?

Maybe that's why these issues ranked so highly in my survey, because parents are frustrated and confused. They probably want confident, independent, thinking kids but can't stand the disobedience that goes with it! I strongly believe that there has been too much emphasis on toddler taming (drugs, detention, TV, videos, giving in, etc) and not enough on child training.

Disobedience

Some years ago, a fellow named Bodenhamer wrote a book, *Back In Control*, that had this classic statement: *'human beings* [and he includes children] *prefer doing things in their own way, in their own time, and given an option, will sometimes do as they please!'*

How right he was. If only we could remember. But we forget. We somehow think that if we fall over backwards for our kids they'll do the same for us. That's not the way it works; the only result of falling over backwards is that we lose our balance.

We shout, scream, smack, nag and remind; all of which do more to raise the blood pressure than to raise cooperative kids. And still they won't do jobs, won't hurry, won't stay in their bed at night, won't go to school, won't get ready on time, won't stay in their room, won't come home when they said they would, won't wash or shower when they should, won't get out of the bathroom, won't help clean up their mess and won't go to time out.

Obedience is a fair ask, particularly for littlies, who can't reason or don't have enough experience to make sound decisions. As they get older and their mind-set matters more, our style should shift from obedience to cooperation so that in time they can make good life decisions for themselves.

If you have young kids and you're after obedience then Bodenhamer has three clear rules.

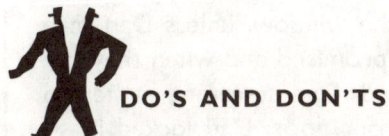

DO'S AND DON'TS

※ **Clear messages**—most of our messages to kids are either so vague, like 'be good', so negative or so threatening that they carry more emotion than message. Tell them exactly what you want and don't harp on what you don't want or that's exactly what you'll get.

※ **Clean follow-through**—you have every right to ask kids to help out so don't be defensive. Just keep it firm but friendly, be quietly determined and see it through.

※ **Consistent follow-up**—kids can't learn if we're giving them different signals—sometimes ignoring, sometimes laughing at and sometimes punishing the same thing.

Cooperation

If we want cooperation it's a slightly different thing again. Obedience is a one-way operation. Cooperation is two-way. It means cooperating; working together.

How you get kids to cooperate depends a lot on their age. You can't use deep and meaningfuls with littles and you can't use star charts with the biggies. And, if you give them the chance, they will push you to the Bodenhamer Brink!

BRINKMANSHIP

If you don't know what brinkmanship is, try taking on a three-year-old. Colin's lesson started at a friend's house when he refused his daughter a ninth biscuit. Jessica performed, so Dad decided enough was enough, packed up and drove her home. On the way she undid the belt and threatened to climb out the window, unless Dad gave her a biscuit when they got home. He promised and when they got home he didn't deliver. Jessica screamed, Dad screamed at her to stop screaming, she took off for the front door, Dad locked it, so Jessica raced around the house slamming every door she could find. So Dad raced ahead and started slamming them for her.

Jessica hid under her bed, Colin said to come out or he'd belt her, so she decided to stay put and does so for two hours, until bedtime. She then cries for another hour because she's hungry. Mum says there's no tea left so gives her a couple of biscuits to see her through till morning. Jessica was finally satisfied and the next day she was as good as gold.

Jessica, like every little kid, was out to test the limits and instead of Dad teaching her, he had joined her and Mum had rewarded her. But we all do it. Go easy on yourself and step back from the brink. Keep your rules and enforce them, but let the consequences do the shouting for you and handle the whole scene with more playfare than warfare.

Job Refusal

Kids who won't do as they're asked ranked consistently in the top 10 problems.

* **Check who is cooperating with whom.** If parents are at war or disagree on what they want from the kids, then the kids are not

being bad kids, they're just good apprentices. If you believe in the goodness of your kids they'll believe they're good and want to prove it to you.

🏃 **Check how they're being asked.** If it's all bark and bully then think how you'd react to someone who used those tactics on you. On the other hand, if it's friendly and inviting in its style then the reaction's likely to be the same.

🏃 **Check when they're being asked**. I've yet to meet the parent who can compete with the TV, the video games or computer. Many families have a slogan in their kitchen which reads, 'ask when my ears are clear'. That shouldn't only apply to parents.

🏃 **Check what they're being asked to do**. If it's jobs that the kids have had a hand in choosing then you can certainly expect them to do it when and how it was agreed.

🏃 **Check that you have their attention first and try to make it less of an order**. We all hate being bossed and, as you're after cooperation, make the ask sound cooperative (eg 'OK, mate, how about we do ... now', 'give us a hand with ... so I can get on with ... ' etc).

DO'S AND DON'TS

🏃 If you're having trouble getting the kids to do jobs they hate, your first remedial action might be to use the 'dangling the carrot' or Grandma principle: 'Please do ... (unliked job) then we can do ... (much liked thing).'

🏃 Cooperation means working together. How you get them motivated depends on *how* you ask, *what* you ask, *who* asks and what they're looking for as rewards. **Babies** learn about life through the senses, so cuddles and kisses and lots of love are the best way to bond them to the cause of cooperation. **Toddlers** are ego maniacs and rabid resisters, so our job is to harness both. All young kids have bigger engines than brakes so:

- tell them what you want, not what you don't want;
- use reverse psychology ('bet you're not big enough yet to ... ') to get cooperation at times;
- use their ego to your advantage—every little kid likes to be big so talk about how big they're growing, what big helpers they are, how kind they are and that's how they'll start to think and act;
- use clear rules, praise, encouragement, diversion, distraction, confidence and energy to get you through. And the more fun and imagination you can muster the better the coooperation.

※ **Preschoolers and primary school-age** kids love tokens—they're like status stripes. They love charts if they're fresh and fun, they still love admiration and hugs and they do understand cause-effect and consequences. As they get older, the tokens have to become more sophisticated and peer approval becomes an increasingly powerful motivator.

※ If they still don't cooperate, switch off or take away whatever is distracting them, don't keep reminding or nagging, because you now have choices on how you want to enforce it.
  a) Suggest that the problem is that their battery has run down and they're too tired. Let them know that you understand, and tell them to have a break in their room and come out when they've found the energy
  b) If you're in a hurry and can't wait, and you're not up to a confrontation, then use the 'Fridge Disk Discipline' (see Appendix, page 351). Get their attention, let them see that you have turned their disk to red/sad side, let them know that you'll do whatever you're asking them to do, but that means they get no favours, no privileges until they've done a few jobs to make up (use the 'Fridge Make Up List' in the Appendix, page 352). And mean it—no TV, no lifts, no favours, call a limited lightning strike!
  c) If you prefer a more up-front approach then don't nag or remind, just use 'Physical Assistance' (see opposite). Take them by the hand, and take them away from the distraction, get them to tell you what you asked them to do and then get them onto it.

The idea is to keep the vibes positive and let the disks do your shouting for you.

✷ Get the kids involved in who does which jobs when so it is a cooperative effort. Some parents use pocket money to reward kids' contribution to housework. If the kids are over eight years, and if you are happy with the idea of paying kids for services rendered, then you may be interested in the 'Pocket Money Chart' in the Appendix, page 360.

PHYSICAL ASSISTANCE

Probably deep down even the purest parent has hit or shaken their kids in frustration. What do you do when you've tried everything else and the kid says 'make me' or 'no' or 'do it yourself'. Depriving them of a privilege, time out, acting hurt, joking them into joining in are top techniques if you can use them, but what if you can't?

With little ones, there's another technique you can use called 'physical asistance'. Calmly, but firmly, help them to do what they won't; for instance physically bring them inside if they refuse, put their fingers around the toys and then walk them across to the toy box and deposit them there if that's what you asked of them. In other words, without any screaming or smacking, show them you mean business.

The big difference between physical assistance and smacking is that physical assistance is aimed entirely at the action (teaching them what you want and ensuring they carry it out), whereas smacking is aimed at the ego (it just shows what you don't want and it's not a good teacher). With little kids, just giving them a hand, making a game of it or if they're stroppy and overtired, leaving it till they've had a sleep and *then* doing it with them, can all save those close encounters of the worst kind. As they say in the classics, more flies are caught with a drop of honey than a litre of vinegar.

Bush Remedies

- Most of the time I let them know that they've just lost a privilege of my choosing unless it's done straightaway.

- I gave them a hug and told them that I still love them, but stuck with whatever I had asked them to do and didn't back down.

- Clarify the rules (ie keep it simple), be consistent with consequences and encourage them when they have helped out.

- Eventually I said, 'Well, I've tried my hardest, I wonder if there's another child out there who would like a Mummy like me?' That seemed to do the trick.

- *Twin Advice:*
  Often it is difficult with twins to get their cooperation as they have each other. What a formidable barrier it is when four eyes are staring at you with four little hands on their respective hips! Time out in different rooms is great because it brings it back to one-to-one and makes your chances of getting their cooperation a little easier.

- This might sound silly, but if you can keep a sense of fun, kids cooperate more. Sometimes when I was not getting anywhere I'd use something as simple as a sock from the clothes basket, stick my hand in it and get the puppet to give the instructions instead of me.

shopping

Although this could hardly loom as a major problem it was regularly rated as a constant problem by many parents in the surveys.

CHECKS

✸ Do you really have to take them shopping? Supermarkets are far too noisy, busy, adulty, pacy and stimulating for little kids. Is there an onsite or nearby occasional care centre for preschoolers or, if they're older, then maybe they can stay with family or friends.

✸ If you must take them, can you go with another adult to help out or can you go at non-peak times for short periods only?

✸ If they're playing up, do you have a history of buying them off with goodies? If so, it's going to take time to teach them that you no longer operate that way.

✸ Have you involved them in the shopping or do they feel you're after the goods and they're just the chattel? If your focus is on the goodies, then expect them to be the baddies.

✸ Have you taken the time to tell them what they can do, how they can help, what they can look for so they feel it's family shopping, not just shopping for the family?

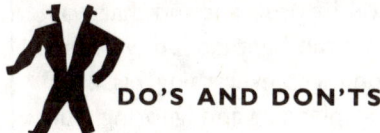
DO'S AND DON'TS

✸ If they're school age and *if* their behaviour and self-control justify the shopping excursion then be very clear up-front about:
   ◆ what you're going for,
   ◆ how long it might take,
   ◆ what they can do to help make the shopping easier (sit in the basket, help you find items, etc),
   ◆ what your rule is about buying goodies on the way,

- what behaviour you expect,
- what privileges (eg going next time) and penalties (eg no treat at the end, no go next time, etc) are hanging on it.

✻ If they're preschool age, save your energy. No matter what they promise, you're asking too much for them to remember, let alone honour.

✻ If the kids are to stay in the trolley top seat then have a few tricky things to occupy them for a while.

✻ If they're going to be up and about, maybe you might like those child-size carts. Personally I loathe them; it gives kids the craze far too early, they tend to want to fill them and they're so dangerous to others, particularly elderly shoppers. If you don't like them but the kids do, remember who's the parent and who carries the responsibility.

✻ Try to make your shopping trip with kids short and to the point so they can learn through success. Make a list before going and, for the sake of the kids, discipline yourself to stick to it.

✻ Remember, if you're up tight about taking them, the chances are they'll be tense and behave that way. If they're good kids maybe they can help you find items. Try to manage the trip so they learn that shopping can be fun, it doesn't have to be torture.

Dear Dr John.

Every Friday I had to take my four-year-old grandson supermarket shopping as his mum was eight months pregnant and that was the only time I had. It was horrible—every time I got landed with the most embarrassing tantrum when he didn't get everything his eyes wanted. I tried bribing, smacking, promising, pleading and ignoring, but nothing worked. One afternoon he was down on the floor, screaming because I wouldn't buy him some lollies and I had had enough. None of my friends were there so I got down on the floor and I cracked a bigger tantrum than his. He stopped, looked at me and then hurriedly pleaded with me, 'Grandma, get up, get up.' I think he was scared his friends would see me. I can honestly say I have never had a supermarket tantrum since!

Bush Remedies

- When I take the kids to the supermarket I give them each $1 and tell them they can buy whatever they like. Shopping takes longer but I have no problems. It's a good maths lesson as well.

- If they wanted something when I was out shopping, my answer was, 'I don't have money for that today.'

- *Twin Advice*:
Shopping with 18-month-olds you never know where they might run off to or what mischief they might be getting up to, so the solution is to place them in a 'backpack'. This was fine till the store detective pointed out that one of them had been helping himself as we walked past some displays that were just the right height.

- Give your child a job to do while you are shopping, eg carry the banana, hold the grocery list, etc.

- Play a game whilst shopping, such as identifying the familiar objects or spotting the grocery first.

- My son, Scott, aged two-and-a-half, kept asking me for lollies in the supermarket and I kept saying 'No, not now,' but the barrage continued. Then he stopped and said to me with hands on his brow, 'Mummy?'
'Yes, Scott.'
'I'm having trouble with that word.'
'What word?' I asked.
'That no word. Don't say it any more.'
What more could one say? The child is two-and-a-half! What am I in for at age 16?
(Would someone care to tell Jodi?)

Time Out Refusal

For some families abuse prevention is but a bedroom away. The problem is that when we lose the plot the kids get terrified and will bust, break, scream or defecate to get out. Others will do the incremental creep, one foot out and down the corridor a bit, till they're back to where it all began.

So, if you want to stay in control, it's best to teach them how to go to their room when the family needs space and before it gets out of hand.

CHECKS

- Is the time out something which all the family uses when they're not coping? If so, it's much easier to train the kids that way.

- Is the time out done with aggression, locking doors, etc? If so, then the kids will be thinking revenge, not remorse and are likely to do some damage.

- If the kids are aggressive, have you taken out anything from the time out area that can do damage?

- Have the kids and family agreed on what area will be their preferred time out area? This area must be a quiet area. If the kids nominate a play area or computer area, then maybe you can let them know you'll give it one try. If it doesn't work, if they don't stay there till the buzzer goes, or if they come out as cranky as they went in, then next pick will be yours.

- Is the time out being overused, going there every time there's an argument or in there for hours each time?

DO'S AND DON'TS

✷ Every preteenage child can be taught to take time out:
  ◆ if you mean business
  ◆ if you send them there, not for naughtiness, but for tiredness, thinking, or whatever their age dictates
  ◆ if the parents are much more positive than negative in their contact with the kids
  ◆ if parents act as if they are in control, if they expect the kids to accept their control
  ◆ if everyone in the house shows them how to take time out when they're upset or needing to recharge their batteries
  ◆ if it's enforced, non-negotiable, and the rules for time out are clear: must be quiet; must stay in time out till time back in signal is given; and must behave in time out zone (ie no damage to property).

✷ Select an appropriate time out area.
  ◆ Use their bedroom if you like. It won't do damage to their love of the room if it's not used to imprison them for hours. It's only meant to take enough time for them to recharge, generally about a minute per year of age—up to 10–15 minutes at most. I don't mind if they have special books or games or whatever in there, it's just meant to be time to unwind. With ADHD problems the time out may need to be more boring as they get distracted and don't reflect on why they're in time out.
  ◆ If you don't like using their room or if the room is shared, then use another room, a time out chair or a time out spot, but it must be quiet and must be away from normal family traffic so they can calm down and reflect.
  ◆ Some families have a piece of cloth which they put on the floor in an out-of-the-way area and use that as the time out spot. The kids must stay on it until the oven timer goes or they've thought of a way to fix the problem or until the parent says it's over. The advantage of this system is that the cloth square is transportable in handbags for use elsewhere. Kids *will* learn and cooperate if the system is consistently enforced.

- ❋ If the kids still won't go or stay in time out then we have to use tougher measures.
    - ◆ Take them yourself if you have time, energy and patience, remind them of the rules for time out and tell them they can come out when the buzzer goes.
    - ◆ Set the timer for as short as one minute for kids not used to waiting long. Congratulate them for successful waiting and gradually build up the time by one-minute increments to shape up their time out tolerance.
    - ◆ When you send them, tell them why they're being sent, and what you want to see when they come out. If they're school age, you might want them to take time till they can make a better behaviour choice that wouldn't break family rules. If they're preschool aged, they may need some help to know what you want when they come out.
    - ◆ Sometimes the 'Think Light' is useful here (see Appendix, page 355). The 'Think Light' does not help them reflect, but it can be useful for bored kids who are getting into trouble or if you just want them to go to their room until they can think of something better to do with their time than what they were doing.
    - ◆ If you don't have the time, energy or patience to enforce it, don't have a confrontation. Let them come out with your blessing (almost reverse psychology), and let them watch you as you put 'staying in time out' on their 'Practice List' on the fridge (see above and 'Practice List' in Appendix, page 354). Then, at a time to suit you, not them, such as when they want TV or mates over to play, use that time to remind them that you can't help out until the 'Practice List' is wiped clean. Then get them to practise going to time out until they're sure they'll be able to go next time you ask.
    - ◆ If it's still a problem, wait till you have better resources to enforce it, such as when you have your partner home to help out with the practice or when they're wanting something desperately from you. It doesn't have to be done in anger, there doesn't need to be any hitting, but it has to be in some form or other or the kids are not getting the boundaries they need to be healthy and confident adults.

The secret to liking your kids has to include temporary absence from them.

COOPERATION, MICROWAVE-STYLE

Jane writes: 'I thought you'd like this story for your new book. I had been to one of your talks and you said to use the 'Fridge Disks' for discipline, with 'Make Up' ideas on the fridge if they'd got themselves in your bad books. You also said that if they wouldn't try to fix it up, then blame tiredness and give them a stint in their room, and if they didn't stay there or kept coming out, use the oven timer starting at one minute to give them the idea of waiting.

But you didn't warn me of the side benefits. Yesterday, my son wouldn't do as he was asked, so I turned the disk to red, but he still didn't. I sent him to his room for five minutes, but he kept coming out asking if time was up. Eventually I had had it so I got up and said, "Right, I'll use the microwave to show you" (meaning the timer). He raced back into his room and flung himself on the bed. "I'll be good," he screamed, "please don't put me in the microwave."'

Bush Remedies

- I count one, two, three. If I get to three I withdraw a special toy or TV for a specified period.

- If the kids wouldn't go to their room, I went to mine!

- At the moment we only have to count to one with number one son, to two with number two and to infinity with number three!

- I made him sit on the bed and not get off or play. Then I'd talk to him and ask him why he was sent there and why we'd punished him.

- There is always a corner to sit in wherever we go. The threat is enough.

Dawdling

This was rated as number nine in the overall list of problems for parents.

CHECKS

- If they're **always going slow**, get a medical check. If that doesn't reveal anything, such as anaemia or thyroid problems, then maybe get advice from a qualified naturopath or iridologist.

- If it's **only on school days** then check what's going on in the classroom or playground.

- If it's **only at home**, check the home tone for some of the following energy sappers:
    - excess pressure
    - lack of one-to-one time with parents
    - unhealthy eating habits (excess sugars, fats, etc)
    - unhealthy lifestyle habits (eg too much TV, computers and other sitting activities), no sport or exercise to the brain, body and blood.

- If it's only with parents, check that it's not their way of putting the brakes on a hurried house that's too fast for comfort.

- If it's only when they're asked to do anything then treat it as an allergy to the four-letter word work and treat it as bad teaching on your part.

DO'S AND DON'TS

- Anyone with a foolproof answer to dawdlers would be worth big money in any average household. But if your Sandy is a dead-set dawdler then here are a few 'Dawdler Deterrent' strategies.

- Talk with him about what jobs he'd like to do and when, but make sure the decisions are comfortable for you as well as for Sandy.
- Keep a note on the arrangements.
- Remember that cooperation means working together, so work with him and try to do a few things together.
- Encourage progress, maybe with a chart.
- Use your family meetings to talk about problems.
- If pocket money is used at your place then include, not just the job, but when it's to be done by and details on what the job involves so there's less frustration (see 'Pocket Money Chart' suggestions in Appendix, page 360).
- If it's not improving, do what you'd do with reading or anything else that he needed to know; practise a few things he has to do till he can do it in reasonable time and hold off breakfast or favourites like TV till basics are done.
- If he's not improving or resisting use of the 'Fridge Disk' and the 'Practice List' (see Appendix, pages 351 and 354) then get Sandy's ideas on how the problem can be beaten and pull out of all privileges until it is.

✗ Forget reminders. They haven't worked for years, so why continue with them. One clever little kid had a motto above his bed that read, 'Never do what others can beat you at or do better, unless you'd better do it because others might beat you if you don't.'

Bush Remedies

- I know kids are messy eaters but with our dawdler the only thing that got him dressed was to be dressed and have everything ready before any breakfast.

- Take them to school in their pyjamas. You'll only have to do it once.

RESISTANCE

Jake was a demon dawdler. He had nice parents, but they were very busy, very successful and very dominating. He couldn't match them so instead of acting up he acted down! That just made him impossible to handle for his high-achieving parents, because he wasn't doing anything wrong—he was just doing the right thing very slowly. He just worked to regulations, pouted, dawdled and took ages to do what he was asked. It was his power kick so the answer was to give him power.

- Power through respect: Mum realised that the pace was too much, that his resistance was like trying to put a brake on the family and she secretly agreed that a brake was needed. She was lucky enough to be able to cut back to part-time work and after school she met Jake with a hug and a big grin and told him that this was a new start and she needed his ideas on jobs and any other things that bugged him.
- Power through choice: she used his ideas on jobs and set up a bit of choice on when and how they were to be done.
- Power through knowledge: they made sure the choices and expectations were all clear and she agreed to give him reasons for wanting something done in a hurry; 'because I said so' is a nice ego trip, but it doesn't help.
- Power through success: at the start she deliberately ignored the odd foot drag and went flat out encouraging the behaviour she wanted.
- Power through control: at times when the agreement on jobs and privileges fouled up, she resisted the urge to take over the controls. Instead, she would ask him what went wrong and what he'd like to do about it and kept holding him to it.

Jake is now 17 and in his final year at school. He has improved with age, but his parents are convinced that they've done the most aging. He's convinced adults are just hurrying their way to the grave. As far as he's concerned the world will go on whether he hurries or not. His mum and I agreed that above his bed she'd hang the sign: 'It'll be Jake!'

Dressing Difficulties

Changing and dressing little kids is like harnessing an octopus. Most parents just struggle through, but, like food resisters, it doesn't pay to make dressing time a battle time or you could have a problem dresser for years to come. If you're having more than average trouble, here are a few checks.

BABIES AND TODDLERS

CHECKS

* Has change time become a battle time? If so, the kids will expect the worst and act the worst.

* Has it become such a fun time that kids think it's all a game and don't understand why you're upset with them?

* Have you provided something novel or interesting to capture their attention while you do change them?

* Is the change table positioned where kids are being distracted elsewhere?

* With toddlers, have you given them a bit of choice (two only) of things they can wear, so their little ego feels that it's choosing?

* Have you made dressing an issue that is angry, hurried or too forced so they feel it's a punishment?

* Have you given so much choice that their little brains just can't cope and so they opt for nothing or something of their choice?

DO'S AND DON'TS

- Some families try to make it a game, but I think the kids tend to like it more than most adults can bear/bare! Use the time for soft talk, rubbing skin, whispering in their ear, and using the time to talk about their body, fingers, why they're wearing particular clothes. Kids tend to react to your confidence, so if you've got their measure they'll usually settle down.

- If Dad's giving it a go, give him space. Recently I received a letter from a playgroup mum telling the hilarious tale of her husband's first tail-cleaning effort.

'Be advised to stay well away of Dad's first solo nappy change. Don't giggle at the rubber gloves or face mask and don't ask, "Whatever is that for?", pointing to the terry towelling nappy which was supposed to be folded into the kite format, but which looks more like a hammock for a baby hippo. It's best to stay out of the room altogether but to make regular visits with cups of coffee, sandwiches and smelling salts.'

That letter shook me to the point that I thought any mere male is treading in dangerously soft territory if he takes on kids' change of clothes. What's more, I received so many good bush recipes on this one I thought I'd let them speak for themselves.

Bush Remedies

- Colour-code your washers, one for bath and one for backside.
- Keep a roll of masking tape handy to mend torn tabs on nappies and mend broken pants.
- Insist on disposables with elastic around the legs to prevent leaks.

- If you're using nappy pins, make sure you use the ones with the plastic-covered end and always place your finger between the baby's skin and the nappy so you don't stick the pin into the baby.

- If you're having trouble getting pins to slide through the bulky material, stick them into a bar of soap first or run the pins through your hair to oil them up a bit for easy entry.

- Attach a few nappy pins to your key ring so you'll always have some spare ones with you when you're out. They're also an excellent turn-off if you're being propositioned at a party.

- Don't ever hold pins in your mouth while you're changing baby as kids are great copiers.

- Get hold of a pair of those bright little jangly socks with a face on the front from Playschool and keep them on the change table to put them on the baby when you're changing him. He's so fascinated by the face and the fact that his toes are making music, he lifts his legs right up to see what's happening and you get a nice neat line to wipe down.

- Cover a boy's penis with your hand or a cloth as you expose it, not for modesty, but to stop the little squirts getting at you.

- Talk very quickly or pull faces or stick some masking tape on his fingers which absorbs him and takes time to take off.

- Buy pants with fasteners in the crotch for easy changing and choose clothes with zippers or velcro rather than buttons.

- When changing or inspecting a child, try whispering right in their ear. Some get so absorbed they forget the rest.

- Put a sultana or piece of rusk into the kid's hand so they bunch their fist to hold it. It makes it easier to slip sleeves on.

- If you have an older sibling, let them change at the same time so the little ones copy. If not, maybe you can dress a puppet or doll while they dress themselves.

- Dress a wriggly toddler on his tummy to get better control.

- If they won't put shoes on, try while they're in the highchair or tickle the sole of their feet to uncurl their toes.

- For nappy changing, make sure you have something they can put in their hand, like a bendy toy or rattle, not the baby powder or they'll use it as confetti.

- Sing to them, pull funny faces and read to them. The kids seem to think my face is funny for some reason. When I look in a mirror I'm surprised they're not screaming.

DRESSING OLDER KIDS

Frequently I'm asked what to do about a child who's such a fussy dresser it turns into a performance every time. These kids tend to be your anxious edgy kids whose skin and sensitivity are easily offended. Some clothes just don't feel right or look right but whereas the rest of us would just wear it, to these little uptight kids it's unbearable, physically or socially.

DO'S AND DON'TS

- Don't try to rush their dressing or you'll get a regular performance.

- Try to go with their small group of favourites so you don't have performances.

- Where they're determined to wear something that's inappropriate for school, rather than have a fight let them wear it and get a message to the teacher to have a chat.

- Where it's inappropriate for the weather, remember that colds don't come from just feeling cold—they're more likely to come from the drop in immune system caused by the fight! Also, some kids' thermostats don't seem to feel the cold or the hot so much. Rather than have a confrontation, go with their stubborn pride and just have something to throw on or swap to if needed.

❋ The sting is that when they want new gear you can tell them that the last choice didn't work so you don't want to waste more money. They can either use their pocket money, so you're not as offended if they don't wear what they've bought, or let them go without for a while till they're ready to be reasonable.

Bush Remedies

🍃 I'm an old preschool teacher. It seems to me that mothers find it easier to dress the kids because they're in a hurry, rather than taking the time to encourage the kids to dress themselves. Give them time if you can.

🍃 When learning to put shoes on, mark the inside of each shoe with an arrow pointing to the inner side. The kids have to put the shoes on the ground first and make sure the arrows are facing each other. Then they know they've got the right one (or the left one, if you know what I mean).

Tantrums

Young kids' tantrums are as inevitable as growing up. From about 18 months to two years, their little egos are up and running, desperate to let the world know that they've arrived and have a will of their own. The trouble is, although they might have the will, they don't know the way—that all takes time. For some, it has been a pattern since they were born; as bubs they may have shown signs of being easily frustrated, more unpredictable, have been difficult to feed, cried more and were more upset by any change. These kids, often boys, need super-patient parents, more routine, set limits, firm and consistent discipline and more comforting than your average kid. They also need, as Steve Biddulph has been telling us in *Raising Boys*, time to horseplay around, learn limits and learn how to curb their aggression.

CHECKS

- **Is it just little egos learning how to cope with frustration?** If so, give them time and don't take it too seriously.

- **Are tantrums a family favourite way to get what you want?** If so, you're in for some beauties as they grow and copy.

- **Do the siblings or parents give in to the tantrums**, so they actually become a very successful strategy? If so, that's where the change has to happen.

- **Are their frustrations being stirred on by someone who enjoys watching them perform?** If so, let that person do all the management of the problem.

- **If it's not their normal style, could they be feeling a bit off?** If so, try the 'T for tantrum test':
  - T—eething
  - T—emperature
  - T—ummy or
  - T—iredness

- **Are they getting mixed messages on rules and behaviour from parents** (one super-soft and the other super-hard)?

DO'S AND DON'TS

- Try to identify the kids' soothers, the things that settle them down when they're upset. For most, it's the natural elements like sand or water; for others, it's music, pets, cuddles, a change of pace or change of space.

- 'Tantrum Rating Scale'
  Keep your sense of humour so you don't sink to their tantrumming level. One way to do this is to see the tantrum as an expressive

performance and rate it out of 10 points as outlined in the 'Parent Pentathlon, Tantrum Throwing Event' below.

PARENT PENTATHLON
TANTRUM THROWING EVENT

RULES: The Tantrum Throwing event is best started in the supermarket. As you wheel them around the aisles wait until they're saying 'Want', 'Want', 'Want'. Then you keep saying 'No', 'No', 'No' and you should have a good one to score.

SCORING: Two points for a verbal refusal like 'No',
Four points for the body stiffen,
Six points for a refusal with horizontal thrashing,
Eight points for full body involvement, and
Ten points for a perfect performance with full family involvement.

✶ 'Tantrum Reduction Tactics'
If Sandy's a top tantrum thrower, here are some tactics to drop his performance.

Minus two points for attitude. If you can see the tantrums for what they are—little systems that aren't getting their way and don't know any other way to get it—then that confidence alone will help.

Minus four points for distraction. If you can distract or divert Sandy, talk calmly, whisper, drop into his ear the name of his favourite pet or fish that he's making sad, or maybe suddenly hear someone he loves coming up the drive, then by the time he works out it's a con, the tantrum is past its worst anyhow.

Minus six points for creativity. If you can use some creative flair in dissolving his tantrum such as hitting the offending furniture, asking to take a photo of him in top tantrum so he has to control it to reproduce it or maybe cracking one yourself, then all of these will tend to take the edge off the tantrum.

Minus eight points for management.
◆ Get down to Sandy's level, talk softly and see if he can calm down enough to tell you what's bugging him.

- If you can give him attention for being good and tell him how big he's getting when he is showing control, that's enormous encouragement for him. For some kids I'll give them a squeeze ball or foam ball to hit out at instead but it depends on the child and their personality.
- If he can't calm down, just leave the room quietly, letting him know you're ready to give a cuddle when he's ready.
- If Sandy's not too good at words yet, that's probably why he's having a tantrum, so help him find words and feelings for how he felt at the time. Use words like sad or angry and maybe colour descriptors such as red, or animal descriptors (ask him what animal he felt like).
- If Sandy's a bit older, then once a tantrum is thrown, there is no negotiation or discussion. Whatever he was after is absolutely not on, even after he has calmed down.
- If Sandy gets totally ballistic and out of control in his tantrum, talk quietly, drop names in that might settle him, and encourage deep breathing. Then do some relaxation or calm scene visualising (see Chapter Two, pages 38–44, for relaxation ideas).

Minus 10 points for perfection. If *you* never crack a tantrum then you may just get rid of them as a domestic pest.

❋ Show the kids how you can be angry, say what upsets you and get at it, before it gets at you and is out of control. But no matter how much you long for peace, don't ever yield to temper blackmail or guess what will happen next time.

❋ Give clear messages and rules on what you do want—the kids mightn't agree but at least they're not confused.

❋ Avoid the big temper stirrers like sweets and tiredness.

Bush Remedies

- I ignored her and made out she was someone else's kid.
- Smile sweetly and pretend it's not happening.

- When my son chucked a tantrum at the supermarket I promptly joined in—I yelled, stamped my feet, went red in the face and went home.

- I've found that the best preventive measure is to never let them get thirsty. If tantrum is in progress, offer a drink of water, if it is refused throw it on them.

- I heard somewhere that when you go shopping, you take a preprinted sign saying 'tantrum in progress, please ignore'. When your child throws a tantrum in public, put the sign on the trolley or near the child and walk away so no-one knows you're the callous parent.

- If my son threw a tantrum I would ask him to yell a little louder because the next door neighbour could not hear him. He stopped.

- When my son was throwing a tantrum, I'd say, 'Don't you laugh,' and he usually did.

- What worked for me was to keep my sense of humour and don't take the tantrum too seriously. When my four-year-old daughter was in the middle of an impressive tantrum I would say, 'Would you mind holding your face that way, it's so fierce I want to take a photo of it.' That stopped her.

Laziness

Nothing drives a family closer to a capital crime than lazy kids. And they're so good at it, aren't they? They've always just started something important when you ask for help, they always feel they're doing more than their brother or sister, they're too tired, or 'sorry, Mum, I didn't hear you.' So you take them for blood tests and hearing tests but it turns out to be an allergy ... to the four-letter word 'work'. Sometimes it *can* be a problem of energy—their only exercise may be the electronic buttons—or they lack friends to motivate them or they feel failures next to smarter siblings. But for lots of lazy kids it's just that they're waiting for a frustrated parent to utter those wonderful words, 'Look, don't bother, let me do it.'

CHECKS

- **Is laziness a problem at school?** If so, then a good thorough check by the school counsellor or educational psychologist is needed urgently.

- **Is laziness a problem only at home?** If so, then check:
  - Are they simply allergic to work?
  - Have they been allowed to develop lazy habits?
  - Do they feel lonely more than lazy?
  - Are they simply unfit and do no physical exercise?
  - Do they have low self-esteem (see page 198)?
  - Do they lack any outside interest to motivate them to be more than lounge lizards?

- **Is laziness a problem both at home and at school?** If so, check their diet for excess junk food, check their lifestyle and check for asthma, anemia or thyroid problems with your doctor. If it's all clear, check with a clinical or child psychologist.

DO'S AND DON'TS

- Remember that laziness is not the problem, it's the symptom. If physically they're okay, then chances are they're failing psychologically.

- Find their niche so they don't feel like the ugly duckling, a disgrace to the human race. Sometimes finding their niche takes a lot of talk, a lot of watching and thinking, and a lot of time. That price is very small compared to the price families pay if kids don't find their niche—poor performance, poor friends, lonely, angry and at risk. (See 'Children's Interest Inventory', page 357 and 'Boredom Beaters', page 358 for some ideas.)

❋ For many boys, as Steve Biddulph reminds us, it's not just their niche they haven't found, it's their identity that's missing in action. They are in desperate need of Dad—not to do anything special, but just to be there, sharing, showing, enjoying, clowning, teasing, talking, learning and whispering. How else do boys get initiated into being motivated males?

❋ Get down to their level, have a bit of fun together, notice the new spring in their stride and the increase in their energy. One mum blames her son's laziness on the fact that he swallowed a teaspoon. Reckons he hasn't stirred since.

LAZY OR LONELY?

Twelve-year-old Dave walked in with this gawky gait, slumped in his chair with head down and no eye contact. This kid's bone lazy, said the note from his dad, so we started checking his little brain out.

It turns out that Dave was devastatingly brilliant in thinking, reasoning and calculating, but the problem was that he wasn't practical. He was all head and no hands, while his dad was a real handyman, a top electrician and very practical. Dad and Dave just weren't on the same wave length. Dad was bitterly disappointed and Dave knew it. This kid had failed the family fitness test; in a sense he wasn't lazy, he was just lonely.

Remember, laziness is just resting before you get tired.

Bath Battles

Here we commemorate the many battles that are fought over the bath—getting kids to get in, to get out, to go to, to share and to clean ... the list of bath battles is endless.

DO'S AND DON'TS

❈ **If you can't get them into the bath**, then check for the following:
- Do you need to use the 'Grandma principle' (that is, they only get something they want after doing something you want)?
- Do you need to rethink the timing?
- Do you need to use the 'Fridge Disk Discipline' (see page 351) and maybe even the 'Practice List', (see page 354) again and again, going to the bathroom at first call? Practising during TV might hasten their attention to the remedy.
- Do you need to use the buzzer and time their bath to the buzzer? Once again, practise that routine if it's not working.

❈ **If you can't get them out of the bath**
- treat it as normal kid fun and just have flexible timing
- if they won't get out then remember there is always a plug-hole that might help (just make sure little boys aren't sitting over it at the time!).

❈ **If they're hogging the bathroom**
- have you worked out times with each that are agreeable to all?
- are they just teenagers? (I recall one little boy thought that pantyhose actually grew in the bathroom till his sister left home.)
- if they're using excess water, get them into the habit of taking a mobile buzzer into the shower with agreed time as a reminder, or let them have showers last. Alternatively, for the over-eights who are earning pocket money, see if they'd prefer to just pay part of the bill.

❈ **If they're leaving a mess in the bathroom**
- work out who cleans up what and when and enforce it. If their part has not been done then they do the whole bathroom or again use the 'Grandma principle'
- have good routines, laundry baskets and disposable areas to help the good habit
- if you can't wait (eg if visitors are coming) then swap a job. You do it, turn the fridge disk to red, and then they have to do the Make Up jobs before they're back into the good books or get any goodies.

- ✻ **If they won't wash or hate washing** (eg their hair)
  - ◆ wash their hair without soap a few times so they lose the fear
  - ◆ tell them favourite stories with lots of expression while you wash
  - ◆ put a large tub underneath the change table, get them to lie down on their back with their head resting over the end of the table, then put a rolled washer on the forehead to prevent water reaching their eyes and tell you what it feels like—in other words make it good feeling fun
  - ◆ maybe let them choose where they want their hair washed: in the bath, at the sink or lying on the table
  - ◆ let them wash your hair first or together
  - ◆ use bubble bath water and share a soapie
  - ◆ give them plenty of playtime before washtime
  - ◆ for older kids, one of the best ideas is to let the kids wear swim goggles, just like in the pool. Some really love both the goggles and their image in the bathroom mirror.

- ✻ **For older children refusing to wash** it can be a mixture of low self-esteem, fear or weak management. Let me share a letter (page 318) I received recently from a mum whose son refused to shower.

Bush Remedies

- I placed them in the shower, clothes and all. I only needed to do it once.
- My two-year-old loves washing dishes, so we now wash her teaset in the bubbles in the bath and then she pours us tea and coffee.
- I told my aromatic daughter with bad BO that 'I'm going to tell you something that not even your best friend would tell you'. I must have done it the right way as she's been okay since. I suppose telling her that she'd lose her friends scared her a bit.
- If they wouldn't wash I would tell them the rats and cockroaches would eat them while they were asleep. Looking back it sounds awful, but it worked.
- When my son wouldn't wash his hands I placed a toy in the bathroom sink, put antibacterial soap in, made it frothy and then

told him to find what I had hidden in there. He started to enjoy washing in the warm water.

- I told them they'd get worms, because they hated worms.

- I lost my leg in an accident well before my daughter was born. But just to demonstrate how much kids copy, let me share a little bathtime story. My daughter began to notice something different about me. When she was three, we were in the shower together and she said, while looking at my stump (and prosthesis leaning against the wall), 'Mummy, when I grow up, I'm going to have a leg just like yours.' I said, 'I hope *not*, darling!!'—Helena Brunner OAM, World Champion Disabled swimmer and single parent.

Dear Doctor,
My eight-year-old son never wants to have a shower. Last night I eventually got him showered at 10.15p.m. He used to be very rebellious a few years ago, but fortunately the teachers found he was gifted and very intelligent and he was accelerated to a much higher class.

My husband can get him to shower but he is often away or late home and if I complain about my son usually we end up having fights.

Hope you can help me.

Leone, I'd say your husband and son are both gifted, especially with their hands. Your son is gifted at twisting you around his little finger and your husband gifted at keeping you under his thumb. It's true that gifted and talented kids often need less sleep, but just give him a good easy routine, a five-minute storytime and off to bed by eight. He can read or listen to tapes from there. Don't have head-ons over his shower, just give him a time and if there is no shower then there is no TV till he's had one. If he's scared of water, let him shower with swim goggles on.

But my bet is, because he's not getting male time, he's making it hard on female time. If I'm right, then tell Dad that it will cost him more than his overtime in time if he doesn't step in. There is no need for smacks—just clear, unconnable rules, consistency, firm determination, and, at worst, one or two fully clad showers to get the message that he's under new management.

But we must act, or the whole family will be in hot water.

School Refusal

For many kids, going to school is even worse than cleaning their teeth. But for families that have this problem (and doesn't every family at some time?) it can be quite traumatic.

CHECKS

* **Is it just a one-off problem?** If it's not normal behaviour for Sandy then work on your best bet.
  1st bet—he's unwell.
  2nd bet—there's something on that day that he feels he can't cope with so he's trying to avoid it.
  3rd bet—there's some incident in the classroom or playground that has freaked him out and he's scared.
  4th bet—his mates won't be there so he's scared he'll be lonely or he wants to have the day off if they do.
  5th bet—he just wants a bit of one-to-one time with you or it may be that Dad's home!

* **Is it a problem that has been simmering away, but is slowly getting worse?**
  - Are sickies a family custom?
  - Have you checked with the school as to how Sandy's keeping up in the playground and classroom?
  - Have you been a bit too understanding of the odd biro spot on the tummy or undiagnosable headaches? If this is the case then the kids will take the easy way out any time that something challenging is happening at school.
  - Have you made the time at home too good an alternative, with TV, computer, a better lunch, shopping with you, etc?
  - Have you had Sandy thoroughly checked out medically to see if he's feeling fit enough to keep up?
  - If he's okay physically, have you checked him out with the school counsellor?

- Are there emotional reasons why he doesn't want to leave home? Is he scared you'll miss him or scared that you'll leave him because of recent separation, divorce or a bad 'domestic', etc?

DO'S AND DON'TS

※ Do some soul-searching, because if you hate the school or the teacher it's very hard for the kids not to.

※ Get up to the school and talk to the teacher. Believe it or not, teachers don't like to see kids going under and a bit of two-way talk can work wonders.

※ If there are learning problems, then it's the school's job to help work out some answers. Just remember that no kid goes to school to fail.

※ If the kid's lonely then it's easy for teachers to find special ways to link groups, change seating or whatever's required if they know the problem (see suggestions under Lonely Kids on page 203).

※ If the kid's getting bullied or bashed (apparently the figures are one in every six kids) then that's now outlawed and the bully needs help as much as the victim.

※ Maybe they're just down because things are bad at home and life has lost any spark. In this case, the whole family needs to get some professional pick-up.

※ Whatever you do, don't let school-sick Sandy win the day or the problem will get worse.
  - Get him to school and tell him it will be okay.
  - Let the teacher know the problems you're having.
  - Set up some ideas together on what you'll both do about it and meet face to face a week later to check how he's going.
  - If Sandy totally refuses to go with you, then maybe call on your partner or a grandparent to help out.

- If no-one else is around to help you, then the school counsellor needs to be informed immediately as there may be some form of home-school liaison officer who could be called on to help out.

※ Perhaps send Sandy with an older primary child he admires or get a neighbour to be the escort.

See if you can get them to share what's bugging them about school. That's what I did; I asked this young kid why he hated school and his answer was: 'Well, I can't read and I can't write and they won't let me talk, so what's left?'

LEFT OUT

Judy writes: 'What goes wrong between home and school? My six-year-old is a good kid who loves drawing, fixing up his bike, building, sport and he plays and mixes well. But since he started school this year he has been complaining that the readers were too hard. When at parent–teacher night, I mentioned how good he was at concentrating, the teacher's jaw just dropped. Apparently, at school, his behaviour is the exact opposite; he's immature, he can't concentrate, he's flitty, he's easily distracted and she asked what did we think about repeating him next year. Now have we got Ben wrong or has the school?'

Judy, you're not wrong and neither is the school. It appears that young Ben might be very mature in what's conveniently called 'right brain' work, but put him in the 'left brain' classroom—that's a wordy, busy avalanche of abstract ideas—and it's a different story. It could be that he can't keep up, he can't keep listening in multitrack or, if he has Attention Deficit Disorder he can't keep concentrating on thoughts because his brain keeps being sidetracked.

Whichever way, six can be a good age to repeat kids if he's a bit too young. But be careful how you explain his problem to him. One mum tried to get through to her kid that he wasn't the only one who got into trouble sometimes. 'In fact,' she said, 'there's a kid getting into trouble on average every two seconds right here in this very city.' The kid just shook his head. 'Every two seconds,' he said. 'Poor kid!'

Bush Remedies

- My daughter had a learning difficulty and as she had special needs sometimes the kids were very cruel to her. Every now and then, in return for good attendance and effort, I will treat her to a day off and we go to the movies, have lunch, get our hair done, and have girl talk. She loves 'wagging' and having me all to herself, so she promptly tells it for news the next day and the cruel teasing just washes over her. Cruel words just bounce off someone who feels like a princess!

- Our son was refusing to go to preschool because he couldn't keep up. We've had success by pushing for early intervention and we got it. It's an excellent program with an excellent teacher and a low staff–student ratio.

- My child is not yet at school. If she cried going to day care I just supported and comforted her and then left.

Late for School

A lot of parents complained about the problem of kids forever running late for school. Most of the comments for Dawdling apply here (see page 302) so I'll just call on 'Bush Remedies' for extra ideas.

Bush Remedies

- I always used a contract system for my child who runs late. I would get my son to write down how many minutes he was late on all occasions and he was able to marvel at his progress.

- The only thing that worked for me was to have school bags, books, clothes and even the lunch cut and ready before they went to bed, so the next morning there was a lot less stress on me.

- Every day we would be running late for kindy, but this time I was determined not to be late, so I arrived 15 minutes early! He asked, 'Why are we still sitting in the car?' because he was used to squealing into the carpark and racing into the centre. But he discovered that he could get the best toys by getting there early, so it's not a problem any more.

- Rather than getting stressed, I just went about my chores and told her to tell me when she was ready. After arriving late a few times, she now is ready on time every day.

- In the mornings there is no TV till everyone is dressed, teeth cleaned, beds made, etc. The rule is, the quicker you are, the more TV you get.

Phone Problems

Kids and phones just don't mix. The minute you're on the phone they want it and bung on the biggest performance if they don't get it. But when they're on the phone, look out. It's their lifeline to life outside the loony bin and they don't let it go lightly. But little kids can be a danger to phones in more ways than one. One mum found her kitchen phone in the sink getting washed because Nanna had sneezed her germs down the phone!

Primary kids are just as infuriating; if it's not for them, then who cares who rang.

CHECKS

- If the kids are forever wanting to take the calls, just remember that it's magic to them—talking to someone who isn't there, wow!

- If the kids are forever giving you a hard time on the phone then maybe your rules haven't been firm enough (see below), or you've let them break through and take over enough times for a regular encore, or your calls aren't short enough and they hate the competition for your attention.

✸ If the kids won't end their calls, then maybe you haven't cleared up the rules on who can phone, when they can phone and for how long. (Call Waiting is not always the cheapest answer!)

DO'S AND DON'TS

✸ With young kids, under five, have a rule that they never answer the phone—use your answer machine instead.

✸ Five- to eight-year-olds only answer when older ones can't and it's by invitation only. If they're too young to write numbers and names easily, then use the answer machine or teach them a 'Please ring back in . . . minutes' line.

✸ Eight-year-olds or older can earn the right to answer if they can show they're good message masters, so have pencil and paper securely attached to the phone table. Good message masters are those who are polite, give their name and number and in exchange, take number, name and date accurately.

✸ Whatever their age, some kids seem addicted to interrupting phone calls. The answer to these characters is not nagging or threats, but 'Phone Practice'.
  ◆ Just get their ideas on what they can do instead of interrupting.
  ◆ Practise on dummy calls over and over again (at a time that doesn't suit them (eg favourite TV show) until they reckon they've got the message.
  ◆ When the real calls come, signal the new game plan, keep the calls brief and applaud their self-control.
  ◆ If they interrupt again, then interrupt their favourite TV show for more practice.

✸ Modern phones can rest on the tabletop or be cup-hooked (not mounted) on the wall. If you don't want young kids dialling, close the cup-hook gap so little hands can't operate the phone.

✸ For young kids left at home on their own (hopefully rarely) who can't phone your number for any reason, the 'easy call' option on most phones can have a delayed hotline. The kids just have to pick up the phone and it can be preprogrammed to automatically dial any number you specify.

✸ For kids who are super-slack on recording messages then either ban outgoing access until all incoming calls are handled well or, as one dad did, act equally dumb. He told his daughter one of her friends phoned all excited and wanting to speak to her urgently, but he forgot to ask her name. Dad reckons he had no problem from that day.

✸ If there's lots of competition for the phone, set up some rules that are seen as fair to all parties. For instance:
- Work out some reasonable phone access times with the kids and keep it consistent. Some families have a 10-minute maximum call time before 9p.m., with teenagers able to make longer calls after that time if agreed.
- Maybe have a rule that calls cannot be made or taken during homework, if that's a problem.
- Allow the kids some privacy, even though it's tempting to eavesdrop.
- If the kids are abusing the privilege with STD or 0055 calls, then get a key lock for the phone.
- If the kids are slow to get off the phone, use an egg timer as a warning that you are now giving them three minutes to finish the conversation.

But the phone can be useful in a crisis. The other day a dad told me his teenage daughter had had enough and was leaving home ... but then the phone rang.

Bush Remedies

🍃 I gave her her own play mobile phone, an animated one to make it fun. She listens in on that when we're talking on the phone.

🍃 With interruptions, I'd ask the caller to hold a moment and get the child on my lap or, if it's a long conversation, set up paint, playdough, pencils or a video.

- The phone has always been an interruption. I don't have an answer, but try and get a cordless phone or longer lead so you can chase them out of the house as you talk.

- I interrupted them when they were playing or watching TV and wouldn't let them alone for two minutes.

- I found a toy phone worked, or better still, a broken one, similar to the family phone, can be obtained free from Telstra. But five minutes can be an eternity for little kids, so keep the calls brief.

- Keep some special activity they love for times when you need to talk on the phone, such as soapy water play in the sink (if the phone is in viewing distance) or a special toy they play with only when the phone rings.

PARENT PENTATHLON
PHONE RING EVENT

RULES: The event starts at the first ring and then the kids race to say nothing or something as inane as 'hello, me big now'. But the game starts in earnest when you grab the phone, because it's then their job to grab your attention away from the phone. They'll fight, argue, hit, kick and pull anything to win you back, and they don't care whether you bellow or belt because they've got your attention.

SCORING: Points go to the parent who can carry on a schizophrenic conversation, saying to the phone: 'Yes, we are lucky, they're all over their colds now', while muttering to the kids: 'Shut up or I'll send you to your room. No, you can't eat that now. No, you can't bite your sister instead.'

Homework

It's amazing really. Teachers, and more recently some education departments, have been able to take two politically correct words like 'home' and 'work' and blend them into an agent of family destruction. Not content to sit on the sidelines and smirk, some authorities have even formalised how much pain parents must suffer each week; two hours for infants, four hours for primary, six hours for junior high school, and at least eight hours for senior high. As the pressure builds on schools to be up with computers, back to basics, clever on communication, frenetic about foreign languages, prioritising child protection, it's no wonder that the curriculum is bursting at the seams and more and more schoolwork spills over to homework. If this is a big problem area at your place, check it out.

CHECKS

* Is it just that there's too much else on after school to be bothered?

* Is there just too much to do?

* Is it that there's no good after-school routine that includes quiet time to do homework?

* Is it that there's no-one home to supervise?

* Is it that the work is too hard?

* Is it that they say they don't know what to do?

* Is it that they keep forgetting to bring books home?

* Is it more a problem for the parent than for the teacher or Sandy?

No homework should be set that the children can't do, that the teacher can't mark, or where the homework contract between teacher and pupil is anything other than watertight.

DO'S AND DON'TS

※ Make homework a cosy, cuddly, fun time for young kids, so they learn to look forward to learning.

※ Have a regular homework time and space.

※ Ensure that homework is finished before any after-dinner play or TV.

※ Keep an eye on how long set work takes—an average of 30 minutes for infants or an hour for primary should be maximum. There are too many other things in life that kids need to learn and that can't be taught sitting behind a desk.

※ Compare with other parents if homework seems to be taking too long.

※ Check with the teacher if your child is having problems. Fights about homework must not be allowed to happen or the long-term costs are high.

※ Reward fast, efficient work, particularly if your child is a daydreamer.

※ Be near enough to help if needed.

※ Check homework, but concentrate on positives. If there's an error, see if the child can find it first, gently point out errors, but avoid criticism.

※ Allow music or radio, whatever helps, rather than hinders the concentration.

※ Make your kids feel important and grown-up when they're working.

- If they keep forgetting to bring it home, then maybe use the 'Practice' technique here. Have them go through all the motions, time and time again, of packing their bag ready to go home and putting the homework book in each time. Keep doing it till they reckon they've got the sequence down pat, but double the practice the next night if they forget.

- Don't do homework for them or it becomes a lifetime job.

- Don't put pressure on them to get top marks all the time or they'll either stop trying or they'll become perfectionists.

- Don't get conned by 'I'll do it soon'.

- Don't allow the TV on during homework.

- Don't allow younger kids without homework to play nearby.

- Don't be conned into conflict. If you get too angry then your partner, neighbour or even a paid senior high school helper would be better. If the work is too hard then the teacher needs to know so she can explain or modify. If the kids would rather play than work after school, then lunchtime might be your offered (unattractive) alternative.

- Don't make them 'study' if they have no homework. If you want them to do extra work then talk to the teacher first for ideas and direction.

- Don't use the old 'in my day . . .'; it ranks second only to 'if I were you' in getting kids offside. Remember that in the eyes of youth, parents are prehistoric.

PARENT PENTATHLON
HOMEWORK MEDLEY EVENT

RULES: This event starts best when the kids burst in and announce that their project is due in tomorrow. Then all hell breaks loose. As one parent races around for snippets on ancient Egypt and their partner traces Tutankhamen, what does Sandy do? He colours in the title page, that's what. And if you dare suggest he should do it, he will scream back, 'I am doing it.' Then, after a midnight marathon, you get it off only to learn that the teacher granted an extension anyhow.

SCORING: Points go to the parent who can cope with their child getting a B without calling the teacher by the same descriptor.

Messy Rooms

If your Sandy, in addition to all his other problems, also has a room that's a pigsty, then join the crowd. This has to be the most common problem in every house.

CHECKS

* Are you being the big martyr and tidying up for him? There's no reason why young kids can't help pick up their own things; they do at day care or school.

* Can he be tidy when he needs to be? If so, he's probably less neurotic than we are.

* Is mess a family style? If so, don't even try to fix Sandy.

* Is he the sort of kid who's spatially hopeless; is good with words, but just hasn't got a clue where he put things or where things go? If so, structure him a bit with set spots and set times to tidy up.

✷ Is he just pretty good at forgetting to tidy? If so, set up a time before TV or play for checking. It's amazing how quickly his brain starts to pick up if the checking is regular and the penalties are consistent.

✷ Is he relying on your frustration to take over and clean up for him? If so, some parents copy the dog catcher—stray gear is impounded and owners have to pay up for its return.

✷ Does he like the mess because it makes him feel cosy and homely? If so, have a few rules such as everything off the floor, no food in his room, washing in the basket and full clean-up each Saturday, before any play, etc. Regular clean-ups are much easier to enforce if it's part of the family's weekly ritual, every week, with no exemptions.

DO'S AND DON'TS

Anyone with a foolproof answer to this one hasn't met my youngest—stuffed toys stuffed everywhere, no room in any drawer to put any washing and drawers hanging over like the Gardens of Babylon. At least I knew she would never be molested by an intruder, they'd never get through the obstacle course!

Here are some techniques to tackle the problem.

✷ The frontal assault technique: all stray items are impounded and locked in a lost property box and the kids pay to bail their clothes out.

✷ The joint attack technique: join forces and clean up with the kids.

✷ The nerve gas technique: these optimistic parents hope that over time, the stench would force the kids into submission, but it doesn't.

✷ The exchange-of-duties technique: parents help clean their room in exchange for kids' help with some other housework (eg hanging clothes out, collecting and folding washing).

- ✻ The starvation technique: children don't get fed until their room is respectable.

- ✻ The cover-up technique: when the room needs to be respectable for visitors, parents simply shut the door (if they can), scrape the mess into a pile or put some attractive drape over it if they can't.

- ✻ The stealth technique: parents warn the kids that an outside attack is on its way if the fortress isn't fixed. When the kids are out, the parents do just that and teenagers hate this outside intervention.

- ✻ The fact is that many kids like cosy, cuddly, messy rooms and other kids don't. Some children, the born organisers and perfectionists, must have everything just right and can be as painful as their messy opposites. The rest of us are in between. But it's good for kids to learn how to sort and arrange so it's worth checking out why they're making so much mess.

- ✻ Some families do strike a truce. This isn't the same as capitulating, but in conflict resolution terms it means you work towards a win-win situation. Children win their right to have some freedom and mess in their room providing it meets the parents' concerns (eg risk of stained carpet, vermin, mildew and mould). This could mean such everyday rules as mess off the floor every day, no food in the rooms and only washing clothes that are put in the laundry basket, etc.

- ✻ With young children, the job is to be helpers together. With older kids, sort out who does which jobs with them and give no assistance on transport, etc till they honour their agreements.

But don't just wait for them to grow up and leave home. As Christopher Morley said, by the time the younger children have learnt to keep the house tidy, the oldest grandchildren are on hand to tear it to pieces!

MESSY MESSAGES

This is a true story about Robyn, our secretary, her bird and her messy kids. It was such a classic I have converted it to poetry in motions.

Robyn, the softie, flung herself down in a lonely mood to think.
'Tis true she was a mother and had three kids but her heart was beginning to sink.
For she had been trying for years to get her kids to clean up,
She had tried and tried but couldn't succeed and so she became fed up.
She flung herself down in low despair as grieved as mums can be,
And after a while she pondered there; I'll give it all up, said she.
Now just at that moment the budgie chirped and around the cage it flew,
And tore and ripped and scattered and flung and this gave Robyn a clue.
She trained her bird to eat scraps of food and to rip up exercise books,
Then released it into the kitchen chaos amidst lots of dirty looks.
Well the bird flew high, the bird flew low and showed it was quite able,
Depositing droppings on open books and nibbling what's left on the table.
Now the bird's quite happy and Robyn's quite happy, as the droppings come off with a broom,
And the kids are tidy, their plates are clean and their homework they now do in their room!

Bush Remedies

- We have a rule in our house that any toys, clothes, etc that are left on the floor at night-time, go into a box or basket and they cannot be accessed for a week. After this time, they have the opportunity to put their items away. The rule is, if they don't empty the basket, the items are thrown out. We have never had to throw anything out yet and very rarely have to put items into a basket. The routine was established in little over a week after years of fighting to get them to pick up their things.—Jan Clark. ADDSUP (Tas)

Discipline Summary

GETTING KIDS TO COOPERATE IS ALL ABOUT BUILDING UP GOOD DISCIPLINE, NOT ONE-SIDED DICTATORSHIP, BUT BUILDING UP GOOD JOINT RULES FOR COOPERATING.

- **D** Dedication and persistence are much more powerful tools than violence.
- **I** Impart clear and consistent rules and get the over-threes to help design the rules.
- **S** See the problem through their eyes. It doesn't mean you agree, but it makes you an ally.
- **C** Concentrate on positives if you want positive kids.
- **I** Ignore or isolate behaviour you don't like. No behaviour continues if it is unsuccessful.
- **P** Praise behaviour you do like and practise behaviour you would like.
- **L** Learn to laugh with the kids and play with life so that problems stay in perspective.
- **I** Insist on some selfish child-free time in your week—martyrs don't make good mothers or fathers.
- **N** Nurture the kid's ego when punishing—quietly, firmly, discreetly and respectfully.
- **E** Endeavour to work as a team. No child, no matter how difficult or clever, can match the strength of a confident couple.

Famous Footnote

A DISTANCED MUM

Cheryl Kernot

POLITICIAN

I'm away a lot and that makes my family different, not unique, just different. The Senate sits for about twenty-one weeks a year and that means I come down to Canberra on Sunday night and I don't go home till Friday night. My husband is more of the full-time parent than I am.

I think you have to talk a lot about sharing responsibilities. We've made choices and we're always working to help the choices work. We do a fairly regular stocktake. For example, it would be easier to have someone come in and clean our house, but we don't do that. We made a choice. I don't want my daughter to grow up thinking that someone else will take responsibility for things that she should do, so we have a constant review of who's doing what around the house and if it's working.

I'm very proud of my daughter's ability to say I'm sorry. I've tried to teach her from an early age that we all make mistakes. I don't want her to have the pressure of feeling she can never make a mistake without people commenting on it. I think it's much more important to acknowledge that you have made a mistake. I've never punished, because I don't believe in punishing for mistakes; I believe in rewarding the courage to be honest, and to say I've made a mistake.

My approach is for resolution, to never go to bed unhappy. I find that resolution is possible with just a little bit of work, but I also think it demands generosity from adults. I think you've got to remember that you're an adult, in a power situation, and that you were a kid once. You've got to trust your children to be honest, and you've got to help them trust you to talk about their emotions freely.

I tried to be positive and sunny when she was a baby and she's now got an optimistic view on life.

I think being a parent is the most important and the hardest job in the world, I really do, and I wish every child in the world was wanted and loved and emotionally nurtured. I'm always distressed when I see children being smacked in supermarkets by harassed parents, and I always feel I want to go up and say,

'Can I mind this child for a little while? Can I take him or her for a little walk while you do your shopping?' because there are so many unsupported parents. People often ask me who I admire. I really admire all those deserted women who stick with their responsibilities of being a parent and who make it work. My daughter has had pretty good health so I really haven't been tested like a lot of other parents, but when it's a hurried trip to the doctor or hospital in the middle of the night, I often think about those parents who are doing it all by themselves.

There is one very important ingredient that makes a family like ours work, and that's my husband. You have to have a pretty atypical male who's happy to do all the things that he does.

CONCLUSION

Who'd Be A Parent?

I have many regrets about my priorities as a father. Not only did I let my wife down and made her carry too much of it on her own, but I also let down my kids. I wasn't there when I should have been. And what disappoints me the most, now I'm older and hopefully wiser, is that I missed out on being part of their growing up, missed out on enjoying the magic of their minds unfolding. I can't get those years back.

PETER 'McDonalds' RITCHIE, businessman
[READ MORE OF PETER RITCHIE'S HONEST SELF-ASSESSMENT AND ADVICE AT THE END OF THIS CHAPTER.]

This book has been a big adventure for Sandy and me. You may not have followed it all the way through, but I hope you enjoyed the parts you did. I've learnt lots from the parents whose priorities and bush recipes have enhanced the book so much. And I've been inspired by some of the great people that have contributed, some well known, some that maybe should be.

What I've been trying to show is that being a parent is not easy for the best of us. It's even difficult for authors of parenting books, as Steve Biddulph shares with us.

> People sometimes think that if you write books about parenting you have 'all the answers', and you never have pain, confusion or struggle! But even after all these years of parenthood, I still have moments when I think to myself, 'What am I supposed to do now?'
>
> Planning a homebirth and ending up with an emergency caesarian—twice. Finding our new baby son almost dead after an apnoea attack and frantically working to resuscitate him. The sheer exhaustion of sleep deprivation in the first years with a new baby. Trying to hold our little daughter screaming and writhing while a doctor struggled to stitch a gash in the back of her head from a dog bite. Going back to a shop with a little child to return a stolen chocolate bar and apologise to the shopowner! Trying to comfort a child who saw a TV ad about children dying of starvation. And that isn't even the teenage years!
>
> There's always something new to challenge and stretch us! But in spite of that, parenthood is still my greatest pleasure.

No-one claims to be perfect, and authentic amateurs are better role models anyhow. But there are a couple of important conclusions which need to be shared at the end of a mammoth manual.

My big concern is that the combination of work and worry, money and materialism, pace and profit, do-gooders and trend setters is making the world an alien environment for families. The human species, the greatest and most successful social animal of them all, has been propelled by the pace of change from his tribal supports. We're on our own; as Pat O'Shane says, it's the age of individualism, with all the excitement, high achievement, loneliness and stress that goes with it.

That individualism has no place for kids. We are in danger of disengaging from the young of our own species and leaving them to the experts and to their own peers for company. Steve Biddulph, in *Raising Boys*, has alerted us to the dire consequences of the missing male in boys' lives. This trend has to be dangerous, but as Jeannie Little reminds us on page 284, as long as they've got one really good parent, they're pretty lucky!

One symptom that we've been disengaging is the rise in abuse statistics. **It is my belief that while we've tried to protect kids through leg-**

islation, **we're not protecting the families or the parents that carry the responsibility to deliver real protection.** In this regard let me share a letter I received recently.

> Dear Dr John,
> Isn't it about time we balanced things up a bit? I mean, all we hear is how to be a better parent, how to listen to your children, how to lift their self-esteem. What about the self-esteem of their struggling parents? The other night when we had friends over I couldn't believe how strongly every parent there felt they were the ones being abused. Some felt the courts were pro-child and anti-parent, especially with this 'Homeless Child Allowance' that kids seem to get at the drop of a hat. Others felt the tax system was anti-parent. The women mentioned the lack of facilities for parents with young kids on buses and other transport and in shopping centres. A few of the guys were angry that you can't even smack a naughty kid any more or you're under threat of child abuse. It's all gone too far. If parents are expected to protect the kids then society needs to be protecting and looking after the parents.

Some years ago, in a Sydney survey of 1000 parents, Dr Shelley Phillips found that one-third to one-half actually felt hostile towards their kids. It's understandable; at times it seems as though kids have the rights and parents have whatever's left.

I hope this book has given some ways we can regain confidence in managing our kids, with more playfare than warfare. But it's not easy. While we struggle alone in our four walls to pick up, keep up and pay up, the kids from very early years now are under the professional eye of marketers, teachers and advertisers. So, instead of criticising each other for being imperfect parents I thought we should have a 'Parents' Bill of Rights' to galvanise some mutual support.

This is *not* an anti-child list and does not condone hitting children. What it's trying to do (tongue in cheek maybe) is to begin to rebuild parent confidence and mutual support so they don't feel the need to hit out their hurt and frustration. Families or countries that rely on violent answers breed violence.

Parents' Bill of Rights

> ### PARENTS' BILL OF RIGHTS
>
> 1. **Parents have the right to raise children**—our society needs kids to survive so politicians must help protect and support that right.
> 2. **Parents have the right to be in charge**—in no species do the kids run the show. We mightn't know much but we've known life and that's what they're learning about.
> 3. **Parents have the right to enjoy child rearing**—let's face it, the hours are horrific, the job's a gerrymander and the pay's pathetic, so why not run it in a way you enjoy? If you're enjoying the family they'll enjoy you.
> 4. **Parents have the right to manipulate children**—it's only by a cuddle for this and a hairy eyebrow for that that kids learn a way through the labyrinth of life.
> 5. **Parents have the right to expect help from the kids**—in today's busy world only families that can work as a team can survive.
> 6. **Parents have the right to their own lifestyle**—loving, caring and sharing are a must, but style is optional. Trying to wear the Jones' lifestyle might be a bad fit.
> 7. **Parents have the right to make mistakes**—as Alvin Toffler said, 'Parenting is the last single preserve of the amateur.'
>
> So face them front-on tonight armed with a new ring of confidence in your right to life. In any family one person plus courage is usually a majority.

Kids have much to learn from us and society can't survive unless they do. Just as we have learnt much in this book about the parts of the child that break down, we need to remember that *we* have many vital parts to pull them back together again: a wise head, a good ear, a soft shoulder, admiring eyes, a positive tongue, embracing arms, forgiving heart, steady hands ... the list could go on. Kids need our *confident* management. They long for loving discipline. But the stress on the parent is too great to deliver this unless we get back into the Balanced Management, as outlined in Chapter One (see page 26).

If we can address our adult needs (for each other, for tribal support and to be valued) and if we can dig deep into our soul to find some peace on this earth then we will be more peaceful and contented parents. I've just been reading Wayne Dyer's book, *Manifest Your Destiny*, and he talks about stages we go through in our journey to find inner peace: the athlete (body-focused), the warrior (success, money and competition-focused), the statesperson (genuine care and interest in welfare of others), and the spirit (the immortal energy and spirit that is within us and not confined or limited to this life). Some may see the parenting triangle as the trinity—father (parent), son (child) and holy spirit (adult). That's for each of us to work out in our own way. One thing is for sure, we're not well-balanced humans unless we do.

But there's another easy way to get back the bounce and the balance in our lives. Let's look at the kids, learn from the kids and watch them at work. Because they play at life, they use their imagination, they can be diverted into fantasy and fun at the drop of a raised eyebrow. Try playing around with life a bit more, and playing at parenting, and watch how easy it will be to re-engage your kids. Maybe the goal of every parent should be to die young but as late as possible!

This manual is my little effort to help parents regain some confidence and regain some easy authority in their kids' lives. If we can re-engage with our kids, and refind the child within us all, then that's great news for families. So who'd be a parent? Sandy and I hope that you wouldn't swap it and that your kids know it!

FAMOUS FOOTNOTE

AN ABSENT DAD

Peter 'McDonald's' Ritchie

BUSINESSMAN

I have many regrets about my priorities as a father. Not only did I let my wife down and made her carry too much of it on her own, but I also let down my kids. I wasn't there when I should have been. And what disappoints me the most, now I'm older and hopefully wiser, is that I missed out on being part of their growing up, missed out on enjoying the magic of their minds unfolding. I can't get those years back but I hope I can be a better grandfather. I have gained some satisfaction from seeing other young executives heed my warning and have better balance of home and work than I had. And it's great to see my very close friend, Bob Mansfield, taking stock and doing his job as a devoted dad.

When my wife had Nicholas, I was present at the birth and then I moved out for three weeks to live in a motel close to where we were opening our first McDonald's. I was a typical Aussie dad. I saw myself as the breadwinner and my wife as the child rearer. I worked hard and set up the family financially and I thought I was doing the right thing. The truth is, if I had the choice to do it again, I'd do it differently.

I woke up to myself in the early eighties, and I realised that I had made some classic mistakes. Firstly, I thought I knew everything you had to know about parenting and I also thought that innately I was going to be a great father.

I also made the most serious mistake of all; I underestimated how important those first couple of years are for a child. I thought they were blobs until they could read and write. The truth is they're sponges!

But the message really didn't hit home until my daughter had her end-of-sixth-grade concert. This was the last primary concert she would ever be in and she had an important role. I had a meeting to go to. Don't ask me now what was in that meeting that made me miss her performance. I wouldn't know. I now say to my executives, there's no meeting that's so vital that it should take the place of something special back home.

I hope other Australian men won't make the same mistake. We are suffering a leadership crisis in Australia at the moment. We're being led by the mediocre and it's largely because of the lack of 'role model' mentoring by fathers.

A lot of children know their fathers consider their work important because they see how much time their fathers devote to work. What they need to see is that fathers also consider them important. It's that kind of contribution from fathers that builds a kid's self-esteem.

If an executive has nothing in his life but work, believing that the more hours he works, the more he will get noticed, then I believe he will not make a good senior executive. You need more in your life than work.

My humble advice to fathers, from my experience, is to listen, spend time, and just *be there*. Have no doubt that families are very important. But you can't just say one thing and do another and get away with it. Your actions must back up your message.

Acknowledgements

My eternal thanks (purely in alphabetical, not political or 'parentally correct' order) to Kim Beazley, Steve Biddulph, Suzanne Chick, Bryce Courtenay, Bronwen Daddo, John Howard, Cheryl Kernot, Kathy Lette, Jeannie Little, Pat O'Shane, Greg 'Wiggles' Page, Peter 'McDonald's' Ritchie and Janine Shepherd—each of whom gave their heartfelt contributions free of charge because they believe in the cause (NAPCAN) and they believe in the family as the cornerstone of our community.

At the same time I'd like to acknowledge the inspiring role so many other role models made to this book. My admiration goes to all the special families coping with special problems that have so much to teach the rest of us. This could include most families, but in this book they are represented by comments from Ms Helena Brunner (world champion para olympian), Ms Joyce McKeogh (Multiple Births Association), Jan Clark and Marina Rosa (ADHD Association), Julie Elliot (ADHD, autism, isolation), Sandra Coster (a disabled partner), Merron Howard (a bereaved partner), Val Travis (an off-shore partner), Joanna Croxon (adoption) and Lynette White (ADHD, aggression). My thanks also goes to the other unnamed contributors.

How do I acknowledge every parent that I've ever met for making me believe that I had something to offer their family? Many I would like to have mentioned by name but it started to look discriminatory and I'm not sure, in the years to come, that the kids would be too impressed. Often good ideas have had to be deleted too, either because others had said much the same or just because I ran out of room. I hope you understand, knowing that even if your personal effort is not here, it has been part of the foundation that inspired me to keep going.

I must thank every parent who has contributed ideas and suggestions in my talks and seminars over the last two years in the following areas: Strathfield West, Woodbury Park, Kariong, Scholastic (Pennant Hills, Epping, Parramatta and Harbord), Burwood, Kincumber, Gorokan, Newcastle, Forresters Beach, Erina, Kurrajong, Southerland, Balmoral, Cronulla, Rooty Hill, Bendigo, Wollongong, Orange, Canberra, Mudgee, Darling Harbour, Mt Isa, Gladstone, North Lakes, Sydney, Umina, Gosford, Drummoyne, Tamworth, Grafton, Coffs Harbour, Kempsey, Hornsby, Bateau Bay, North Ryde, Crows Nest, Bondi, Tumut, Wagga

Wagga, Forbes, Albury, Bankstown, Belmont, Liverpool, Perth, Brisbane, Adelaide and Toowoomba.

Then there are some special people and groups that must be thanked for their contributions. Those marked with an asterisk (*) are mentioned in the Help Reference page at the back of the book.

- Multiple Births Association*
- The ADHD support groups*
- Playgroups throughout Australia*
- The Nursing Mothers Association
- The family night congregation of Umina Uniting Church
- the Post Adoption Resource Agency
- Camp Quality
- The Tough Love group*
- Family Day Care*

I also thank the following child care centres and schools for their contributions in the various surveys:

- Gosford Preschool kindergarten
- Kariong Community Preschool Kindergarten
- Woy Woy Peninsula Child Care
- Kids Factory, Kincumber
- Terrigal Long Day Care Centre
- Papalya Long Day Care Centre, Erina
- Clovelly Child Care Centre
- Eyers Close Preschool, Kariong
- Hillside Preschool, Avoca
- Highland Grove Preschool, Green Point.
- Umina Public School
- Central Coast Grammar School
- Empire Bay Public School

Then there are those in the engine room that fire the book up and get it going. I would particularly like to thank Brett Brennen, my manager; Jane Knight, my wonderful niece and phantom typist; Prof. Alan Knight for his quantitative assistance; Ms Leanne Knight for library searches; Alan Fowler, friend and computer buff extraordinaire; and Brad Baker, head of design at the Powerhouse Museum, a fabulous friend and illustrator who created Sandy. Nancy Wiley, a wonderfully spirited person who recently retired as a highly respected preschool director, knows this book backwards. She believed in it, she carried out many of the surveys for it, she read the menu script, she criticised the menu script and she helped me interweave the special stories. I can't see how I could have finished it without her.

This book has taken enormous effort. My publishers, Pan Macmillan, have given me the encouragement to go on and two wonderful ladies, Rosemary Sinclair and Jane Ewins of NAPCAN, made me feel that the cause—helping child abuse prevention—was worth the effort. Thank you to everyone who helped.

Then there's Jean, my wife, who has had to put up with the necessary obsession that goes into any book. But she has done more than that. She believed in me. To you, Jeanie, I offer humble and totally inadequate thanks, for all you've done for the family, often with little help, probably too much criticism, but you've done it and the kids and I are eternally grateful.

Finally, there's the kids the book is all about. Not just my three—Jenny, Heather and Rosie—who have made being a parent just the hardest and bestest thing I have ever done. But to all our kids, every one of them pains in the aorta. To them and their families I dedicate this book. But I'd like to add my own special tribute to the parents who have lost their little Sandys. This is a special dedication to all the Phoebes & Timmys that are no longer with us (see Appendix for Phoebe's story).

Appendix

Phoebe's Story

Here's one story that might make each of us realise just how lucky we are and to treasure the kids we have for the few short years we have them.

This is the brief story of Phoebe's three-year fight to live, after being diagnosed with the most common and treatable form of childhood leukemia.

Many may view our family's story as one of great sadness, grief and despair. At times it was all of these, but it was, and still is, one of great love, caring, learning, increasing knowledge and personal growth.

Phoebe's illness brought hope and despair. A bone marrow transplant was scheduled but she relapsed five days prior to the transplant. The day before she died, she asked to watch our old home movies and laughed at her antics as a two-year-old. Hours later she began to deteriorate quite rapidly and died peacefully in her own bed listening to her favourite Beethoven violin concerto. Her final words to me were, 'I don't need you any more, Mum!'

Phoebe's influence lives on.

I have in my kitchen a small sign which I read frequently: 'Some people come into our lives and quickly go. Others stay a while and leave footprints on our heart and we are never the same.' Our daughter has certainly left footprints in the hearts of many, for I know the imprint Phoebe's life had, and still has, on our family, friends and all those who knew her. For those of you who have a child who is battling a life-threatening disease, I send my heartfelt wish that no matter how hard the road ahead, you will find the resources deep within to meet each new challenge and to find strength to grow from each experience.

—Merron Howard, editor of the Family Newsletter for the Oncology ward, Sydney Children's Hospital, and FDC coordinator.

Preferred Social Rewards and Punishments by Age

	BIRTH TO EIGHTEEN MONTHS	EIGHTEEN MONTHS TO FIVE YEARS	SIX TO 11 YEARS	12 YEARS AND OVER

R E W A R D S	smiling face
	cuddles
	stroking
	singing
	conversing
	attention
	whispers
	reactions
	movement
	impact
	physical play
	one-to-one time
	good taste
	physical play
	rhythm
	power
		attention
		smiling face
		hugs
		admiration
		talk time
		one-to-one time
		impact-reaction
		pretend play
		success
		problem solving
		bigness
		   recognition
		favourite food
		rides-rhythm
		approval
		'happy disk'
		TV/video
		computers
			attention
			adult approval
			tokens
			name mention
			peer approval
			mastery
			winning
			competency
			problem solving
			competitive
			   success
			cooperating play
			badges
			privileges
			status symbols
			respect
			explanation
			friends
			one-to-one talk
			front seat of car
			'green disk'
			TV/video
			computers
				peer attention
				peer approval
				independence
				freedom
				mature symbols
				status symbols
				winning
				public
				   recognition
				respect
				money
				car
				parent-free time
				friends
				phone calls
				group inclusion
				sexual attraction
				social competent
				   approval
				trust
				TV/video
				computers

P U N I S H M E N T S	sad face
	waiting
	stern voice
	hairy eyebrow
	'no'
	ignoring
	sharp clap
	frustration
		sad face
		waiting
		stern voice
		hairy eyebrow
		'no'
		ignoring
		time out
		adult
		   disapproval
		toy deprivation
		attention
		   removal
		scolding
		'sad face'
		no TV/video
		no computer
			logical
			   punishment
			natural
			   punishment
			time out
			grounding
			detentions
			privilege stop
			'red disk'
			stern voice
			peer disapproval
				logical
				   punishment
				natural
				   punishment
				grounding
				privilege stop
				peer disapproval

Fridge Disk Discipline

HOW TO USE FRIDGE DISK DISCIPLINE
1. Trace around the base of a glass to create two disks and cut them out. Colour one green and the other one red. If the kids are preschoolers then draw a happy face on the green one and a sad face on the red one. If they're high school age you may care to just use just ordinary rectangles of paper with their name on each, one featuring a tiny happy face down the bottom right-hand corner and one featuring a tiny sad face.
2. You can use them separately or paste back-to-back.
3. Use a round magnet for the nose, or hold to fridge with any form of magnet anywhere unobtrusive.
4. Have one set for each child over two years of age.
5. When the child is cooperating the disk is on the green/happy side. When the child doesn't cooperate, tell the child what you're sad about and then make sure they know that the disk has been flipped to red/sad side.
6. Let the kids know you won't be able to cooperate (or give help) because you're not getting cooperation (or getting help) and pull out of any favours until they have made amends.
7. The way to make amends is to do one or more of the jobs on the Make Up List (see next page)—as nominated by parent—so they pay their dues and everyone is happy again. Then flip the disk back to green/happy side.
8. If they won't do the Make Up it means their battery is too tired to have a go, so give them time out in their room for a battery recharge. They can come out when they feel ready, or when the oven timer goes, or whatever system you decide on.
9. If there is no Make Up, then there are no favours until it's all sorted out. The line of attack is that they're good kids and want to sort it out, so what's gone wrong?
10. The idea is to keep it fun and let the disks do your shouting for you.

Fridge Make Up List

SELECTION *Put a cross in the ones to be done*	KID'S NAME	MAKE UP IDEAS
☐		help bring in washing
☐		help set the table
☐		help tidy up toys
☐		help get dinner ready
☐		please do as you were asked
☐		help tidy up lounge
☐		help tidy up bedroom
☐		help get Mum a drink
☐		help get Dad a drink
☐		help tidy up bathroom
☐		help play with the baby
☐		*Home brewed favourites:*
☐		
☐		
☐		
☐		

HOW TO USE MAKE UP LIST

1. To be done with fridge disks—perhaps cover in contact, stick on fridge and use whiteboard pen to cross the ones you want done, or add your own.
2. When done, erase crosses, flick fridge disk to green and you're back in action.
3. Add some more ideas of your own in the blank squares.

Success Charts

1. This is only an example; families can devise their own.
2. Remember, charts only work if the kids are keen to play the game.
3. It's best not to have kids competing on their charts or it spoils the fun.
4. The first thing to get ready is the Lucky Dips—these are just cheap, fun things they can win when they reach the Dip and help to maintain their interest.
5. Common lucky dips are a favourite food, special privilege or some little adventure.
6. Points are not given for being 'good', but for the specific behaviour you're trying to encourage (beating temper, waiting, accepting NO, beating fear, etc).
7. At first give the points easily, so the kids get the idea and get keen. As you go on, you can make the points a bit harder to get.
8. Always tell the kids what they got their points for and preferably write down the reason and when they earn their next point, check what the last few have been for.
9. Although your focus might be on one child, others can be involved, either by getting points on this chart, too, or by having their own Lucky Dip cards for drawing when Sandy hits the Dip.
10. Points can be noted by writing in the square, colouring in or using a sticker of some sort.
11. When they get to the end, Sandy gets some preagreed prize; again not too expensive as it's meant to be a game, not a bribe.
12. The idea is to use the chart to shape the behaviour towards what you want by building in better habits.
13. Remember, charts work on novelty so don't be disappointed if, after a few weeks, their interest softens. That is the time to sit down and create another that interests them, or, if they're sick of charts, think up some other game, eg on the computer, or building a happy face on the fridge, feature by feature (like Hangman).

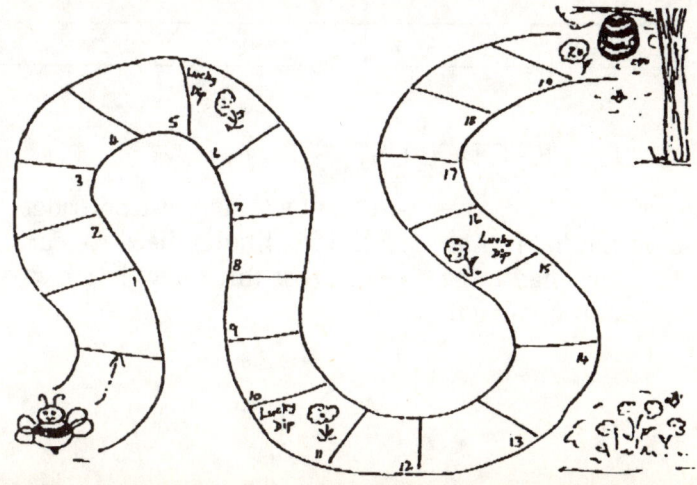

Practice List

SELECTION	KID'S NAME	PRACTICE LIST
Put a cross in the ones to be done		*Good habits needing more practice*
☐		hearing Mum/Dad first time
☐		going to room when asked
☐		staying in room till buzzer goes
☐		doing as asked, no back-answering
☐		finding something useful to do
☐		waiting
☐		speaking nicely to people
☐		keeping hands to self
☐		doing something quietly when parent is on the phone
☐		coming when called
☐		waiting when someone else is talking
☐		'freezing' when asked
☐		letting others go/choose first
☐		*Home brewed favourites:*
☐		
☐		
☐		
☐		

HOW TO USE PRACTICE LIST

1. Amend to suit, then cover with contact, stick list on fridge, and put a cross on the habit that your child is finding hard to learn.
2. If the habit has had to be given a cross three days in a row, then use the sad face in conjunction.

Think Light

1. With a pencil, trace around a dinner plate onto yellow cardboard.
2. Cut out the cardboard.
3. Share ideas with the child on things they would like to do that would stop them getting into trouble when they're bored or being a bit of a pest.
4. With preschoolers, cut out pictures or draw these ideas (even stick figures) onto pieces of paper and maybe subtitle so they get to learn the words too.
5. Cut out the pieces of paper you've written or drawn on and use Blu-Tack or equivalent to stick the ideas onto the cardboard.
6. Hang their Think Light in their time out area.
7. When they're bored or being a pest, they can go (or be sent) to their time out area and pick out one of the activities listed on their Think Light.
8. If they say they don't like those ideas or they're sick of them, then tell them to think about some other ideas that could be swapped for some of the ones already there. That way the yellow light stays fresh and useful as ideas for time out.
9. When they've thought of what they want to do, they ask for the green light to do it.
10. If they're school age and they've been sent to time out as punishment, you may not allow them out until they can indicate what they will do next time the same problem arises.

Travellers' First Aid Kit for Families

CAR
- Set of cassette tapes of car games and activities.
- Special tapes of favourite songs, heard only in the car.
- Pad with plastic lift-up flap (the children draw, lift flap to erase).
- Age-appropriate jokes, comic or picture books (for kids who don't get carsick).
- Pocket games, both manual and electronic.
- String for cats' cradle.
- Knitting Nancy—French knitting spool.
- Resurrect Rubik cube—maybe paste on appropriate pictures to make block jigsaw.
- In the glove box: a small container or sandwich bag of tasty finger food or dried fruit, which could be handed out for not asking how far to go till we hit the next town or whatever.
- Bi-carb soda to take the smell out of carsick spots.
- Sticker fun book.
- Road Safety activity books, etc—supplied by Macquarie University.
- Plastic cups and fresh water bottles for hot days to stop dehydration.
- A stable table.
- Colouring-in books and pencils or colour-by-number style.
- Talking books (from libraries) or books that you read along with tapes.
- Walkmans with headphones!

HANDBAG
- A few bandaids (preferably those with animal and colourful strips), useful to give kids to try to open them to fill in time such as when they're in a supermarket trolley.
- An old wallet (maybe with play money).
- A small inexpensive working calculator.
- Some little handheld computer game.
- Old set of keys.
- A spare pack of baby wipes or moist towlettes.
- Maybe a small safe container with dried fruit.

Children's Interest Inventory

acting	electricity	poetry
aeroplanes	electronics	puppets
aquariums	fishing	puzzles
art	football	radio & crystal sets
astronomy	gardening	reading books
balloons	geography	remote control cars
barbies	handyman jobs	rollerblading
baseball	hair brushing	running
baseball cards	hiking	science fiction
bike riding	history	scouts & guides
bird watching	insects	seashell collecting
board games	Internet	sewing
boats	kites	singing
bushwalks	Lego blocks	skateboarding
card games	lizards	skating
carpentry	magic	soccer
cars and trucks	magnets	stamp collecting
chemistry	make-believe	storms
clay modelling	make-up	storytelling
climbing	map reading	stuffed animals
clock collecting	marbles	swimming
clothes	martial arts	T-Ball
coin collecting	mechanics	telephoning
colouring in	microscopes	television
computers	miniature soldiers	telling jokes
cooking	model making	travelling
cubby building	money making	video games
dancing	movies	water
digging (sand play)	music	weather forecasting
dinosaurs	pet care	writing stories
dolls	photography	yo-yos
drawing	photo framing	yo-yo diablo
Home brewed favourites:		

Boredom Beaters

play touch footie	visit a museum
go bushwalking	play a sport
play Monopoly/Battleships, etc	go fishing together
listen to music	do a science experiment
read and tell jokes	solve a puzzle
look at family photo albums	fiddle with cards/stamps
draw pictures	write a birthday card together
play catchings or frisbees	phone a relative
sing songs	put on music and dance
go for a trip in the car	meditate or pray
go to the zoo	build a cubby together
just talk (best present, best memory)	go putt putt golfing
go out for dinner	browse the encyclopedia
cook something, make bread	surf the Internet together (see opposite for list of sites)
repair something around house	play video games
play one-on-one basketball	read magazines
go on a picnic	work with clay, playdough, Lego
visit historical site	ride bikes
do a multi-piece puzzle	make music
build something crafty	play with toys
play with pet	help elderly neighbour
solve brainteasers	learn magic tricks
Home brewed favourites:	

Web Sites

There are some 2000 children's games and activities web sites. Some useful and appropriate ones include the following:

> KIDSGAME.PRN andSEARCH.PRN
> 5 Geokids Home Web Page - http://www.geocities.com/Enchanted Forest/1254/
> Family Games: Shareware, Freeware, Educational... - http://www.familygames.com/
> Jed Yang - http://geocities.com/EnchantedForest/2207/
> Nikolai's Web Site - http://www.nikolai.com/
> Surf Point (list of web sites) - http://www.surfpoint.com/Games--Children's Games.html
> Welcome to the Kids and Teenz Zone II - http://www.toptown.com/hp/kids/index.htm

Pocket Money Chart

Week Beginning _____

TASK	VALUE	NAME	NAME	NAME
KITCHEN				
clean breakfast bar				
wash up				
wipe up				
put dry dishes away				
pack dishwasher				
empty dishwasher and put away				
DINING				
set table				
clear table				
fold up washing				
take clean clothes to rooms				
BEDROOM				
make bed				
put clothes away				
put dirty clothes in laundry				
tidy up dressing table				
tidy up floor				
BATHROOM				
clean bath/shower				
tidy up vanity				
clear the floor				

TASK	VALUE	NAME	NAME	NAME
LOUNGE				
tidy up toys				
tidy up chairs				
clear the floor				
dust and clean the room				
water indoor plants				
OUTSIDE				
mow lawns				
tidy up yard				
do lawn edges				
weeding				
water garden and pot plants				
clean up carport/garage				
take out rubbish to bin/otto				
take out bin/otto				
bring in empty bin/otto				
Home brewed favourites:				

Family Meeting Form

WHAT'S HAPPENING   Week beginning _____
- LEFT OVERS FROM LAST WEEK
- PAY UP (POCKET MONEY)
- CAR COVER
- NEXT WEEK'S SPECIALS
- CODE BREACHES
- CODE CORRECTIONS
- OTHER BUSINESS

FAMILY MEETING RULES

1. Choose a night once per week when everyone can be home and try hard to keep that regular night, no matter what, for the family meeting.
2. Make the night a take-away, finger food or even cheap eat-out night so domestic kitchen staff can attend. Maybe start or finish with an activity everyone enjoys (eg a game of cards).
3. Preset a finishing time and get someone to keep notes on decisions made—if others don't want to do this job they can't complain if it's recorded the wrong way.
4. Make the time light and easy, but have a rule that anyone trying to take the mickey out of the meeting can be silently suspended and has no further say in decisions that night and has to put up with decisions made by others.
5. Make sure that everyone feels this time each week is for everyone to find out what's happening, to collect their dues and to settle complaints. It's not just for Mum and Dad to dish out the discipline or load them with lectures.
6. **Left-overs** means just checking business from last week to see how it all worked out and what needs more attention.
7. **Pay up** means pocket money dues are paid from pocket money sheet (see page 360).
8. **Car cover** means finding out and coordinating transport for what everyone's got on over the next week.
9. **Next week's specials** means any special jobs needing to be done over the next week and any special things coming up at school or work that others need to know about.
10. **Code breaches** means a review of the rules over the past week to see how they worked and what areas need tidying up.
11. **Code corrections** is where any new conduct rules are covered and consolidated into written form so everyone knows what's involved.
12. **Other business** refers to any odds and ends or any beefs about other individuals needing to be aired. If it only involves one or two people then it can be sorted out after the meeting perhaps.

Angry Parents' First Aid Guide

Place this list by the phone for fast access in times of emotional emergency.

Anger Rating/10	Action
10	DON'T TOUCH your child. Just go outside for a walk and say 'Hi' to anyone, even a dog will do, to break the pain cycle.
9	DON'T TOUCH your child. Just shake or belt a pillow, and keep doing it till the tears flow and you're both safe. Then take some deep breaths and have a cuppa in another room.
8	DON'T TOUCH your child. Use your phone, not your fist, and let someone know you're in pain. If you need a number phone any Helpline, eg 13 11 14.
7	TAKE your child out into another room, put on soothing music and just keep rocking together to reassure each other.
6	MASSAGE your child with baby oil. Using warm hands, do the 'Weather Report Massage' on their back: little pitter pat of raindrops followed by the bigger spots, swirl your hands slowly around their back for the big wind, cup hands and pat all over the upper back for thunderclaps and then around the shoulders for the big tides surging. Eventually go slower and softer and calmer as the storm passes.
5	TAKE your child in the car or go for a walk to visit friends, favourite shops or a favourite neighbour. Or just keep driving (if you're not dangerously angry) till you feel better.
4	TALK to your preschool teacher or phone family day care and let them know you're doing it a bit tough from time to time and need a break and ideas. Remember that people like to help, it makes everyone's life worthwhile if they think they're useful.
3	THINK up some fun things you can do together to get you both laughing, and think up ways to stop you feeling trapped in your own house. Join the Nursing Mothers Association, playgroup or join a parenting course through the local health centre or Community Education Course.
2	PLAY music, burn oils and make your home feel comfortable. Find some company, preferably for yourself and your child, but either will do.
1	WRITE out your ideas and share them, because you're ahead of the rest of us!

Remember, your child will be all right if you're all right, so look after yourself first.

Contact Numbers

NAPCAN
(National Association for the Prevention of Child Abuse and Neglect)
Level 1/17 Newland St
Bondi Junction 2022
Ph: 02 9369 4572
Fax: 02 9364 4579

ADHD Network of Australia
ACT   Canberra/Queanbeyan
       Support Group
       Ph: 02 6290 1984
       Fax: 02 6286 4475
QLD   Ipswich ADD Support
       Group
       Ph: 07 3817 2429
       Fax: 07 3817 2453
TAS   ADDSUP (Tas) Inc.,
       Ph: 03 6429 3332
NSW   Hyperactivity/Attention
       Deficit Association
       Ph: 02 9411 2186
WA   Joondalup Parent Support
       Group
       Ph: 08 9300 3153
VIC   ACTIVE Inc.,
       Ph: 03 9650 2570
       Fax: 03 9650 3689
NT   Darwin ADD Support
       Group
       Ph: 08 8981 2444
SA   PLAD
       Ph: 08 8260 4420
Raymond Terrace ADD booklet
       Ph: 02 4987 3249

CAPS
Ph: 1800 688 009

Parent Helpline
NSW   Ph: 13 20 55
SA   Ph: 1336 4100
WA   Ph: 08 9272 1466 (Perth)
       Ph: 1800 654 432 (country)
QLD   Ph: 1330 1300
ACT   Ph: 02 6278 3995

Lifeline
Ph: 13 11 14

Family Crisis Lines
(names of services differ between states)
NSW   Ph: 1800 066 777
QLD   Ph: 3235 9999
VIC   Ph: 13 12 78
       Ph: 03 9329 0300
         (counselling)
ACT   Ph: 1800 688 099 (CAPS)
NT   Ph: 1800 019 116
SA   Ph: 13 14 78
TAS   Ph: 1800 633 937
WA   Ph: 1800 199 008 (Crisis
         line)
       Ph: 1800 654 432 (Parent
         help line)
       Ph: 1800 643 000

Poison Information
Ph: 13 11 26

Tough Love
Ph: 02 4950 2390

Multiple Births Association
Ph: 02 9875 2404
Callers will be directed to local no's.
Offices:
NSW   Ph: 02 9686 4141
QLD   Ph: 07 3844 6488
Helplines:
QLD   Ph: 07 3844 8977
ACT   Ph: 02 6258 8928
NT   Ph: 08 8988 4616
SA   Ph: 08 8339 6783
TAS   Ph: 03 6223 2609
VIC   Ph: 03 9885 0653
WA   Ph: 08 9309 5393
NSW   Ph: 02 9639 8686

Child Care Access
Ph: 1800 670 305

Playgroup
NSW   Ph: 02 9632 8577
VIC   Ph: 03 9388 1599
SA   Ph: 08 8346 2722
QLD   Ph: 07 3371 8253
WA   Ph: 08 9221 3142
TAS   Ph: 03 6223 4814
NT   Ph: 08 8985 4968
ACT   Ph: 02 6285 4336

Family Day Care
NSW   Ph: 02 4599 6000
       Fax: 02 4588 6028
ACT   Ph: 02 6254 5244
VIC   Ph: 03 9686 9797
       Fax: 03 9686 9798
QLD   Ph: 07 3395 7044
       Fax: 07 3899 2271
WA   Ph: 08 9272 6985
       Fax: 08 9370 5409

References

Aisbett, Bev, *Living With 'It'*, Harper Collins, Sydney, 1993

Aisbett, Bev, *Living 'It' Up*, Harper Collins, Sydney, 1994

Angus, Jane, Brennan, John & Keaney, Leonie, *Free Stuff for Kids*, Roland Harvey Books, Melbourne, 1996

Armstrong, T., *The Myth of the A.D.D. Child*, Penguin Books, N.Y., 1995

Balson, Maurice, *Becoming Better Parents*, ACER, Melbourne, 1997

Biddulph, Steve, *Raising Boys*, Finch Publishing, Sydney, 1997

Bodenhamer, G., *Back In Control*, Prentice Hall, N.J., 1983

Blaker, K., *Born to Please*, Grapevine Press, N.Y., 1988

Byrne, R., *Let's Talk About Stammering*, Unwin, London, 1995

Chick, Suzanne, *Searching for Charmian*, Picador, Sydney, 1994

Clarke, I.C., Davenport, G. Et al, *Help: For Parents of Infants, Birth to Six Months*, Harper & Row, San Francisco, 1986

Cornelius, H. & Faire, S., *Everyone Can Win*, Simon & Schuster, Sydney, 1989

Courtenay, Bryce, *April Fool's Day*, Mandarin, Melbourne, 1994

Covey, S., *7 Habits of Highly Effective People*, The Business Library, Melbourne, 1990

Cue, Kerry, *Born To Whinge*, Penguin Books, Melbourne, 1988

Dengate, Sue, *Different Kids*, Random House, Sydney, 1994

Dyer, Wayne, *Manifest Your Destiny*, Harper Collins, Sydney, 1997

Ekman, P., *Why Kids Lie*, Schwartz & Wilkinson, Melbourne, 1990

Fowler, C., & Gornall, P., *How to Stay Sane in Your Baby's First Year*, Simon & Schuster, Sydney, 1991

Garth, Maureen, *The Inner Garden*, Harper Collins, 1994

Garth, Maureen, *Inner Space*, Harper Collins, Sydney, 1995

Garth, Maureen, *Moonbeam*, Harper Collins, Sydney, 1992

Garth, Maureen, *Power of the Inner Self*, Harper Collins, Sydney, 1996

Garth, Maureen, *Starbright*, Harper Collins, 1994

Garth, Maureen, *Sunshine*, Harper Collins, Sydney, 1994

Green, Christopher, *Babies*, Simon & Schuster, Sydney, 1988

Green, Christopher & Chee, K., *Understanding A.D.H.D.*, Doubleday, Sydney, 1997

Green, Christopher & Roberts, Roger, *Toddler Taming*, Doubleday, Sydney, 1990

Greenspan, S., *The Challenging Child*, Millennium Books, 1996

Hall, Janet, *How You Can Be Boss of the Bladder*, Globe Press, Melbourne, 1989

Hall, Janet, *Easy Toilet Training*, Globe Press, Melbourne, 1995

Hay, Louise, ***The Power is Within You***, Hay House Publications, 1991

Hay, Louise, ***You Can Heal Your Life***, Hay House Publications, 1988

Hills, A. & Stone, P., ***Breast, Bottle, Bowl***, Harper Collins, Sydney, 1993

Hills, A. & Stone, P., ***Good Food For Kids***, Harper Collins, Sydney, 1995

Hines, T. & Ritchie, K., ***Beating Sneaky Poo***, Canberra Pub. Co, Canberra, 1985

Hunford, Martin, ***Where's Wally***, Walker Books, London, 1987

Irvine, John, ***Coping With School***, Simon & Schuster, Sydney, 1992

Irvine, John, ***Coping With the Family***, Pan Macmillan, Sydney, 1994

Irwin, A., ***Stammering in Young Children***, Harper Collins, London, 1988

Jones, S., ***Crying Baby, Sleepless Nights***, Viking O'Neill, Melbourne, 1985

Kuols, Kathryn & Riedler, Bill, ***Redirecting Children's Behaviour***, Parenting Press, 1997

Lane, A., ***Mum's the Word***, Bantam, Sydney, 1988

Lansky, V., ***It Worked For Me***, Exley Press, London, 1985

Last, C., & Herson, M., ***Handbook of Child Psychiatric Diagnosis***, Wiley, N.Y., 1989

Leach, Penelope, ***Baby and Child***, Penguin, London, 1989

Lette, Kathy, ***Mad Cows***, Picador, Sydney, 1996

Mackay, Hugh, ***Why Don't People Listen?***, Pan Macmillan, Sydney, 1994

Matthews, Andrew, ***Making Friends***, Media Masters, Singapore, 1990

McGrath, H., ***Friendly Kids, Friendly Classrooms***, Longman Cheshire, Melbourne, 1991

Miller, Alice, ***The Drama of Being a Child***, Virago, London, 1995

Mullinar, G., ***Not Just Four Letter Words***, Harper Dove, Melbourne, 1992

Readers Digest, ***How To Do Just About Anything***, Readers Digest, Sydney, 1987

Rowe, D., ***The Depression Handbook***, Harper Collins, Sydney, 1990

Saxelby, C., ***Busy Body Cook Book***, Hodder & Stoughton, Sydney, 1995

Schaefer, C.E. & Petronko, M. R., ***Teach Your Baby to Sleep Through the Night***, 1993, Harper Collins, Sydney

Seligman, Martin, ***The Optimistic Child***, Random House, Sydney, 1995

Shepherd, Jeannine, ***Dare to Fly***, Random House, Sydney, 1997

Shepherd, Jeannine, ***Never Tell Me Never***, Pan Macmillan, 1994

Welford, H., ***Successful Potty Training***, Harper Collins, London, 1987

Weston, D. & Weston, M., ***Playful Parenting***, Putnam, N.Y., 1993

Wallace, Ian, ***You and Your A.D.D. Child***, Harper Collins, Sydney, 1997

York, P; York, D. & Wachtel, T., ***Tough Love***, Bantam, N.Y., 1982

Zigler, Z., ***Raising Positive Kids in a Negative World***, Ballantine, N.Y., 1989

Index

abuse 2, 227–8
achievements, personal 201
Active Attention Demanding Disorder 72
activities *see also* games
    boredom-relieving 164–5
    car trips 171–2
ADD *see* Attention Damaged Disorder; Attention Demanding Disorder; Attention Digested Disorder; Attention Disabled Disorder
ADHD *see* Attention Deficit Hyperactivity Disorder
adolescents *see* kids, older
aggression problems
    aggression 228–32
    anger 233–7
    bad temper 233–7
    bullies 248–51
    competitive kids 245–8
    destructive kids 242–5
    reasons 227–8
    sibling rivalry 238–42
    stealing 252–4
    summary 255
anger *see also* screaming; tantrums
    bush remedies 237
    checks 233–4
    classic style 12
    do's and don'ts 234–6
    energy outlets 235
    facing our own 234–5
    management 233, 237
    parental 26
    'reframing' 235
    triggers 233
Angry Parents' First Aid Guide 363
answering back *see* back-answering
anxiety *see also* panic; separation anxiety
    classic style 10
    environment check 38
    self check 37
    situation check 37–8
    symptom check 37
arguing
    bush remedies 179–80
    checks 176–7
    do's and don'ts 178–9
    singing arguments 215
assault, sexual 273

Attention Damaged Disorder
    bush remedies 80
    do's and don'ts 79–80
    symptoms 78
Attention Deficit Hyperactivity Disorder
    Attention Demanding Disorder comparison 72–3
    bush remedies 91
    checks 86
    concentration span 90
    cyclonic behaviour 12
    described 85–6
    diet 84
    do's and don'ts 86–90
    identifying 71–2
    listening problems 93, 94
    real-life tasks 88
    rules 90
    showing off and silly talk 192
    stealing 252
    time out 88–9, 299
Attention Demanding Disorder *see also* interrupting problems
    ADHD comparison 72–3
    attention seeking behaviour 11
    diagnosing 74
    do'and don'ts 74–6
    showing off and silly talk 192–3
Attention Digested Disorder
    bush remedies 84
    do's and don'ts 83–4
    food intolerances 82–3
    symptoms 83
Attention Disabled Disorder 82
attention problems *see also* Attention Damaged Disorder; Attention Demanding Disorder; Attention Digested Disorder; Attention Disabled Disorder
    attention seeking behaviour 11
    biggest problem 71–2
    interrupting problems 96–100
    listening problems 91–5
    summary 101
babies
    close contact 222
    cooperation 291–2
    crying 158–60
    dressing difficulties 305–8
    immaturity problems 260

babies (cont...)
    learning 22
    masturbation 279
    shaking 168
back-answering
    bush remedies 179–80
    checks 176–7
    do's and don'ts 178–9
bad dreams
    bush remedies 119–20
    checks 117–18
    do's and don'ts 118
bad habits
    checks 276–7
    copying 276
    do's and don'ts 277–8
bad temper *see* anger
Bananas in Pyjamas 119
banter *see* teasing
bath battles
    bush remedies 317–18
    do's and don'ts 316–17
    washing refusal 316, 317–18
Beazley, Kim 71, 102–3
bed departure
    bush remedies 112–14
    checks 110
    do's and don'ts 111–12
    toddlers 109–10
bed pooing 267
bed wetting
    bell pad system 270
    bush remedies 271–2
    checks 268–70
    do's and don'ts 270
    expectations 268–9
    medication 270
    retention 270
    twins 272
bedtime routines 110, 112–17
behavioural problems, top 20 3
Biddulph, Steve 21, 338
biting
    bush remedies 150
    checks 148–9
    do's and don'ts 149–50
    flooding technique 149
bladder control *see* bed wetting
bladder tap 271
Body Check 185
body contact 219–22
body parts
    behavioural problems 4–5
    discovery 272, 275–6
    euphemisms 184
boredom
    Boredom Beaters 358
    bush remedies 166
    checks 162–3
    do's and don'ts 163–6
    holiday 164–5
bossing
    back-answering 177
    checks 209
    classic kid style 10
    do's and don'ts 209–11
    reasons 208–9
    selfishness 216
breathing relaxation 41
budgie solution, messy rooms 333
bullies
    bush remedies 251
    causes 249
    management 249–50
    school 251
    victims 250
Busy List 76

car whingeing
    bush remedies 171–2
    cause 169–70
    checks 170
    do's and don'ts 170–1
carsickness 139–40
Chick, Suzanne 197, 224–5
children *see* kids, little; kids, older
Children's Interest Inventory 200, 357
cleaning up techniques 331–2
colic, evening 160, 260
communication
    bad 17
    demanding 178
    good basis 93–4
    skills summary 194
    styles 177
communication problems
    arguing 176–80
    back-answering 176–80
    boredom 162–6
    car whingeing 169–72
    crying 158–61
    lying 180–3
    most hurtful 157–8
    screaming 166–9
    showing off 192–3
    silly talk 192–3
    smutty talk 184–7
    swearing 173–6
    teasing 188–91
    whingeing 162–6
competitive kids
    bush remedies 247
    checks 245–6
    do's and don'ts 246
    peaceful activities 246
complaining *see* whingeing
compulsive behaviour *see* rituals

computers
    games 79
    obsession 78
condoms 274
contact, body 219–22
cool image 11
cooperation problems
    bath battles 315–18
    dawdling 302–4
    disobedience 288–9
    dressing difficulties 305–9
    homework 327–30
    job refusal 290–4
    late for school 322–3
    messy rooms 330–4
    microwave-style 301
    modern trend 287–8
    phone problems 323–6
    school refusal 319–22
    shopping 295–7
    tantrums 309–13
    time out refusal 298–301
    twins 294
    two-way cooperation 289
Courtenay, Bryce 105, 128–9
crying
    bush remedies 161
    do's and don'ts 159–60
    types 158–9
cuddle-shy
    bush remedies 222
    checks 219–20
    do's and don'ts 220–1
    family style 219

Daddo, Bronwen 157, 195–6
dawdling
    bush remedies 303
    checks 302
    deterrent strategies 302–3
    power play 304
daydreamers 122–3
death, thought of 36
demanding behaviour 72–7
denial management style 14
depression
    bush remedies 36, 46
    home tone check 33
    little kids 33
    medical check 32
    older kids 34
    parental 24–6, 34
    perception check 33
    situational check 33
    symptom check 32
'desensitising' technique, worry 39
destructive kids
    bush remedies 245
    checks 242–3

    do's and don'ts 243–4
    family background 244
developmental problems see immaturity
    problems
diets
    elimination 83–4
    weight reduction 144
discipline
    definition 76
    summary 334
dobbing in 183, 184
'Down There' problems see immaturity
    problems
Dream Jar 116
dreams see bad dreams
dressing difficulties
    babies and toddlers 305–8
    older kids 308–9
dummies 280, 281

'ear problems' see attention problems
early wakers 120–2
eating out 151–2
eating problems
    biting 148–50
    car sickness 139–40
    eating disorders 143–4
    food refusal 140–4
    fussy eaters 132–8
    junk food 144–7
    overeating 144–7
    restaurant rebels 151–2
    slow eaters 132–8
    summary 153
elimination diets 83–4
epilepsy 122, 124
'eye problems' see sleeping problems

faeces, impacted 265–7
Family Meeting Form 362
fashion consciousness 9–10
fast foods 136, 145, 146, 147
fear see anxiety
feelings, talking about 235
fighting see sibling rivalry
flooding technique
    bad habits 277–8
    biting 149
    masturbation 279
    rituals 55
    sex play 273
    thumbsucking 280
food see also diets; eating problems
    comfort eating 145
    craving sweets 145
    daily intake 141
    fast food 136, 145, 146, 147
    intolerances 82–3
    self-serve 134–5

food refusal
    little kids 140–2
    older kids 142–4
'foot problems' *see* cooperation
forgetfulness
    bush remedies 126–7
    cause 124
    classic style 11–12
    do's and don'ts 125
Fridge Disk Discipline 211, 292, 351
Fridge Make-Up List 76, 352
friendships 205–8
fussy eaters
    10 top tips 136
    bush remedies 137
    checks 133
    do's and don'ts 134–7
    tense mealtimes 138

games
    As If Game 38–9
    Bed Settlers' Program 111
    Carpe Excreta 264
    Cooperation Chart 239
    Desk Disks 87
    Face Lifter 43
    Fridge Disk Discipline 211, 292, 351
    Fridge Disks 77
    Garden Massage 116
    Guess Where? 221
    Habit Chart 97
    Imagining the Cure 65
    Look And Listen 210
    Magic Macaroni Tin 34
    Magic Power Stones 47
    The Mike 190
    Mind Muscle Chart 58
    Mind Muscle Management 236
    Noise Nobbler 193
    Poo Exhaust System 263
    Sneaky Poos 267
    Stirrer Monster 247
    Stretching the Friendship Chain 48
    Teasing Tossing Tactic 191
    Think Light 75, 230–1, 300, 355
    This Is Me 201
    Traffic Lights 89, 230
    Weather Report Massage 44
    'What if' Worry-Winning Game 38
    Word Lifters 40
    'Worry-Unloading' Game 43
    Worry-Winning Ladder 39
gender difference 272, 275–6
'Give it a Rest' drawer 43
'Good Kids Gauge' 240
grazing 134
grizzle countdown 163
grown-up image 11

hair pulling 276, 277
'hand problems' *see* aggression problems
hearing problems 82, 91
'heart problems' *see* relationship problems
hitting
    as punishment 227–8
    solution to 232
holidays activities 164–5
homework
    checks 327
    do's and don'ts 328–9
    forgetting 329
    parental involvement 330
    pressure 327
Howard, John 9, 29–30
hugging 219–22
hurt, sharing 235
hypochondriacs 64–6

Imagination Worriers 40
immaturity problems
    by age 259–60
    summary 283
incarceration management style 15
inquisition management style 15
intellectualisation 14
Internet Web sites 359
interrupting problems
    bush remedies 100
    checks 96
    do's and don'ts 96–7
    practise waiting 97

jealousy
    becomes unity 215
    bush remedies 214–15
    checks 212–13
    controlling 213
    do's and don'ts 213–14
    reducing 214
    twins 214
job refusal
    bush remedies 294
    checks 290–1
    do's and don'ts 291–3
    twins 294
junk food 136, 144–7

Kernot, Cheryl 287, 335–6
kids, little *see also* toddlers
    bad habits 276, 277
    depression 33
    food refusal 140–2
    immaturity problems 260
    learning stages 22–4
    masturbation 279
    meal size 136
    obedience 289
    phones 324

kids, little (cont...)
    right and wrong 181
    self-esteem 217
    selfishness 217
    stealing 253
kids, older
    bad habits 276–8
    cooperation 292–3
    depression 34
    dressing difficulties 308–9
    food refusal 142–4
    immaturity problems 260
    learning stages 22–4
    masturbation 279
    panic 50–2
    phones 324–5
    right and wrong 181
    self–esteem 217
    stealing 253
    washing refusal 316, 317–18

late for school 322–3
laziness
    checks 314
    do's and don'ts 314–15
    or loneliness 315
    reasons 313–14
learning ages and stages 22–4
'left-brain' kids 124, 125
Lette, Kathy 131, 154–5
listening
    active 94
    mechanics of 91
    practice 81
listening problems
    bush remedies 95
    checks 91–2
    do's and don'ts 92–4
Little, Jeannie 259, 284–5
loneliness
    bush remedies 206–8
    cause 203
    checks 204
    do's and don'ts 204–6
    laziness 315
    'reframing' 205
    suggestions 208
lovemaking 274
lying
    age factor 181
    building trust 182–3
    bush remedies 183
    checks 180–1
    do's and don'ts 182–3

Make-Up List 352
management instructions
    balanced 26–8
    kids' styles 9–12

management styles 14–17
parenting styles 12–14
martyrisation management style 15
massage
    Garden Massage 116
    making contact 220
    panic relief 52
    Weather Report Massage 44
masturbation
    by age groups 279
    flooding technique 279
    stopping 277, 278
'me first' philosophy 216 see also selfishness
mealtimes
    routines 135
    tension at 138
messages, phone 324, 325
messy rooms
    bathroom 316
    budgie solution 333
    bush remedies 333–4
    checks 330–1
    do's and don'ts 331–2
milk, full cream 136
mind problems see up-top problems
monsters see bad dreams
mood problems see up-top problems
morning kids 120–2
'mouth problems' see eating problems
muscle relaxation 40
music
    background 80
    making contact 220
    singing arguments 215
music relaxation 42

nagging management style 15
nailbiting 276, 277, 281–2
night monsters see bad dreams
Ninja versus Killer 100
noise levels 78–9
nose picking 276, 278

obsessions see rituals
Obsessive Compulsive Disorder (OCD) 53, 54, 56
one-track thinkers 123
O'Shane, Pat 7–8
overeating
    bush remedies 147
    checks 145–6
    do's and don'ts 146–7
    effect 144–5
overweight problems 143–6

Page, Greg 227, 256–7
panic see also anxiety
    checklist 51
    do's and don'ts 51–2

panic (cont...)
    triggers 50
parent pentathlon
    Disabled Orienteering Event 126
    Food Foils Event 132
    Homework Medley Event 330
    Midnight Madness Sprint Event 109
    Phone Ring Event 326
    Tantrum Throwing Event 311
parenting
    balanced management 26–8
    body language 39
    challenges 338
    obsessive problems 54
    overcontrolling 180–1
    playful 44
    praise 199
    styles 12–14
    time out management 298–301
    tough 66–7
parents
    hostility 339
    Parents Bill of Rights 339–40
Passive Attention Demanding Disorder 73
perfectionism
    bush remedies 58
    classic style 10–11
    do's and don'ts 57–8
    handling mistakes 59
    symptom check 57
pets, cuddly 220, 221
Phoebe's Story 349
phone problems
    bush remedies 325–6
    checks 323–4
    do's and don'ts 324–5
    house rules 325
    kids' attitude 323
    messages 324, 325
'Physical Assistance' technique 292, 293
pocket money 253
Pocket Money Chart 360–1
poo refusal
    bush remedies 265
    checks 261–2
    do's and don'ts 262–5
    management 268
    parental pressure 261
potty training 261–5
Practice List 354
preschoolers *see* kids, little
private space 182
problem solving
    ADHD 88
    family 202
    loneliness 205
    styles 14–17
property damage 243, 244, 245
psychological problems *see* up-top problems

punishment
    effect 16–17, 19
    effective rules 18
    preferred, by age 350

'quality' time 21
quiet 79

Ranting Parent Test (RPT) 170–1
reading to children 79
red colouring 85
'reframing'
    anger 235
    loneliness 205
    self–esteem 200
    stealing 254
rejection
    anger 233
    cause 203
    handling 206
relationship problems
    basis 197–8
    bossing 208–11
    cuddle-shy 219–22
    jealousy 212–15
    loneliness 203–6
    self-esteem 198–203
    selfishness 216–19
relaxation techniques 40–4
restaurant rebels 151–2
restraint, body 243
rewards
    appropriate 17
    preferred, by age 350
'right brain' kids 123
rigid personality 60
Ritalin 74, 84, 85
Ritchie, Peter 337, 342–3
rituals
    bush remedies 55
    do's and don'ts 54
    symptom check 53–4
rooms, messy *see* messy rooms
Royal Prince Alfred Hospital's Simplified
    Elimination Diet 83–4

salt 136
saturation management style 15
school
    bullies 251
    lateness 322–3
    repeating classes 321
    separation anxiety 48, 49
school refusal
    bush remedies 322
    checks 319–20
    do's and don'ts 320–1
school sick
    do's and don'ts 63–4

school sick (cont...)
    manifestation 62
    symptom check 63
screaming *see also* shouting
    bush remedies 169
    checks 166–7
    do's and don'ts 167–9
    lower voice 167
    toddlers 167
self-esteem
    bush remedies 203
    do's and don'ts 200–3
    little kids 217
    parents 218
    'reframing' 200
    school-age children 217
    summary 223
    symptom checklist 198–9
selfishness
    bush remedies 219
    causes 216
    do's and don'ts 217–18
self-talk skills, positive 200–1
separation anxiety
    bush remedies 49–50
    checks 46–7
    do's and don'ts 47–8
sex obsession 187
sex play and talk *see also* smutty talk
    bush remedies 275–6
    checks 272
    discovering gender 272, 275–6
    do's and don'ts 273–4
    exploration 272
    flooding technique 273
sexual assault 273
sexual difference, discovering 272, 275–6
sexual intercourse 274
shaking babies 168
Shepherd, Janine 31, 68–9
shopping
    bush remedies 297
    checks 295
    do's and don'ts 295–6
    twins 297
shouting management style 15–16
showering *see* bath battles
showing off 11, 192–3
shyness 10, 122
sibling rivalry
    bush remedies 241–2
    checks 238
    competitive kids 245–8
    do's and don'ts 239–41
    Lego jar 239
    management 240–1
sick thinking
    avoiding school 62–4
    hypochondriacs 64–6

silly talk 192–3
Simplified Elimination Diet 83–4
skin contact 220–1
sleep interruptions
    checks 106–7
    do's and don'ts 107–9
sleeping problems
    bad dreams 117–20
    bed departure 109–14
    early wakers 120–2
    sleep interruptions 106–9
    slow sleepers 114–17
    summary 127
    twins 113
slow eaters *see* fussy eaters
slow sleepers
    bush remedies 116–17
    checks 115
    do's and don't 115–16
    non-settlers 114
smacking
    alternatives 20
    management style 16–17
    prevention 21–2
smutty talk
    bush remedies 186
    checks 185
    do's and don'ts 185–6
    euphemisms 184
    peer pressure 186
snacks, healthy 134, 135–6
sneaky poos 265–7
social skills 209–10
soiling 265–7
'spoilt' *see* stubbornness
stages of development 260
stealing
    bush remedies 254–5
    checks 252–3
    do's and don'ts 253
    impulse control 252
    'reframing' 254
stimulation levels 78–9, 161
stroking 222
'strong-willed' *see* stubbornness
stubbornness
    bush remedies 62
    checks 59–60
    do's and don'ts 60–1
    harnessing 60
Success Charts 353
sugar 136, 145
supermarket shopping 295, 296
swearing
    attraction of 173
    bush remedies 175–6
    checks 173
    curry powder 179
    do's and don'ts 173–4

'Swearing Saturation Strategy' 174

tantrums *see also* screaming
    bush remedies 312–13
    checks 310
    do's and don'ts 310–12
    inevitability 309
    rating scale 310–11
    reduction tactics 311–12
    supermarket 296
teasing
    boredom 188
    checks 188
    destructive 189
    do's and don'ts 189–91
    'Practice' cure 189
    victims 191
teenager learning stages 24
teething 161
television *see* TV
temper *see* anger; screaming; tantrums
Think Light 75, 230–1, 300, 355
throwing up in car 139–40
thumbsucking 276, 278, 280–1
tidiness *see* messy rooms
time out
    ADHD 88–9
    appropriate area 299
time-out refusal
    bush remedies 301
    checks 298
    do's and don'ts 299–300
toddlers *see also* kids, little
    bad habits 276
    cooperation 291–2
    crying 158–60
    dressing difficulties 305–8
    immaturity problems 260
    learning 22
    masturbation 279
    phones 324
    right and wrong 181
    screaming 167
    selfishness 216
toilet training 261–5
'tongue problems' *see* communication problems
touch
    early importance 222
    good and bad 273
    learning 219–22

'Traffic Light' aggression management 230
Traveller's First Aid Kit for Families 356
trust 182–3
tummy ache remedies 35
TV
    limited 79
    obsession 78
twin advice
    as individuals 208
    bed wetting 272
    getting cooperation 294
    jealousy 214
    shopping 297
    sleeping together 113
up-top problems
    anxiety 37–46
    depression 32–6
    hypochondriacs 64–6
    Mind Muscle summary 67
    panic 50–2
    perfectionism 57–9
    rituals 53–6
    school sick 62–4
    separation anxiety 46–50
    stubbornness 59–61
    types 31
urinary problems *see* bed wetting

vomiting in car 139–40

waiting
    difficulty with 96
    practising 97
waking problems *see* sleep interruptions
washing 315–18
water
    drinking 136
    relaxation 42
Web Sites 359
weight problems 143–6
wetting the bed *see* bed wetting
whingeing
    bush remedies 166
    in cars 169–72
    checks 162–3
    do's and don'ts 163–6
Word Worriers 40
worry *see* anxiety
worth, sense of *see* self-esteem